THE TIMES
OF MY LIFE

For Rosemary Courtney

With warmest best wishes

Betty Ford

Gerald R. Ford

October 4, 1979

THE TIMES
OF MY LIFE

BETTY FORD

with Chris Chase

HARPER & ROW, PUBLISHERS
AND
THE READER'S DIGEST ASSOCIATION, INC.

Portions of this work originally appeared in the *Ladies' Home Journal*.

The lines on page 32 are from "Chant for Dark Hours" in *The Portable Dorothy Parker*, copyright 1926, 1954 by Dorothy Parker. Reprinted by permission of The Viking Press.

FIRST EDITION

Designed by Eve Kirch

Library of Congress Cataloging in Publication Data

Ford, Betty, 1918–
  The times of my life.
  Includes index.
    1. Ford, Betty, 1918–   2. Presidents—United States—Wives—Biography.
3. Ford, Gerald R., 1913–   4. Presidents—United States—Biography. I. Chase, Chris, joint author. II. Title.
E867.F66   973.925′092′4 [B]   78–2131
ISBN 0–06–011298–0

78 79 80 81 82 10 9 8 7 6 5 4 3 2 1

To Jerry

CONTENTS

Photographs follow pages 84, 148 and 212.

PROLOGUE

When I was a young girl, I went to a fortuneteller who read tea leaves and who told me I would be meeting kings and queens. I interpreted that to mean I was going to be a great dancer. I was wrong.

When I married Jerry Ford, I really thought I was marrying a lawyer, and he would practice law until it was time for him to retire, and we would spend the quiet life of a medium-sized city in Grand Rapids, Michigan. I was wrong again.

Both of these errors can be laid to a failure of imagination, but I make other kinds of mistakes too.

When we married on a Friday, because it was fall, and in the fall we couldn't miss a Saturday football game, I chose Friday, October 15, and all the ushers were furious because they were duck hunters and October 15 was the opening of the duck season.

That's one of the reasons I first thought about calling this book *Whoops!* (I also wanted to get some sex into it, so it would outsell Jerry's.)

A while ago, a woman wrote in the *New York Times* that Jerry and I had got "his-and-hers book contracts. Which was more than

any previous First Lady ever got for just smiling nicely." It's a
funny crack, but it begs the question, and misses the point.

The point is I am an ordinary woman who was called onstage
at an extraordinary time. I was no different once I became First
Lady than I had been before. But, through an accident of history, I
had become interesting to people.

It began after Jerry was nominated to be Vice President. I was
deluged with requests for interviews. I put everybody off. "Until
my husband is confirmed," I told them. Once Jerry was confirmed,
they all called back, reminding me of my promise. I phoned my
husband at his office. I was in tears. "What am I going to do? I don't
want to give interviews!"

"You can't go back on your word," he said.

So suddenly, at fifty-six, I was a public person.

I had thought I would hate being First Lady. Wrong again. I
loved it. I loved it when we'd ride down the streets in a motorcade
and people would yell, "Hi, Betty" or "Hi, First Momma" (a name
I was given courtesy of Flip Wilson, and which later became my CB
name). I took it as a compliment, a sign of affection, not of
disrespect. Those people identified with me, they knew I was no
different from them, it was just that fate had put me in this
situation. Same with my husband. There were times when he had to
be Mr. President, when protocol demanded it, but if you yelled,
"Hi, Jerry!" at him, he'd "Hi" you right back.

I thought he was a terrific President, and I worked hard for his
election—I don't suppose I can say re-election, since he wasn't
elected in the first place—and I think when they didn't send him
back to the Oval Office the American people missed the boat.

But that boat's sailed. And anyway this is not going to be a
political book. (If you want to know the secrets of Watergate, don't
come to me.) Neither is it going to be a book about etiquette, or—
though I lived to meet the kings and queens promised by the
fortuneteller—how to set the tables at a state dinner. It's going to be
a love story, and a story about a woman and her family and how
they wound up in the White House.

And out of the White House. As soon as we were out, I decided to write the book. I'm restless, and I thrive on activity, maybe even struggle.

Struggle is educational. I remember after we built our house in Virginia—I'd struggled with the interior, with the landscaping, with the crabgrass—I said, Never again will I build a house. I'll buy, I'll decorate, I'll have things changed to my specifications, but I just can't imagine starting from scratch again.

I was wrong one more time, because here I am starting from scratch again. New house, new life, new work.

If I can bring it off, this book will be personal, and it will also be, from time to time, amusing.

I'd like not to be wrong about that.

1

~

THE SADDEST DAY

Having decided in favor of the light-hearted approach to autobiography, I will now turn around and describe the saddest day of my life.

It was Friday, August 9, 1974, the day my husband took the oath of office as President of the United States.

I had not let myself see it coming. I think the possibility so terrified me that I was blocking it out. I wasn't totally unconscious, of course. I had watched John and Mo Dean on television. I'd heard rumors about how President Nixon couldn't sleep and was playing the piano at two o'clock in the morning, and how people in his Cabinet had gone to him and said, "Don't put the country through this; resign," and he'd said no.

I knew Jerry was worried, and I knew it would be terrible if the President had to be impeached, yet I avoided facing the consequences of this knowledge. I didn't see because I didn't want to see. The Nixons were friends of ours, and at the end they were holed up in the White House, cut off from everyone, and I thought of calling Pat to try to talk to her, but even about that I was hesitant; it seemed wrong to want to invade her privacy.

Besides, I was frantic with trying to be the wife of the Vice President. Since Jerry had replaced Spiro Agnew, the demands on our time had increased but my staff had not, and that summer our oldest son, Mike, married his wife, Gayle, and I was busy with the wedding, and redoing Admiralty House for us to live in. (Before Congress decided to fix up Admiralty House as the official residence of the Vice President, Vice Presidents had lived where they liked, and done their entertaining at the State Department.) I'd already selected the silver, and the china with its cobalt blue and gold trim and the Vice Presidential seal on the borders rather than in the centers of the plates, and on Thursday, August 8, I had scheduled a trip to New York. I was going up to look at furniture at Kittinger's, which makes very good Early American reproductions.

On Monday, August 5, Jerry told me I'd better cancel my reservations.

Now it hit me that Nixon was really going to resign.

He did it, on television, on the night of August 8.

Up until then, I'd kept hoping that something would happen which would save the President, save the office, save all of us, hoping it wouldn't end the way it ended.

From Thursday night through Friday, I was like an actor on a set, being told where to go and what to do. The children had to be reached. Mike and Gayle were on their way to Boston, dragging a U-Haul full of wedding presents, and when they got there, the Secret Service met them and gave them tickets to fly back to Washington. Our second son, Jack, had been working as a ranger in Yellowstone National Park, and he was on a horse in the back country. A helicopter had to find him and lift him out of there; he barely made it home in time for his father's swearing-in. The telephone kept ringing, people were racing around me, and I was numb. There was no time to think about what impact this was going to make on our lives; there wasn't even time to get haircuts for the boys.

Friday morning, at our house in Alexandria, I remember discussions about clothes for Susan, Gayle, the boys—they couldn't show up in blue jeans—and Gayle finally wore one of my dresses and Susan another, and Jack put on a perfectly decent shirt and tie, but if you look at the official family portrait, you'll see he's in his cowboy boots.

Limousines took us to the Vice President's office. We watched on television. In the East Room President Nixon was saying goodbye to his Cabinet and staff under the painted two-hundred-year-old eyes of George and Martha Washington. The President was talking about his father being a great man and his mother being a saint, and people were crying, and it still seemed impossible to me that this was happening, though later I could admit to myself that I should have known it long ago, that it had been in all the newspapers I hadn't let myself read, it had been in the faces of all those people marching with signs outside the White House.

Before President Nixon finished talking, Jerry and I were taken to the White House. We joined the Nixons and walked with them toward the helicopter. The President and Jerry were in front, and Pat and I were walking arm in arm, and she said, "My heavens, they've even rolled out the red carpet for us, isn't that something?" And then she said, "Well, Betty, you'll see many of these red carpets, and you'll get so you hate 'em."

The men were waiting for us, and we formed a phalanx and walked on, four abreast, between the two rows of a military guard standing at attention for the last time in President Nixon's honor, and we all stopped halfway down the carpet. The two men shook hands, and my husband said, "Goodbye, Mr. President," and Mr. Nixon said, "Goodbye, Mr. President," and then the Nixons walked the rest of the way alone, and we stood and watched while the helicopter took off. It was about 11 A.M.

At 11:35, President Nixon's formal note of resignation was delivered to Secretary of State Henry Kissinger, and at noon Jerry and I came into the East Room behind the Chief Justice of the United States, Warren Burger.

There were more than two hundred people waiting, some of them smiling and clapping, some of them with swollen eyes. There were old Congressional friends, Democrats and Republicans, there were friends from Michigan, there were generals and reporters and members of the Cabinet. I was holding a Bible opened to the Book of Proverbs, to a passage Jerry says every night as a prayer: "Trust in the Lord with all thine heart; and lean not unto thine own understanding."

"Mr. Vice President, are you prepared to take the oath of office as President of the United States?" the Chief Justice said, and Jerry said, "I am, sir," and raised his right hand, with his left hand on the Bible. Then he repeated after the Chief Justice, "I, Gerald R. Ford, do solemnly swear that I will faithfully execute the office of President of the United States, and will, to the best of my ability, preserve, protect and defend the Constitution of the United States, so help me God."

The words cut through me, pinned me to the floor. I felt as though I were taking the oath with him, promising to dedicate my own life to the service of my country.

I was the wife of the President of the United States.

What an astonishing place for Elizabeth Ann Bloomer to have come to.

2

GROWING UP
IN GRAND RAPIDS

I always wanted to be called Elizabeth, but it didn't happen. Once in a while my parents, hoping to make an impression on me, delivered both barrels: "Elizabeth Ann, you stop that!" and my husband, when he's trying to hurry me along because I'm late, will occasionally say, "Ee-liz-a-beth, come on now," but mostly I've been Betty or Bet or Bets.

I was born in Chicago on April 8, 1918, a year brought to my reluctant attention in March of 1977 by my daughter Susan. She telephoned and said, "Well, you're going to have a birthday pretty soon," and I said, "Yes, I'll be fifty-seven," and she said rudely, "You'll be *what?*"

"I'll be fifty-seven," I said.

"Mother," she said, "get out a piece of paper and a pencil and subtract eighteen from seventy-seven and find out how old you're really going to be—"

Obviously, I did not care to be fifty-nine, so I had lost a couple of years. It didn't do me a bit of good. No sooner had I hung up on Susan than I got a whole load of birthday greetings sent to me by a very nice fifth-grade class. Their teacher wrote that they had been studying the Presidents and their wives, and had thought it would be a good idea to send me cards, and every darn one of those cards said 59 on it. If it didn't say 59 once, it said 59 in all four corners, or it had a cock-eyed picture of a big cake with what looked like 150 candles on it.

When I was a baby, my family lived in Chicago and Denver, but we came to Grand Rapids when I was two, and my memory starts there.

My mother's name was Hortense Neahr Bloomer; my father's name was William Stephenson Bloomer. He worked for the Royal Rubber Company, and he traveled, selling conveyor belts to factories. My mother wrote him every single night. I can remember coming downstairs after my homework was done, and my mother would be at the desk writing to my father. Jerry and I are the same way: we've always communicated daily; the only difference is we've used the telephone.

One of my father's favorite pastimes was fiddling with an old crystal set. I can see him sitting hunched over that crystal set, earphones on, and all of a sudden crying, "Wow! I got Chicago, I got Chicago, come listen to it," and we'd all run and take his earphones and listen to WKMG or whatever that famous old station was in Chicago.

I had two older brothers, Bill Junior and Bob, for whom I felt sorry because I didn't believe any girl would marry a man named Bloomer, despite the evidence that my adored mother had done so.

(There aren't too many Bloomers around the country. After I got over being embarrassed about the name, I started trying to uncover a relationship with Amelia Bloomer, who'd invented the divided skirt. I never could find a connection, but for years, when I traveled anywhere, I'd look in the phone book to see if there were Bloomers in that town.)

My brother Bill was seven years older than I, my brother Bob five years my senior, and I think I was an accident, the result of an unplanned party. Mother, who was thirty-five or thirty-six when I came along, always said I'd popped out of a bottle of champagne. I liked that idea.

My mother was an attractive woman, my father was a good-looking man, and I was a fat little kid. We had a cottage up at Whitefish Lake, where we went every summer, chugging off in an old Cole Eight touring car.

We left for the lake the day school let out, and we didn't come home until school started again, so we had dozens of friends up there. (It wasn't until I was a teenager, and my brothers were grown, that we began to lose interest. By that time, the Depression was on, and we all wanted to work during the summers, and our cottage was sold.)

I can still feel my mother's arms around me, holding me, as she stood out on the porch and we watched a storm come rolling in across the lake, waves swelling, thunder crashing, lightning slicing the sky, and my mother telling me how beautiful it was. I found out later she was scared to death, but she taught me not to be afraid; I was safe in those arms.

Almost forty years later, I tried to do the same thing for Susan. It didn't work. She's twenty-one now, but at the first crack of thunder she goes straight down into the cellar with a candle. I thought Mother's method was good; maybe I wasn't so strong-willed as Susan.

There was a hotel near the cottage, Hart's Hotel, which featured picnic grounds. Being a baby who liked to wander, I'd find my way to the picnic grounds—there's a snapshot of me out there in my rompers, with the Dutch–boy bob many children sported in those days—and I'd stagger from table to table, and everybody had a cookie or a piece of cake or some ice cream for me. I just got fatter and fatter until finally my mother hung a sign on my back. It said, PLEASE DO NOT FEED THIS CHILD.

I much preferred the cuisine at the picnic grounds to eating at our cottage, because my father was a great fisherman. He spent his entire vacation fishing, and we were served fish and fish and fish until I hoped I would never see fish again. To this day, I don't like it. Once in a while in a restaurant I'll order Sole Véronique, with the grapes, but I won't prepare fish. They say it's good brain food, but I don't know how they know.

Brain food notwithstanding, we passed wonderful months at Whitefish Lake. When I was tiny, I had to go out on a snipe hunt. The older kids take the little ones into the woods in the dark and say they're going to catch snipes, which only come out at night. And all day long the older kids have been working, setting up booby traps and scary things to pop out of the bushes at you. Once you've been on a snipe hunt, you're considered a veteran, and you can join the group and torture some other little kid.

In Grand Rapids, we lived at 717 Fountain Street, right in the middle of the city. The house had a front porch and vines and a hanging glider. It was frame, as were most of the buildings in town. When I moved East, I was surprised to find so many houses were brick. In Michigan, the furniture industry flourished because of the plentiful supply of wood. At one time, lumber barons stripped the northern part of the state of its trees, flattening out acre after acre, and where they went through nothing came up again but scrub oaks and pines. Now it's changed, the forests have been replanted, and there are beautiful woods, just as there used to be.

Named for the mile-long rapids in the Grand River, Grand Rapids grew out of a trading post founded by a French Canadian named Louis Campau who wanted to barter with the Indians. The year was 1826. By 1836, there was already a cabinet shop in the village. Dutch woodcarvers came to settle, and the thrifty, hard-working Dutch were largely responsible for the stable character of the developing city, in which every factory worker seemed to have his own neat little house with tulips planted out front.

We used to brag that Grand Rapids had more privately owned houses than any other place in America.

I recall our house as being filled with light, probably because I was happy there. Certainly the furniture wasn't light; in that period, they used a lot of heavy oak. Many of my friends' parents had done well in the furniture business; they had couples working for them, and chauffeurs to drive their cars, but I was never made to feel inferior.

I started dancing lessons when I was eight years old. I'd have liked to study the piano, too; but although we were reasonably comfortable, there was just so much money to go around. As it was, I tried to play the piccolo in the school band. That was the instrument they loaned me, and I lasted about two weeks. I think I learned to play "America, the Beautiful," and got bored. I wasn't born to be a piccolo player.

I was a terrible tomboy and the bane of my big brothers' existence. I trailed them around and tried to make them let me play football and ice hockey with the guys, and sometimes they had to babysit me, and I was always interfering in their fights. When they got to rolling on the floor, I'd be trying to pull off the one who was on top. It didn't make any difference which one was on top; I was for the guy on the bottom.

We didn't have a bathroom for every bedroom at 717 Fountain Street—not many people did in those days—and I had to share one with my brothers. For years I darted across the hall in my birthday suit. Finally my mother said I couldn't do it any more. "You've got to start putting something on."

I couldn't understand what she meant. We'd grown up together like puppies, and it didn't make sense to me. "Well," she said, "you never know when the boys are going to have friends over, and they may be coming up the stairs or out of their room, and you don't want to be caught running around bare nekkid."

She put me into a robe, but I thought she was being foolish. My daughter, Susan, having also been brought up with older brothers (we threw them into the bathtub together), has, for better or worse, equally unconventional ideas about what constitutes propriety. "I'd rather have a guy see me naked than in curlers," she says.

My children speak their minds in a way that might have surprised my mother. She was a rather formal woman, and whenever she took me shopping, I had to wear a hat and white gloves. If I said that my friends weren't made to dress this way, Mother pointed out that she had lived in big cities, not only in Chicago and Denver but also in Seattle, and her mores were not necessarily those of Grand Rapids. She'd loved Seattle, even though it had rained there just about every day. "You carried an umbrella, that's all," she would say.

Mother was particular about table manners too. You weren't permitted to butter an entire slice of bread at one time, and if you wanted to eat an apple, you were banished from her hearing. "You sound just like a horse," she would say. "Go into the kitchen or go to your room." Same thing with gum. If you insisted on chewing it, you were asked to go off by yourself.

We tend to think we're more easygoing than our parents, but I was imprinted with some of my mother's prejudices. I could never stand to see anyone chew gum either.

Because he was gone so much, my father came home bearing gifts, trying to make up for his absences, and when I was little he seemed to me to be a cornucopia from which stuffed animals poured. He brought me a teddy bear, which I fastened onto and dragged everywhere. He was just a typical brown teddy bear, but I thought the world of him. In fact, I thought all the stories I read about teddy bears were true; that bear was alive to me.

It's funny, I swore all the time I was growing up that I would never marry a man who traveled, but it must have been in my stars. My first husband traveled and then Jerry ended up being gone from home two hundred days a year throughout much of the time when our kids were growing up. "I love my father, but I didn't know I had a father until I was ten or twelve years old," Susan says. "Everybody was supposed to be home for dinner Sunday night because Daddy always made a point of being home for Sunday-night dinner. Well, it meant nothing to me. Just a man sitting there at the table."

In the play *The Glass Menagerie*, the absent father is characterized as "a telephone man who fell in love with long distances." I've known a few men like that, and they didn't all work for the telephone company.

As a child I did a bit of short-distance traveling myself. The little girls I knew liked to weekend at one another's houses (what kids today call sleepovers). Mary Adelaide Jones and I invented a game we thought was hilarious. We would stand in the shower in her house and stick our bottoms under the hot water, to see who could outlast the other and get her fanny reddest.

Mary Adelaide's mother, whom I called Auntie Flo, was a stunning woman, very strict. I revered her. I guess I liked the discipline. The Joneses' house had a ballroom in which we children weren't permitted. It held a grand piano and a few throw rugs, and the floor was waxed so shiny you could see the electric lights reflected in it. Auntie Flo did not want us walking across that floor with our muddy feet.

Auntie Flo Jones was only one of a vast circle of aunts and uncles who were not really related to me at all. One night, when I was staying over at the Jones house, and Mary Adelaide and I were saying our prayers under her mother's supervision, I was going on and on about God bless Aunt Gussie and Uncle Armand, and God bless Aunt Leona and Uncle Arthur, and God bless this other uncle and that other aunt, when Auntie Flo said in some wonderment, "Betty, where do all these aunts and uncles come from?" "Oh," I said, "my mother gets 'em for me."

My actual family was small. All the grandparents had died before I was born, but I have pictures of them. They look like they were fun. They smile out of photograph albums, the women in skirts down to the floor and high button shoes, the men in bathing suits with sleeves and stripes. I don't know how they ever swam in those things.

We were all demon swimmers up at Whitefish Lake. It was a tight-knit community; most of the people we knew there have held on to their families' cottages, and today they go up with their grandchildren. The members of my generation feel a closeness that comes of our parents' having been friends, and of our having shared long summers when our world was as green as our hopes. Mostly we haven't seen each other for years, but if by chance two of us meet we start right in to chatter as though we'd been together yesterday.

Home from the lake each fall, we'd find, or make, new mischief. On Halloween, instead of trick-or-treating, we'd go on a rampage called "garbage night." We tipped over everybody's garbage pail, whitewashed everybody's porch, soaped everybody's windows. We did things so terrible I would be furious if my children had ever tried them. One Halloween night, my brother

Bob and his friend Bobby Bill Roe waited until the trolley car had stopped to let some people off, and then they ran out and pulled the trolley off the line, breaking the electrical contact. The conductor had to get down out of the car and come and wrestle the thing back into place.

I'm grateful it's different now. You just buy candy and hand it out, or moppets come around with UNICEF boxes, and that's a pleasure. We were really nasty kids.

Fountain Street was regal, with beautiful old houses and huge old trees, and in the fall, after the raking, there would be great piles of leaves to jump in. People were still permitted to burn leaves then, and the smell was gorgeous. Even today, when I think of Grand Rapids, I think of fall and the things that go with fall—the wood smoke, the crunch and smell of the leaves, the pumpkins, and the football games.

When the stock market crashed in 1929, my dad lost a lot of money, and after that my mother said we had to cut back, and she became chief cook and bottle washer.

Still, there were few shadows over my childhood. Even our animals led charmed lives. We had a German shepherd named Teddy, a dog I believed to be brilliant. By the time he was fourteen years old, he was so slow crossing the street we were afraid he was going to get hit by a car; he'd wander out with perfect confidence, like those ancient ladies who hold up one imperious hand to stop the onrushing traffic. So we gave him to friends who lived in the suburbs. Once these friends took a ferryboat across Lake Michigan from Muskegon to Milwaukee, and they dropped Teddy off in a kennel on the Milwaukee side, some sixty miles from the pier, and then continued on a motor trip. When they returned some days later, Teddy was missing. He'd leaped the wall of the kennel. They felt awful, but there was nothing they could do, so they drove back to the ferry, and there was Teddy waiting, his poor feet blistered. He'd traveled the sixty miles on foot. That dog was a genius. Or at least he had a good nose.

All of us in the gang I grew up with went to social-dancing class together. We started, as I mentioned earlier, when we were eight years old. The girls wore white gloves and ankle socks and black patent Mary Jane shoes. (Funny how that never changes. In the seventh grade, for her Junior Assembly, my daughter Susan still wasn't permitted to wear stockings; it was socks, Mary Janes, and white gloves all the way.)

Our dancing teacher was named Calla Travis. Calla was an old woman even then—she lived to be ninety-three—and we were the great-great-grandchildren of her first students. (Considering that I began giving lessons when I was fourteen, I probably could be teaching the great-great-grandchildren of *my* first students. Bill Seidman, one of the advisors my husband brought with him to the White House, was always telling everybody I'd been his dancing teacher, and I could have killed him for it.)

Calla kept us under control with castanets. I can still see her shaking her unnaturally red hair, flashing those clattering castanets, calling boys and girls to order and attention.

Every year she put on a show featuring her pupils. The recital came in the spring, and for the big event Calla took over the stage of the St. Cecilia's Society building. My debut there was not auspicious. A bunch of us were skipping around the stage, sand buckets from the five and dime decorated to look like baskets of flowers in our hands, and I dropped my basket, which went clunk, clunk, clunk, down toward the footlights, while everybody in the audience roared. My mother decided then and there that I was a total flop, and might as well give the whole thing up.

It was after one of Calla's shows that I got my ring from Bud Wilmarth. I was ten years old, and my girlfriends and I were already engaging in romantic rivalries. The big thing was to get a boy to give you an engagement ring. The ring had to come from a good Woolworth's, one that carried the finest ten-cent jewelry, and it had to have something that looked like a diamond in it. A lot of girls were after Bud Wilmarth, but it was I he promised the diamond ring. He said he would bring it to the recital at St. Cecilia's. We dressed in the rest rooms—there were mobs of children to be costumed—and then you had to walk through a tunnel to get to the stage. That tunnel, black as a coal bin, was where I elected to wait for Bud after the recital, I guess so that nobody would see if he stood me up. Outside, my poor mother was sitting in the car, wondering what was keeping me, but I had no intention of leaving until Bud showed up with the ring.

When I was in fifth grade at the Fountain Street Elementary School, I got my first kiss from a boy. We were taken on a class picnic, a bunch of us piled onto the back seat of a car, and John Sears got me under a blanket and I felt a peck on my cheek. I was stunned. I thought, Oh my heavens, this is really big stuff.

At twelve, I went to my first dance with a boy. He was a friend of my brothers, and as it turned out, I married him when I was twenty-four. Those were the days of the big bands touring the country. Wayne King had come to Grand Rapids, and I was thrilled to be asked to go. I think my mother permitted it only because my brothers were also going, and she felt they would be keeping an eye on her baby. Little did she know that all they wanted to do was lose me.

I wore my first long dress, pink net with little rosebuds on it, and a full, scalloped, tiered skirt. It wasn't nearly sophisticated enough to suit me; I wanted one of those that were slit to the waist in the back. But my mother was firm: either the pink number or nothing, take it or leave it. I took it.

When you say you've had a sunny childhood, the assumption is that you're smart enough to know you've been lucky. I did know it. But, for even the most fortunate, there are intimations of mortality. A friend just my age died when we were both so small the grownups wouldn't tell me what she died of. That frightened me. And my mother was president of the Mary Free Bed Home for Crippled Children—run by a group of ladies who raised funds to support it—and I would go there with her and see babies who'd had polio, or who were in casts for some other reason. By the time I was a teenager I found I could entertain them. We'd bring all of them into one big room, and I'd work with a record player and beat out rhythms. If the children's legs were in casts, but their arms were free, they would clap. If their arms were crippled, sometimes they could tap their feet. Denied normal movement, they exulted in whatever movement was possible. I would dress up in a leotard and long skirt and try to make the whole event festive and dramatic, and the children would work very hard and laugh very freely.

I was one of the fortunate people who slip into adolescence easily, turning from tomboy to girl without paying any particular price. Teddy the bear and Teddy the dog had been the cherished companions of my childhood, but as I came into my teens, I was looking around, figuratively speaking, for Teddy the boy. And, even more fervently, I was looking ahead to a career as a very important dancer. I had aspirations, but I wasn't smart enough to have fears.

3

THE GOOD CHEERS

Fourteen was a watershed year for me. For one thing, my mother stopped making my clothes. Up until then, I had been able to think of nothing that would be more fun than to have a store-bought dress. Store-bought dresses weren't as nice as what my mother made me, but when you're brought up by a fine seamstress, you don't appreciate handwork. I barely got through sewing class in school. (It was a required subject in the seventh grade. The boys had to take shop and the girls had to take cooking and sewing. Miss Gillette didn't think much of my seams, and I certainly didn't care.) It skips a generation. Susan sews beautifully.

When I was fourteen, I chose to be confirmed an Episcopalian. I'd been christened, but not confirmed. My father was a Christian Scientist, my mother an Episcopalian, and I liked the Episcopal services. I also had a couple of friends whose father was dean of the church, but that didn't affect my decision; those girls were devils. Like sewing, piety seems to skip a generation; I wonder if my grandchildren (Mike's as yet unborn babies) will be hellions just to pay their daddy back for being a minister.

I was one of those goody-goodies who liked school, and Central High was one of the best schools in Grand Rapids. I knew very few students who went away to boarding school; from Central, you could get into almost any college without taking college boards. I particularly admired my Latin teacher, who was stern (again, my liking for discipline), and I was fond of my French teacher and also the guy who taught math and coached the Central High football team.

Every afternoon, right after school, I went to dancing class. Because I'd loved the social-dancing classes, I'd persuaded my mother to send me to Calla's studio for other kinds of instruction. Calla offered a complete program—Spanish dancing, ballet, tap, acrobatic—with excellent teachers, and I signed up for everything. I adored it all.

I dreamed of going to New York to ballet school until I encountered modern dance. I think Calla herself had first heard of the Dalcroze System of modern dance during a visit to the University of Wisconsin, which was one of the few colleges that taught it. I immersed myself in books about Mary Wigman in Germany, and Ruth St. Denis and the Denishawn dancers. I loved the freedom of movement they preached. In ballet, each *jeté*, each arabesque, was totally prescribed, and I was probably the worst ballet dancer who ever came down the road. I couldn't get my knees straight enough. When I had to do a solo ballet number—you couldn't complete Calla's courses and become a full-fledged teacher until you did a solo ballet number—I wisely designed my own costume. Instead of a tutu, I wore a thing with scarves hanging down and covering my knees so you couldn't see whether they were bent or straight. I got out there and pirouetted to the "Waltz of the Flowers," and presto, I was a professional.

There was no kind of dance that didn't fascinate me. I'd hear about some boy who'd been out West among the Indians and learned a rain dance, and I'd go to him and make him teach it to me. I was insatiable.

Last year I heard Beverly Sills on a television show. "I don't sing because it's my career," she said. "I sing because it's my happiness."

Dance was my happiness.

The year I turned fourteen, the Depression was in full swing, and from then on I worked at various jobs, trying to contribute to my upkeep. Saturdays, at lunchtime, I made three dollars working as a teen-age model at Herpolsheimer's Department Store. I would wander through Herpolsheimer's tearoom wearing an outfit from stock, and ladies at the tables would stop me—"Just one moment, dear, let's look at that"—and I would say, "Twenty-five ninety-five, third-floor sportswear." I'd leave my paychecks with the cashier for a month or so, and by the time I went to collect there would be enough to amount to something.

Saturday afternoons I gave dancing lessons. Having gone into the business of teaching social dancing to tykes, I naturally had to charge less than Calla, the master. Calla got a dollar, so I think I charged fifty cents. Our house didn't have a room large enough for classes, and I rented Auntie Flo Jones's basement. Her ballroom was still out of the question—she wouldn't permit all those Mary Janes on her satin-finished floors—but the recreation room was okay.

She took a dollar from me for the use of the hall. "It isn't the money," she said, "but if you're going into business, you have to start right, and understand how businesses are run." I paid Wally Hook a dollar too. He was a good piano player. And, once in a while, Walt Jones, Mary Adelaide's brother, would sit in and blow his saxophone or bang his drums. On those days, we felt we had a really classy band. My pupils learned the foxtrot, the waltz, and the Big Apple.

In Central High, we all belonged to fraternities and sororities and had to go through the pledge business of being scuts. If an older member told you to crack yourself like an egg and scramble, you had to knock your head on the edge of a chair and get down on the floor and flail about. Two weeks of this; it was the snipe hunt all over again.

My sorority was Gamma Delta Tau, but we were called The Good Cheers. When I told Sis Hall (now Mrs. Benjamin Fisher) that I was going to write a book, she offered me only one piece of advice: "Don't forget The Good Cheers," she said. Nowadays, sororities and fraternities aren't too highly regarded, unless they have a purpose like debating clubs or French clubs. I think schools are trying to get away from pupils' feeling—and being—excluded, and maybe that's a better way, but the societies were big in my day.

When my brothers' friends began looking at me with calf eyes, asking if they could take me to the movies—again, I date this pretty much from my fourteenth year, despite a couple of previous long-dress parties—my brothers were put out. Why, instead of pole vaulting, or playing tennis, were these heretofore perfectly sensible guys suddenly mooning over dopey Betty Bloomer?

I loved it. And I was bad. I would set my cap for somebody and work at it until I got his fraternity pin. As soon as I'd got it, I was satisfied, and I moved on to the next victim. I was scrupulous about giving the last fellow's pin back, that's the only good thing I can say for myself.

Sometimes there was a boy who wasn't interested, and that annoyed me. I had crushes on boys I couldn't get dates with. I actually fought with another girl over a boy named Dick May. Dick May just didn't care. Once he did something to me that his father considered rude, and Dick was made to ride his bicycle up to our house and bring me a box of candy. That didn't help our relationship either.

Bud Wilmarth, who'd given me the diamond engagement ring, was sent away to Howe Military School, and when he came home on holidays, his family would throw parties. The whole crowd from Calla's ballroom class would go, and we'd be so impressed with Bud in his uniform and his brass buttons. We'd dance in the dark—the lights were turned out, but you didn't stay with one partner all evening, you kept changing partners—and you could always tell when you were dancing with Bud; you could feel those brass buttons against your chest.

The boys of my youth.

Bud Wilmarth.

Walt Jones.

Jack Stiles, who went to a different high school and had a

beautiful silver car, and who would sometimes come by Central and pick me up and drive me home.

Monty Welch, who was a prankster. He took me to a birthday party where the ice cream was frozen very hard, and he was so determined to conquer it he cut through the ice cream and kept right on going through the china plate. Everybody else thought it was funny, but I was completely mortified.

Louis De Lamarter, whom I dated but who—thank the Lord—hadn't invited me to go with him when he went down to the Majestic Theatre where they were showing a Boris Karloff movie and took a duck or a goose in under his coat. Just as Boris Karloff was climbing out of a well, his great dripping hands looming up out of the darkness, Louis let go with this duck or goose or whatever it was off the balcony of the theatre, and it fluttered down and landed on a woman, who practically had a heart attack. Louis had to go to court. Somehow he managed to get off with a reprimand.

We girls didn't have steadies—I wouldn't have gone steady for the world, looking forward as I was to my big career in New York—and mostly we double-dated. The truth is you were glad if your date was driving because then you didn't have to rassle in the back seat with a boy who had more hands than you could control, when you weren't in the mood for going six rounds.

We did play kissing games (I played Spin the Bottle, and my children after me played Spin the Bottle) and we listened to the radio (there wasn't any television, of course) and kept notebooks in which we wrote down the words to popular songs like "Smoke Gets in Your Eyes." Just about every weekend a name band would come to town—they traveled from school to school—and we'd go to the dances and sigh over the vocalists. There was one fellow with Fred Waring who had a divine voice.

Once in a while, the De Lamarter family took me to Ann Arbor to a football game, and since my father worked out of Chicago, where the Royal Rubber Company had its main office, I sometimes got over there to see a dance performance in a theatre.

We had lots of snow in Grand Rapids, which is just a bit south of the snow belt, and I was used to ice skating and tobogganing.

We'd hold toboggan parties at the country club on nights when the hills were covered with crunchy powder. We'd go out in the moonlight, build jumps, then pile maybe six people onto one of those long flat sleds with their runners curling up in front. The more people who got on, the faster it went, and we'd go whizzing over these jumps, half the time flying off and landing in a drift. It was very exciting, and afterward we'd go in and sit by the fire and drink hot chocolate.

I've said I had a sunny childhood. I also had a wonderful girlhood. Then, the year I was sixteen, my father died of carbon monoxide poisoning. He had gone out to the garage to work on the car; it was a summer day, very overcast, very humid. The garage doors were open, he had the engine running, and he'd got under the car to fiddle with something.

A couple of friends from Detroit had stopped by the house to visit and Mother went out to the garage to get Dad to come in, and she found him. The ignition was on, but the motor wasn't running any more. The car must have run out of gas, and the air was so heavy.

They called an ambulance and took him to the hospital, but it was too late.

I'd been out with Ev Thompson, a girlfriend who had her own convertible, and we came wheeling up to my front door with the top down on this hot, hot day. Ev was honking the horn and we were waving and yelling and showing off the way sixteen-year-olds do, and my cousin Shine, who was the same age as my brother Bob, came racing down the front walk to the car and said, "Shh, just calm down." And I said, "Why? What's wrong? What's happened?"

"Well," Shine said, "they had to take your father to the hospital."

She didn't tell me he was dead. Maybe she didn't know.

4

BENNINGTON

It was rougher for everybody after that. Because he was gone, and we'd loved him. And afterward, because the Depression was still on. There was insurance, so Mother didn't have to work—although she sold real estate for a while—but we'd all been pitching in to help ourselves anyway. (Until I started giving dancing lessons, I'd been paid an allowance of twenty-five cents a week, and I knew I wasn't going to get to New York on that.)

My brother Bill, who was already twenty-three, enrolled in the General Motors School of Technology, and two years afterward, in 1936, I was graduated from Central High.

Forty years later, I went back and spoke to another graduating class, which was so big that the ceremonies had to be held at the Civic Auditorium. The school had changed since 1936; the central city had become predominantly black.

I tried to put myself in those kids' shoes, not to talk down to them, but to talk with them. I didn't know how many were going on to college, how many would be entering trade schools, but after acknowledging the gulf between their ages and mine, their experiences and mine, I still felt that more things bound us together than

separated us. Because kids, unless they've been brutalized, are
eternally optimistic, and I remembered very well the optimism of
my own senior year. And my junior year. And every year since I'd
turned eight and started thinking about being a dancer.

I hadn't got too far with my mother when I'd talked about
New York. "You can't go until you're twenty years old," she'd said.

It wouldn't have done me any good to fuss, and I wasn't the
kind to run away; the bond between my mother and me was strong.
We struck a compromise. For two summers, the years I was
eighteen and nineteen, I went off to Vermont, to the Bennington
School of Dance, which held its classes at Bennington College.

The township of Bennington sits in the southwest corner of the
state, between the Taconics and the Green Mountains. There are
deer in the woods and trout in the streams, and toward autumn the
trees begin to burn with color; the leaves of the silver birches turn
yellow, the crowns of the maples are already dappled with yellow
and crimson.

But the gorgeousness of nature was secondary to the gorgeousness of my life, to the ecstasy of being able to dance eight hours a
day. I was exposed to Louis Horst and Martha Graham. Doris
Humphrey and Charles Weidman were there, dancing together,
and José Limón and Anna Sokolow were there, and Hanya Holm. I
studied with every one of them. All day long I took classes, and at
night I danced more, rehearsing with the Anna Sokolow group.
Anna was a young choreographer, and she'd chosen a bunch of us to
teach her new routines to.

That first summer, after some of those strenuous days, Natalie
Harris (she still calls me Skipper, because when we were at
Bennington I always wore a yachting cap) and I discovered we
could walk up the stairs to dinner but we couldn't walk down again.
Our thigh muscles had knotted up, our knees wouldn't flex, and the
pain was so bad we had to sit on our tails on a landing and slide
down, step by step, jarring ourselves as little as possible.

I was more stuffy than some of the girls I'd grown up with, and
I didn't drink and I didn't smoke. Since sixteen I'd been asking dates
to light cigarettes for me so I could hold them and look as though I

were smoking, yet I wouldn't have dared to take a drag on one. I don't know whom I thought I was fooling, waving those cigarettes around like a demented teen-age Bette Davis. Same with liquor. If anyone handed me a drink at a fraternity house, I'd switch with my date, take his empty glass. Or, if I didn't think that was going to work because I didn't want him plastered, I'd just pour my libation into the nearest potted plant. Better a potted plant than a potted escort.

But when I was at Bennington four of us went into town one night—all girls—and we had a few beers and came back to the campus giddy. We were doing leaps and bounds all over the green, and finally one girl said we'd better all go take cold showers, and the others agreed. That was a big event, my first fling.

It's almost impossible to describe the impression made by Martha Graham on a girl who came to her straight out of high school. I worshiped her as a goddess. She was a tough disciplinarian; believe me, if you got her knee in your back when you weren't sitting up straight enough during an exercise, you never forgot it. But, as I've said before, I admired that kind of strictness. You can't be a dancer without it; not only your body but your mind must be disciplined.

It's forty years since I first set eyes on Martha, and she was in her forties then. Her body was such a beautiful instrument, and she used it with such strength. When she did an extension, she'd be up on the ball of one foot, and the other leg would be straight up behind her head, I swear. Small though she was, she could wear sweeping skirts, great circles of skirts, which fit close to her hips and then spread out. She wore her hair down, long, flowing, and she brought into a room a presence that was riveting. To this day, I feel that shiver of awe and delight when she comes on the scene.

A couple of years ago, a friend sent me an old quarterly from Bennington—by that time, I was in the White House—and in this magazine was a picture of a teacher named Martha Hill, surrounded by a group of girls sitting on the floor watching one of their number perform. The picture was captioned "Martha Hill with Students." I glanced at it, glanced away, then did a comedy double take. The student in the middle, big as life, standing with arms outstretched and a deadly serious expression on her face, was Elizabeth Ann Bloomer. I passed the magazine to my secretary. "You know who that is?" She studied it for a minute. "My God," she said, "it's you."

Martha Hill gave me some of the toughest assignments of my life. "Okay, tomorrow I want you to come back with a pavane," she'd say, and I wouldn't know what a pavane was, I'd have to look it up before I could come back with it. As for dance notation, I could not learn it; it's ghastly hard. I could write my instructions out in words—"take a quarter step forward"—or I could draw little stick figures in various attitudes, but that's not dance notation. Dance notation is like music, with lines on the paper, and you put your little notes on these lines, and the notes are supposed to tell you whether the person is in a lined-up position or a prone position or has his or her leg extended—oh, it was terrible stuff for a booby who wanted only to soar, and who didn't care a fig for recording how she'd done it.

After the first summer in Vermont, I went back home and got busy doing all sorts of things. I was biding my time. I joined the Junior League, because they were always putting on Follies to raise money for charity and they needed a good dancer. I did some modeling. I did some teaching, not just in Auntie Flo's recreation room, but also at the YWCA. Weekends there were dances at the country club and football games at Ann Arbor; lots of the boys I went around with were still in college there, so I was no stranger to Ann Arbor. (Shortly before Christmas of 1976, I was made an honorary lawyer by the University of Michigan, and in my acceptance speech I told everybody I deserved the distinction. "I never attended classes," I said, "but I put in my hours. I spent enough time here to get a degree.")

My second summer at Bennington I had prepared myself. I was in better condition for the rigors of the training, and I knew by then that Martha Graham was the person with whom I wanted to cast my lot.

But I didn't ask her until I was back on my home ground the

next fall. She was giving a concert in Ann Arbor, and I went. What Martha was doing was so completely new that I don't think a lot of people understood it. I think they wondered what in the world they'd seen, the way some people come away from an avant-garde play and wonder what in the world that play was about. (In 1934, a Vermont newspaper ran a headline saying, "Bennington Campus Seethes with Women Who Jump in Odd Fashion," and when Martha and her troupe—all women, until 1938—appeared in Billings, Montana, they were referred to as the Graham Crackers.)

But for me modern dancing was exhilarating, it was release, it was the freedom to be able to express myself through my body. That night in Ann Arbor, I ran around backstage, grabbed Martha's hand, and blurted out, "If I come to New York, can I be at your school?"

Half amused and, I suppose, somewhat pleased, she said yes.

5

NEW YORK

My mother drove me East. We stopped and saw Niagara Falls, because it was one of the seven wonders of the world, and we spent the night there. Next morning, we went on to New York.

Natalie Harris, my roommate at Bennington, and I got along well, and we'd decided to take an apartment together when we came to the city. Nat's family lived an hour and a half away, in New Haven, so she'd already been down looking around. She'd found a neat place in Greenwich Village—a walkup in a house in an alley—but my mother took one look and said no. "I'm sorry, girls, you cannot live here. It's just too dangerous."

Even in those days, the Village had a healthy reputation for colorful goings-on, and my mother started talking about the Barbizon Hotel for Women. The Barbizon was a fine place, but it didn't appeal to Natalie or me. Martha Graham's studio was on Fifth Avenue, down near Washington Square. "We don't want to go way uptown," I said. My mother stuck around until she saw us settled in a one-bedroom apartment in a big building with an elevator. It was on Sixth Avenue, near the old Chelsea neighborhood, and Nat and I were within walking distance of Martha's studio.

In 1938, Erick Hawkins was the first—and only—male dancer to be working with Martha's troupe, and that pleased my mother too, because she was very suspicious of New York men. She told me all kinds of stories about what could happen to me if I wasn't careful. (Sort of like Lily Tomlin's mother explaining to Lily that "only tramps have pierced ears.")

It must sound strange to modern young people to think that a woman of twenty should listen so dutifully to her mother, but my mother was loving and supportive, and I didn't resent her advice. On the other hand, I wasn't afraid. Not of anything. I was quick, I was intelligent—when you have two older brothers you have to be quick and intelligent—and I was strong-willed. I wasn't going to let anyone walk over me. I believed I had my place in this world just the same as anyone else, and my place at that time seemed to me to be New York City.

In order to make a living, I worked days and took my dance classes at night. Even when a girl got good enough to appear with the Graham troupe, Martha could only afford to pay her ten dollars a concert, so most of the dancers had to find other ways to feed themselves.

My mother helped, since I couldn't entirely manage alone, and I remember the first day I went to look for a job. I got dressed fit to kill. I wore my best gown and a silver fox cape, and I started out to make the rounds of the modeling agencies. It must have been priceless. You could tell I was straight from the sticks.

But you learn fast in New York. By the time I went to see John Robert Powers, who was important in the modeling world of the thirties, I was wearing a tailored brown Chesterfield coat with a brown velvet collar and a large-brimmed brown felt hat pulled down over one eye and flipped up on the other side. It was a good-looking hat. There was a crowd of girls in Powers's outer office waiting for the great man, and he came out and walked around the room and looked at everybody. And he stopped in front of me and said, "Come into my office."

In trepidation I followed him. We both sat down, but only he talked. He said I would have to get pictures made, carry a portfolio. "Stand up," he said. "I want to see how tall you are."

I stood up.

"Okay," he said, "now pull your dress up. I want to see your legs."

I pulled my dress up about two inches.

"I don't mean your knees," he said. "I want to see your legs."

My desire to work was warring with my mother's warnings. I phumphed around for a couple of seconds, then yanked my dress above my knees and glared at Mr. P., a good-looking man who was trying hard not to laugh out loud.

"Well," he said, "they're pretty heavy, but I guess they'll do."

And that was how I came to be registered with John Robert Powers. Through him, I got a few photographic assignments, but nothing very exciting. I had better luck on Seventh Avenue. I wore hats well so I did some millinery modeling, and I did some modeling in fur houses, and I got a steady job at a dress house called Sacony. That was a break. Sacony made dresses, bathing suits, sportswear, and I had a chance not just to work in the showroom, but to do an occasional fashion show.

Everything you model requires a particular adjustment, but I caught on quickly, and the dance training helped. I could glide across the floor without too much wiggling and waggling, and in those days you didn't have to be as tall as the girls are now.

I enjoyed Seventh Avenue, maybe because I love clothes. (Anyone who sees my closets knows I love clothes. In the new house in Palm Springs, I asked for one whole room to be built on, and that room is nothing but a closet, with spaces for my shoes and pocketbooks and sweaters and blouses so I'll never again have to move my winter wardrobe to the attic.) I also enjoyed eating in those good kosher restaurants near the office. I used to take the subway to the job, marveling, as generations of girls have done, at the New York experience—the subway, the Automat, the first apartment away from home. Nat and I split the rent, lived frugally, and welcomed any hometown boys who showed up at our door.

Some of the boys I knew were going to Harvard and Princeton, and on weekends they'd come to New York and phone me, and of course I was happy to go out for dinner and dancing. It was a treat, something I couldn't afford to do on my own. Once John Sears—the boy who'd given me my first kiss—materialized, and we went dancing at a hotel that had a band (I don't remember which one; I didn't expect to have to put it down for posterity) and a man came up to me and gave me his card. He said he wanted to screen test me.

I was flattered, and took the card. Later on, after my head had cleared of wine and cigarette smoke and pipe dreams, I thought, Elizabeth, you don't want to go in the movies. And, what's more, that guy may be handing you a big bunch of baloney. I'd heard about schemes where men lured a girl on, and then, having caught her, suggested less respectable activities. From my mother, for openers.

In the euphoria of the talent scout's first attentions, I'd given him my name and Sacony's phone number, whispering it over John Sears's shoulder on the dance floor, and for a week after that he kept calling me at work. Finally I made a date to meet him at a place called the Circus Bar, and I got a friend—a tall, good-looking redheaded girl—to go in my place. Movies weren't my game. Dancing was.

At least I believed that at the time. Even so, some weeks my social life got in the way of my dancing, and Martha and I had talks about it. "You can't carouse and be a dancer too," she said. I wanted to have my cake and eat it, but Martha, who'd lived a long time on "a crust of bread and liberty," wasn't sympathetic to cake eaters. She said I had ability, a nice animal-like movement that was appealing, and that I could have a future, but I would have to give up everything else.

For me that was hard. I enjoyed seeing friends, having dates, and if you're really committed to dancing, there's no time for friends and dates. Dance is your religion. I guess I was somewhat deficient in the dedication department.

I remember that first Thanksgiving in New York. Nat had gone home to New Haven—I don't know why I didn't go with her—and I'd never been alone on Thanksgiving before. I was miserable. Down on the street below our living-room window, an organ grinder was wheezing away at "Come Back to Sorrento," while his monkey scampered around with a tin cup, and the sight and sound were so mournful I wrapped thirty-five cents in a piece of paper and threw it down to them.

Later on, a boy phoned and asked me if I wanted to come to Brooklyn and have dinner with his family, so the day was saved. I'd gone out with this boy before, a good-looking blond who worked at a hotel in the city, but in Brooklyn any visions I might have had of a possible flirtation faded. He was an only child, and he was Momma's boy.

Momma's boy and nobody's girl. I was feeling a little lost, and more than a little homesick.

Next year was better. I didn't socialize so much, I settled down to my classes. I began to think maybe I was ready to make whatever sacrifices it would take to be a concert dancer, the obsession of my late teens seemed to have returned.

But I didn't make it into Martha's main group. Nat Harris did; I didn't. Still, I was chosen for the auxiliary group, and while we didn't go on the road when Martha traveled—she never could afford to take all her people with her—the auxiliary dancers did appear whenever the Graham troupe played a New York concert. I remember my first time as a member of the ensemble at Carnegie Hall. Martha danced "American Document," and she filled the place. I thought I had arrived.

But the person who'd really arrived was my mother. She came to New York, stayed for two weeks, and got scared. She'd never expected me to get so deeply engrossed in this career. The whole time she was with me, she talked about what was going on at home, who was getting married, who'd given which parties. She tried to make me wish I was back there in Grand Rapids having a good time with my friends. It went right in one ear and out the other. Wisely, she gave up. Even more wisely, she offered me a deal. "I can see I've made no impression on you," she said, "but if you'll come home for six months, just to humor me, and at the end of that six months you find you still want to come back here and go on with your dancing, I will never say another word against it."

If I'd been a genius, I couldn't have been swayed, but I wasn't a genius. I never thought I could be as great a dancer as Martha

Graham, and yet I felt that if I had put my mind to it, paid the price it would have cost, I could have made it. I had confidence. Whether or not my confidence was justified is another question.

I couldn't turn my mother down. I went to Martha, and it was awful. I felt I had to tell her personally. I was sure I'd be back, yet when I said I was going home for six months, I felt sick. Martha took it calmly. She had seen many girls come and go. "I think it's a wise thing for you to do," she said.

Reporters are forever asking Martha Graham what she remembers about me. She always says, "She had a very straight back."

In the play *The Cocktail Party*, T. S. Eliot contrasts the life of ordinary joys and sorrows of people who marry and have children with the life of vocation. About those who choose the first road, he says,

> They may remember
> The vision they have had, but they cease to regret it.

About the other road, he says,

> It is a terrifying journey.
> Neither way is better.
> Both ways are necessary. It is also necessary
> To make a choice between them.

I never dreamed, when I went back to Grand Rapids with my mother, that I had made my choice.

6

BACK HOME

Briefly, I was the Martha Graham of Grand Rapids. I started my own dance group, I choreographed for it, and my friend and former teacher Kay Clark credits me with introducing religious dance to the city.

Well, my company did perform something called "Three Parables" on the wide cement steps leading up to the altar in the Fountain Street Baptist Church. We used a voice choir and three very strange instruments, old instruments that were hollow sounding and shrill, filling in the places where the voice choir stopped to catch its breath.

We were all deadly serious, despite some pretty funny accidents, like the one where a member of the group arched back and stuck her finger straight up another dancer's nose.

Calla Travis hired me to teach modern dance at her school, and without my noticing it the six months my mother had asked for passed. I was enjoying not only my work but the freedom to go out with lots of boys and not feel guilty about it. My mother got my brother Bill to invite me up to Petoskey, Michigan, where he and his wife (also named Betty) were living, and they introduced me to a lawyer. By the time I came back to Grand Rapids, I'd met the lawyer's family, and we considered ourselves engaged. Not officially, exactly, but he'd bought a ring, and I'd accepted it.

Then he showed up in Grand Rapids. Whoops! He was a very sober fellow, and we went out with a group of my wild friends, and when we got home at about 4 A.M., we had a brief conversation.

"I won't talk to you now," he said. "I'll talk to you in the morning." His tone was just like the tone of the Ralph Bellamy character who always tried to get the heroine to come to her senses and not go back to Cary Grant in a thirties movie.

"That's all right," I said. "You don't have to talk to me. Here's your ring."

I knew he was going to tell me I had to change my ways, and I couldn't see settling down to the kind of existence that suited him. I didn't think his mother liked me anyway.

It was embarrassing. That lawyer was a very good friend of my brother's, but I realized I'd become engaged to him only because I didn't know what else to do. My friends were getting married, and I thought I ought to get married too. Bad reason. And Mother was no help. One minute she'd say she didn't think I should get married, the next minute she'd be wondering when I was going to get married. Fortunately, for him and me both, I came to my senses before we went through a ceremony.

Speaking of marriage, another interesting thing had happened while I'd been in New York. My mother had fallen in love. She was darling, like a sixteen-year-old girl with her first beau. She had been single for five years, and pretty much alone. My brothers had gone first, then I'd left to study with Martha. Now Mother would once again have someone on whom to lavish her considerable energies and affection.

Arthur Meigs Godwin. He had his own house right down the street, in the next block from ours. To me, he'd been Uncle Art, and his wife had been Aunt Leona—some of my mother's friends that she'd got me for relatives. A banker who'd retired when he was forty-five years old, Arthur Godwin was an omnivorous reader and a compulsive traveler. He and Aunt Leona had been driving in Mexico when their car went over a cliff and she was killed. He lay in a gully practically dead himself, and a Mexican farmer found him and took him home. The people there sewed him up as best they could with some kind of animal gut, and one man set out on foot for the nearest village to get help. Uncle Art was in Mexico a long time before they were able to move him, alive because of the kindness of strangers.

When he was finally brought back to Grand Rapids, my mother and father took me to visit. I was still a small child and I remember my mother saying, "Now don't touch the bed because he's in a great deal of pain, and we mustn't do anything to jar him."

After he got better and was able to go out, my father used to drive him to the hospital once a week for his therapy treatments.

I loved Arthur Godwin, and now I was so happy he and my mother were going to be married that I asked if I could call him Dad. He said he'd be delighted. He'd never had any children. As for Mother, the thrill of this new romance rendered her reckless. So far as our house was concerned, she couldn't have cared less. We'd lived in it for twenty years, but when she left on her wedding trip— it took a whole year, they went around the world—she told me to get rid of the place and everything in it.

I was marooned with all this stuff, and I didn't know what to do. I can remember hurling things out the attic windows into the backyard for the Salvation Army to pick up. All I wanted was to get the job done. I had no conception of the worth of antiques, the salad bowls, the creamers and sugars I'd been using all my life; they were just pieces of glass as far as I was concerned. I sold off that heavy cut crystal that had been on the table every day, and now I kick myself that we don't have it.

After the house was sold, I took an apartment. It had a bedroom, a kitchen, a living room with a pull-down bed so someone could stay over, and I had a maid who came in once a week. I still wasn't much of a cook. I knew how to bake a cake, but the only main dish I ever attempted was pork chops. I took pork chops, put them in a pan and browned them, then put some onion slices in with them and poured a large can of tomatoes over the whole thing. It was really very good.

(When I got married for the first time, those pork chops, and hamburgers, were my entire repertoire.)

I found a job at Herpolsheimer's again, this time as assistant to the fashion coordinator. I trained models to show clothes, and nights I taught dance classes. It was the time of the craze for the conga, the first South American dance to make it big in the United States. Everybody wanted to learn the conga. Husbands came with their wives, and we all lined up and kicked in one room of an old mansion that a brother and sister I knew had turned into a theatre workshop.

I got by with a little help from my friends, as always. Often I was wined and dined by the local bachelors, among them Bill Warren. He was the same Bill Warren with whom I'd gone to my first dance the year I was twelve. Bill was in the insurance business with his father. He was blond with curly hair, he was a good dancer, a good tennis player, he liked a good time, and unlike some of the men I dated, he wasn't a bit stuffy. (Bill had never been stuffy, and he wasn't always a dependable date. Once, when I was in high school, I'd gone to a dance with him, and he'd left me in the lurch while he stepped out with some boys to have a beer. I was furious. As soon as he came back, I slapped his face. "You're not a gentleman," I said. "Don't ever bother to call me again." That was my mother's training. Lots of boys went out in the parking lot and tippled, but not when they were with me.)

When my mother and stepfather got back from their wedding trip, I gave up my apartment, stored my furniture, and moved into their house at 636 Fountain Street. It was a darling house, with a bedroom downstairs where my mother and my stepfather slept, and a dining room with gorgeous hand-screened wallpaper, and specially woven rugs that fitted neatly around the hearthstones of the fireplaces; up on the second floor there were two bedrooms and a sewing room.

My mother and my stepfather were not enthusiastic about Bill Warren, which made him all the more alluring to me. Much as I adored my folks, I was always testing my judgment against theirs. Sometimes I was wrong, sometimes they were wrong. For instance, one night a week I worked in a school in an all-black district. Grand Rapids had the same kind of de facto segregation you find in many cities, and at that time there just weren't any black dance teachers in that district. I was performing a community service for children who were talented and enthusiastic, but my stepfather, a generous-natured man, was in this one area narrow-minded. Tuesday nights it was always very quiet at the dinner table because Dad knew I was going off to teach at the black school.

Where Bill Warren was concerned, I was sneakier. I would lie about our dates. (I was of age, of course, and parental requests were not binding, but I was also living under my mother's and stepfather's roof, and had no wish for confrontation.) I'd say I was going dancing, or to the movies, my mother would say, "With whom?" and I'd say, "Oh, John Locke." "That's nice," she'd say. Then John Locke would come to pick me up, he and I would go out the front door and climb into a car, and there would be Bill waiting for me.

By 1942 the whole world was changing. At General Motors, where my brother Bill worked, they were turning out tanks and jeeps, and half the boys I knew were in uniform, my brother Bob among them. He enlisted in the Seabees, and got right into the middle of the action in the Philippines. We used to get those little V-mail letters, with words and phrases blacked out so you couldn't tell where they came from, and we fell on them with avidity and a relief which was never spoken. Everywhere you went in Grand Rapids, the war had touched people. The butcher's son was overseas too; the butcher and my mother exchanged commiseration.

Bill Warren had diabetes and he wouldn't be going off to service. We finally decided to face my family and tell them we were serious about each other, as serious as either one of us got in those days. I brought Bill home, said, "We're going to get married," and waited for the blowup.

There wasn't any. Mother and Dad never said another word against him. As for his family, they were pleased. They thought I'd be a good influence on their lightfoot lad.

We were married out of my stepfather's house, in the spring. I was twenty-four years old, and I wanted a garden wedding. The minister of St. Mark's wouldn't marry me except in church, so I found a Presbyterian minister who was willing to perform an Episcopal service.

We exchanged vows in the living room and then went through the French doors into the garden for the reception.

A while ago somebody asked me what was in bloom.

"I was," I said.

7

THE FIVE-YEAR
MISUNDERSTANDING

My family gave us a week at Lake Michigan for our honeymoon. It was early, before the real vacation season started, and we stayed in a cottage and I had to do the cooking. No, we didn't have pork chops three times a day; sometimes we had eggs.

Then we moved to Maumee, Ohio, a suburb of Toledo. Bill wasn't working for his father any more; he'd taken a job with an insurance company in Maumee. We rented an apartment, in a house right on the river, from a schoolteacher who lived upstairs. I managed to get a job down in Toledo in a big department store, and I also taught dance at the university. I didn't have the required college degree, but Martha Graham wrote a letter for me, and that did the trick.

Dozens of rabbits hopped around the house in Maumee, and once I cranked a window open, took aim, and shot our dinner with a 20-gauge shotgun. I'm sure it was illegal. I didn't do the cleaning and skinning; I left that to Bill. I couldn't shoot a rabbit now.

We moved around, pillar to post. That was the story of the marriage. Bill decided he didn't want to be in the insurance business any more, and we went home to Grand Rapids and stayed with his family until he found another job.

Our next move was to a suburb of Syracuse, New York, where Bill went to work for the Continental Can Company. The company flew him East, and I followed on the train. The trains were crowded with soldiers being moved across the country; I sat on my suitcase in an aisle until a salesman offered me his seat. When I found out what went with his seat—namely him—I went back to my suitcase.

In the town near Syracuse, we rented an apartment full of cheap maple furniture, and I got myself onto a production line in a frozen-food factory. During the war, factories needed any help they could get; you could work as many hours a day or days a week as you wanted to. I spent four-hour shifts sorting peas, spinach, different vegetables, putting them in boxes, closing the boxes, placing the boxes on a conveyor belt and sending them off to be sealed. One time, picking over spinach, I found a worm. You had to go through the stuff and throw any bad leaves on the floor, and in order to make it limp enough so it could be packed the spinach had been dunked in a quick bath of boiling water. That worm had been partially cooked. I still eat spinach, but from that day to this I approach it very carefully.

We liked New York State. One night we were walking around and we spotted a sign in the window of a wonderful old house, but we couldn't make out the printing in the dark. "Maybe it's for rent," Bill said, and we crept closer.

When we got to the porch, we burst out laughing. The sign had been lettered by a very proud Girl Scout, junior grade. A BROWNIE LIVES HERE, it proclaimed.

Bill's job with Continental Can didn't pan out, and we went back to Grand Rapids, where he was hired by the Widdicomb Furniture Company. Widdicomb trained its salesmen thoroughly. You had to go through a six-month course, work in the factory, learn every step of how the mahogany was bleached, how the sofas and chairs were put together, so that when you went on the road, you'd know exactly what you were talking about and could explain anything a prospective customer might want to know.

We took an apartment and got the furniture out of storage again. Then, his training period over, Bill started traveling. He had the whole East Coast—Maine to Florida—for his territory, so he was gone a lot. I wonder what Dr. Freud might have had to say about it. I'd loved my father, who'd gone away and left us, and here I was married to another good-looking traveling salesman.

I went back to Herpolsheimer's. This time they hired me as *the* fashion coordinator, not just an assistant. I worked with buyers, with the advertising department, I trained models, put on fashion shows, I was sent to New York to check out the new styles. But I wasn't happy. Even when Bill was home, I wasn't happy. The things that had made our dating so amusing made the marriage difficult. Every night I'd leave work, go to the apartment, fix dinner. About ten o'clock, Bill would phone from a popular spot where all the guys from the showroom went. "Why don't you come down here, and we'll go somewhere to eat?" After a while I gave up. Why go to the trouble of fixing dinner and then throw out all the food? I might just as well head straight for the bar.

But I didn't want to sit around in bars any more. Dorothy Parker once wrote a poem which included the lines:

> Some men, some men
> Cannot pass a
> Bar-room.
> (Wait about, and hang about, and that's the way it goes.)
>
> Some men, some men
> Cannot pass a
> Woman.
> (Heaven never send me another one of those!)

This wasn't Bill Warren to a T, but he was certainly a man for a good time. I began to feel more sympathy for what my poor stodgy lawyer from Petoskey had gone through. Here I was, ready for a house and children, and Bill was by no means ready to settle down. No matter how many somersaults I turned, it wasn't enough to keep him home.

I felt as though I were dangling in space, like a puppet with nobody working my strings. I finally got to the point where I thought, He can do what he wants with his life, but, damn it all, this is not for me.

I was writing him a letter telling him not to come back to the apartment, that I was sending his things on to his family's house, the night his boss called to tell me Bill had been taken ill in Boston, and was in a diabetic coma.

They didn't think he was going to live.

I flew to Boston. He was alive, but one side of his face was paralyzed. I stayed with friends because to have stayed in a hotel would have been very expensive, and I went to classes at the hospital to learn how to give insulin injections. And all of the time the question kept snaking through my mind, What am I doing here when I no longer love this man?

But I told myself I had no choice.

After I'd been in Boston six weeks, Bill's father drove East to take him home. The only way he could be moved was by train. They carried him on a stretcher to an ambulance and in the ambulance to the train. And I drove Mr. Warren's car back to Grand Rapids.

I don't remember the trip. I must have stopped someplace because you couldn't do Boston to Grand Rapids in one stretch; the roads weren't that good. But I honestly can't recall anything about it.

Bill's parents had rented a hospital bed and moved it onto the sunporch of their house. I slept upstairs and wondered what was going to happen to us. I was there the day Dr. Tom Akin came to examine Bill. Afterward, I walked to the door with the doctor. "How is he?" I said. "I'm sorry," Tom said, "but I don't think he'll ever walk again."

My heart sank to the bottom of my boots. I was twenty-seven years old, and I saw the rest of my life as a series of jobs through which I would try to support him and me. All I could think of was, This must be my cross. There are plenty of people who've been stuck like that. There's nothing to do about it but work so hard you don't have time to think.

Every day I went to Herpolsheimer's and came home at night on the bus, dog-tired. I didn't have to give Bill his shots after all, because his mother knew how to do it; his father was diabetic too. My own mother was certainly understanding, there were no I-told-you-sos, but she had a new life now, and she was busy with it. Sometimes I spent a weekend with her and my stepfather up at the cottage at Lake Michigan. It made a break in the dreariness.

Eventually Bill was moved to the hospital, and I went back to our apartment. Every night after work I visited him. It was such a terrible experience, the whole thing, that I only remember the bare facts, and it lasted two years.

Then, miraculously, Bill recovered. As soon as he was all right, back at work again, and could take care of himself, I went to a lawyer and started divorce proceedings.

Bill didn't put up much of a struggle. I took a dollar in settlement (you had to have some sort of settlement to make it legal) and it was finished. I was twenty-nine years old, and I didn't want to hear from anybody about my marriage having been a failure. I didn't fail, but it's a long time ago and nothing's gained by going into the details. Lots of Bill's friends resented the fact that I'd divorced him. That was only natural, but frankly, by then I didn't give a hoot. From bloom to bust in five years.

I knew I had to make a life for myself and figured I'd probably do that in the fashion field. Maybe I'd head for Rio de Janeiro, which I'd heard was one of the biggest fashion centers of the world. I was so fed up with marriage that I knew I'd never consider another one.

Those were pretty much my colors at the time I met Gerald Ford.

8

A FRESH START

After it came out that I was a divorced woman—Jerry had already been named Vice President—Bonnie Angelo, a correspondent for *People* magazine, asked me why I'd never told anybody. "Well," I said, "nobody ever asked me."

Initially, I'd thought of starting this book at the most exciting part of my life, which was when I married Jerry. He was running for office for the first time, so it was the beginning of his career as a politician, and it was also the beginning of us, of him and me.

In 1947, Gerald R. Ford was probably the most eligible bachelor in Grand Rapids. He was good-looking, smart, and from a fine family. They weren't especially wealthy—his father had the Ford Paint and Varnish Company—but they were active in civic affairs and in the church guild. (Once my marriage had ended, I'd started going back to church myself. Bill and I had hacked around so much, been out so late on Saturday nights, we'd found church just too difficult on Sunday mornings. Once in a great while we would make it down to Grace Episcopal, which was where Jerry and his family went, but I never saw Jerry there. He was away in the war.)

Jerry's mother, Dorothy Gardner, had first been married to Leslie Lynch King, the brother of her roommate in boarding school. The match was unsuccessful. She was gregarious, he was possessive. She once told me that if she even nodded to a gentleman on an elevator her husband practically had a fit. He wouldn't let the milkman deliver milk. He was just insanely jealous.

Jerry, born Leslie King, Jr., on July 14, 1913, in Omaha, Nebraska, was a fat yellow-haired baby (we probably resembled each other as infants), and after his parents were divorced in 1915, his mother brought the little boy back to Grand Rapids to her family.

I've collected a bit of that family's history. We have a set of twelve pearl-handled knives that Jerry's maternal great-grandfather, John Varnum Ayer, won in a shooting contest with the then Prince of Wales someplace in Pennsylvania. Great-grandfather Ayer was quite a betting man. On March 29, 1872, he noted in his diary that he had "bet Jesse Boynton a basket of champagne" over some now illegible difference of opinion, and he bet a man named George Kimball $5 "on each state that will go for [Ulysses] Grant," and he and a Colonel Bethel bet on the probable yield of certain sugar and pecan crops, the loser to forfeit "a fine suit of clothes."

I love all that. The Ayers lost their family-owned steel company a long time ago, but we've still got Great-grandfather's pearl-handled knives.

Anyhow, J. V.'s granddaughter, Dorothy King, met Gerald R. Ford at a church social in Grand Rapids, and they fell in love and got married. Mr. Ford adopted his new wife's child, and they renamed him Gerald R. Ford, Jr. Then the couple proceeded to have three more sons of their own. I'm not going to go into a lot of Jerry's early history (I'm sure he'll tell it in his own book) except to say that I admire the elder Mr. Ford. He was really caring, and he gave his ready-made son a lot more than his name.

All through my growing-up years, I'd heard of Jerry without ever knowing him. He'd been a football hero at South High and at the University of Michigan, so everybody in town pretty much knew who he was. After the war, I'd seen him at the Kent Country

Club dances on Saturday nights, but he was always with other girls, and I was married, so if we spoke it was only to say how do you do.

While I was in the process of waiting for my divorce, I didn't date. But one night in the fall of 1947 my friend Peg Newman called me and said, "Jerry Ford wants to know if you'll come out and have a drink."

Peg's husband, Frank, and Jerry were involved in a drive to raise money for cancer research, and Jerry had put Peggy up to phoning me.

I said I was working on a style show for the next day, and I expected to go right on working until two o'clock in the morning. Suddenly the voice on the other end of the telephone changed. Bashful Jerry had taken the instrument out of Peg's hand, and he was giving me this big harangue about how it would do me good to stop for a few minutes, and he'd come by and get me and we'd go around the corner and have a beer, and I'd be much more refreshed when I went back to work.

I said no, I couldn't possibly. "What's more, I'm in the process of getting a divorce, and you're a lawyer, you ought to know better."

"We'll just go to some quiet little spot where nobody'll see us," he said.

"I don't think that's quite cricket," I said. Although my divorce was uncontested, I wasn't going to take any chances, do anything to put myself in a defensive position.

He ignored my scruples and went back to pushing his theory of the pause that refreshes. It was easier to say all right than to waste the time talking on the telephone. "But I can only be gone twenty minutes," I said.

He picked me up at my apartment, we went down to a place on the corner of Division and Hall streets, and the next time I looked at my watch, an hour had passed.

That's how it began.

In weeks to come, though I still wouldn't venture out much, Jerry and I occasionally slipped off for a date, and one night we were standing on a movie line to buy tickets to the second show at nine o'clock when who should come walking out of the theatre but my mother and stepfather, who'd been to the seven o'clock show. There was nothing for me to do but introduce everybody, and I think my mother was quite shocked. To her, I was a married woman until I got the official paper which said different.

(You have to keep in mind the era and the town. By Grand Rapids standards, my mother was positively liberal. The Dutch population had two strong church groups, one more strict than the other, and their children weren't allowed to go to the movies, to drive, even to come to the Y to take modern dance lessons.)

Once my divorce became final, Jerry and I continued to see different people. He'd been dating many girls because, his friends said, he was carrying a torch for a model he'd been sweet on, yet we seemed to prefer one another. I was going out with various fellows, most of them young lawyers (one of the boys who wanted to marry me was a widower with children, but I wasn't ready for that kind of responsibility), and coming to the decision that Jerry was really the top of the heap.

One night he came to my apartment, and three other boys had stopped by before him and brought beer with them. They were sitting on the living-room floor shooting craps and drinking, and Jerry marched in and plunked himself down on the couch and opened up the evening paper. Like a stern father. Never said hello. Pretended to be reading the baseball scores. Gradually, the guys on the floor began to feel this cool blast coming from behind the sports pages, and two of them got up and left. Not the third. He was going to sit it out. So was Jerry. Neither of them would go home. Finally I said, "I don't know about you guys, but I've got to work in the morning, so I'm going to bed."

They walked out of the apartment together, still silent. I was living on the corner of Washington and Prospect, on the ground floor, and my bedroom window was open. I could hear every word as they stood under the streetlight, communicating at last. Jerry asked exactly what the other guy's intentions were toward me. The other guy said he was very interested. "Fine," Jerry said. "I just wanted to find out."

It was pretty nervy of him to be asking anyone's intentions, since right from the start we'd assured each other that neither of us meant to get serious. I think in a crazy way it may have been the thing that brought us together. Once I'd said marriage was the last thing on my mind, and he'd made it clear it was no part of his program either, we could relax, have a good time, go to all the football games. He wanted a companion, and I filled the bill. As for me, I liked handsome blond men, I found him physically attractive, I enjoyed his company and his friends. What was more, my parents approved of him as heartily as they'd disapproved of Bill Warren.

My interest was put to the test when the snows came. Jerry had done a lot of skiing in the East; he'd gone to Yale Law School and he liked to ski every weekend of the winter. I had never skied. Skiing was not yet popular in the Midwest when I was growing up.

Jerry took me shopping—we decided I wouldn't invest in the most expensive equipment because we didn't know how successful this experiment was going to be—and I got the poles and the skis and the boots and the pants and the sweaters and the parka and the long underwear. Then we headed way up to the northern woods of Michigan. Once we got there, he took me out, had me herringbone up a hill, turn around, and slide back down. Then he said, "Now you practice that while I go over to the Bowl and take a few runs, and I'll come back and see how you're doing," and he disappeared. Well, he never came back to see how I was doing until the end of the day. I had herringboned up the hill and slid down a good many times and I finally gave up and went into the cabin and got warm.

We'd built that cabin with our own hands, while the weather was still mild, before the ground froze. Jerry, Jack Stiles (the boy who'd once owned the silver car, and who'd been a fraternity brother of Jerry's at the University of Michigan), Bud Wilmarth (of the brass buttons and the Woolworth ring), and another friend named Neal Weathers had got together and bought some property at this place called Caberfe, and they and their wives and I put a log cabin on it. We called it a lodge, but it was just one room with eight cots and a pot-bellied stove, which not only kept us warm, but on which we also cooked breakfast. The only bad part was if you had to get up in the middle of the night you had to go out to a freezing cold outhouse, which was a primitive one-holer. (My folks had had a plush two-holer up at Whitefish Lake, before we put in plumbing. I can still remember all those pictures of the Chicago World's Fair stuck up on the inside walls with thumbtacks.)

Three of the male partners in the cabin were lawyers. I was up to my neck in lawyers. (Jerry had come back from the war and gone into an old established law firm headed by a man named Julius Amberg, a firm in which Phil Buchan, another college friend of Jerry's, was already established.)

Fortunately for me, Jack Stiles's wife Phoebe was no great shakes as a skier either, so the two of us stuck together. After a few weekends, Phoebe and I got so we were taking the rope tow and going all the way up. Having Phoebe with me made it congenial. Then at night all eight of us would go out to dinner, usually at a nearby tavern with a jukebox and a tiny dance floor. It was our big Saturday bash, and we reveled in it.

I had a terrible time getting away for those winter weekends because Herpolsheimer's had brought in a new president who'd decided to reinstitute the custom of Saturday fashion shows in the tearoom (shades of my teens). Jerry had to wait for me to get through before we could take off, and I ran that Saturday lunch show so fast it was just a blur of clothes—"How much was that?" "What was that?" the ladies would be saying—and then I was out of there and gone.

I'm not sure at what point I began to question the ground rules Jerry and I had laid down. We'd agreed not to get serious, but now I found myself wondering if I was going to ruin everything by falling in love with a man who didn't want me to love him, and worrying that maybe he was still a little moonstruck over the New York model.

He'd told me about her. They'd met while he was at Yale Law and she was going to a women's college in Connecticut. They'd gone steady for four years, but she'd refused to marry him because he was going to go back to Grand Rapids and practice law, and she didn't want to settle down in Grand Rapids.

While Jerry was away at war, his model had married—and divorced—somebody else, and Jerry had decided he wasn't the marrying kind, whether out of hurt or conviction, nobody knew. But the relationship between him and me was slowly changing. He'd taken me to meet his family (I'd gone there for Thanksgiving dinner, bounced his brothers' babies on my knee), and while I don't think I was their favorite—Mrs. Ford was fond of a young widow whom Jerry had known since they were both children, and I think she was hoping for them to get together—his parents accepted me with friendliness.

Christmas of 1947 was coming, and Jerry was going to Sun Valley for three weeks—he always went to Sun Valley for the holidays—and I had to stay behind in Grand Rapids. There were good reasons. One was that he hadn't asked me to go to Sun Valley. Another was that Herpolsheimer's Department Store didn't give its employees long vacations at one of the busiest times of year. And a third was that I was due to go to New York on January 2 and scout Seventh Avenue, because the fashion houses would all be having shows that week.

But it was going to be a blow to me to have Jerry gone for so long. I knew darn well that he would have a good time out there because ladies followed him wherever he went, and I was jealous. I had a woman who was a seamstress at Herp's (we used to shorten the name of Herpolsheimer's the same way people in New York call Bloomingdale's Bloomie's, but Herp's sounds like a fever blister to me now) make up a Christmas stocking. It was very elegant, of red corduroy with a black velvet cuff (we still have it; the red has faded to orange), and I filled it with silly presents for Jerry to take with him.

He was going to Sun Valley by train, so I put in a little choo-choo, and I got a pair of dark glasses and fastened blinders on them, and I knitted him a pair of Argyle socks—it turned out they were too big, they didn't fit—and I bought him a very nice pipe lighter. I conferred with a friend about whether I should simply have it monogrammed with his initials or if I dared do something more personal. I'd thought of a line—"To the light of my life"—that I wanted to use, but I was fearful about sticking my neck out. I went ahead and did it anyway, had the words engraved around the bottom of the lighter in letters so small the inscription looked just like a design, and then I put the lighter in the toe of the corduroy stocking.

I'd been thinking hard about our situation. All his friends kept telling me that Jerry was a bachelor in his soul, he'd be a bachelor all his life, I was barking up the wrong tree. No matter whom I spoke to, they offered the same opinion: you're wasting your time.

Well, it was my time, and I had plenty of it.

New Year's Eve I went out with another lawyer; when I didn't have you-know-who, I took what I could find. We celebrated at the Blythfield Country Club, and I got home at about four o'clock in the morning. Before I went to bed, I called Jerry to wish him a happy new year, but I hadn't been thinking about the change in time. His room in Sun Valley didn't answer, so I left word for him to call back. Why I did that I don't know, because at seven o'clock the phone rang, and it was Jerry. I was trying to wake up and make sense, and all I could think of to talk about was that I had to go to New York and look at the new spring lines.

"Why don't you call Brad Crandel when you get there?" Jerry said.

Brad Crandel was an artist—that was in the days when a lot of magazine covers were not photographs, they were illustrations—and he and his wife had been close friends of Jerry and the model, so I wasn't wild to socialize with the Crandels. "If you think I'm going to call him up, you're crazy," I said, none too sweetly. "If you want me to meet him, you can call him yourself."

He did. From Sun Valley he arranged the whole thing. When I got to New York, to the Waldorf Towers (I stayed in the Junior League rooms there because Junior Leaguers got a discount), Brad Crandel had already left several messages. We made a date for cocktails. I was to come to his studio over on the East River.

I guess I didn't have to cover any shows that afternoon, because I had lunch with Walt Jones, Mary Adelaide's brother, the one who used to play drums for our classes in his mother's basement. Walt was depressed; he'd just separated from his wife; so lunch lasted clear until the cocktail hour.

"Look," I said, "I have to go to Brad Crandel's. Why don't you come along?"

Walt said okay, he had nothing to do, and he'd like to meet Crandel, who was a kind of celebrity. We got a cab to the studio and found Brad alone. His wife, Mickey, was away at their country house. We sat down and talked for about fifteen minutes, and then the doorbell rang.

"I wonder who that can be?" said Brad, and he went to the door, and we heard him doing this kind of phony-sounding "Darling, what a surprise!" and in she slinked, Jerry's model. It hit me like a ton of bricks. Crandel must have phoned her as soon as he knew I was coming, and suggested she drop by and get a look at old Jerry's new flame.

She was a gorgeous blonde, skinny as a rail, and when she peeled off her mink coat and threw it on a chair, she was revealed— and I mean revealed—to be wearing a black satin dress cut down to her bottom rib. Until she arrived, I'd thought I looked pretty fashionable in my striped taffeta petticoat peeping out from beneath my maroon-colored suit, with a blouse that matched the petticoat. Now I shriveled up under my hat, while she proceeded to cross-examine me about friends of Jerry's in Grand Rapids, and about Jerry's family, and how was his mother, and did they still have barbecues up at the cottage, and in between these questions, which appeared to me to be staking out a prior claim to Jerry, she was somehow managing to vamp Walt Jones. She'd touch his fingers, throw him a glance, cross her long legs, and he was besotted. She took him right out from under my nose. He told her he had to escort me to my hotel, but then he'd be right back to pick her up for dinner.

That night I wrote Jerry a letter filled with spleen. (We'd been corresponding daily, which had given me heart. I hadn't expected him to take time out from skiing to write.) I told him he could have his Brad Crandel and his model. I didn't want any part of them. To me they were 100 percent synthetic, and if they were the kind of people he wanted to associate with, that was his privilege, but he could count me out.

The big mistake I made was to drop my letter in the mail chute as soon as I'd finished it, because when I woke up the next morning I thought, What a dumb thing to do; you should have played that a little cooler. But there was no way to get the letter back; it was gone.

When we had our reunion in Grand Rapids, I waited for Jerry to say something about my diatribe. He didn't utter a word. He'd brought me a present from Sun Valley, a hand-tooled leather belt with a silver buckle, and we got off onto other subjects. After a while I couldn't stand it any more. "Listen," I said, "did you by any chance get a letter from me that mentioned something about your artist friend and the model?"

"Yes, I did," he said. "I gather you didn't care much for them."

And that was all he said. He claims he's still got my letter in his safety deposit box ("I thought that was a good place for it"), but he won't show it to me.

I think it was the three weeks' separation which had made the difference. Everything moved very fast after that. Still, some of Jerry's courting habits didn't change. He seldom showed up at my apartment until somewhere between 10 and 12 P.M. because he was connected with every civic organization in town.

"I'd like to come by and see you tonight, but I've got to go to a meeting first," he'd say. (As one of my brothers pointed out later, when I was looking for sympathy because Jerry was away so much, "You knew what you were getting into. You knew he was a hard worker and that work came first.")

In February he proposed. He's a very shy man, and he didn't really tell me he loved me; he just told me he'd like to marry me.

I took him up on it instantly, before he could change his mind.

9

RUNNING

He told me we couldn't be married till the fall because there was something else he had to do first. I didn't question him, and he didn't tell me what this other thing was. Not until spring. Then he said he was going to run for Congress. By that time, his mother knew too. About Congress and about us. "If you're going to announce for Congress, you'd better also announce your engagement," she said. "Voters are going to want to know that you're planning to get married." I always accuse him of marrying me to give himself a respectable image.

We chose the engagement ring together. He phoned me at Herpolsheimer's one day and asked if I could meet him, and he sounded very excited. On our lunch hour, we went to a jewelry store and picked out a ring—a round diamond in a square setting—that we both liked, and one that a lawyer of modest means who was about to run for public office could afford.

In July, after we were officially engaged, he finally broke down and admitted that he loved me. I knew it was something difficult for him to say, and that if he ever said it he would mean it, so the words thrilled me. I was thirty years old, Jerry was thirty-five, but I was feeling like a girl again, strong, full of hopes, equal to anything.

Which was good, because the next few months were frantic. The Republican primary came in September (Jerry had to run against the incumbent, a Congressman named Bartel—but called Barney—Jonkman), we were married in October, and the election took place on November 2.

Jerry's father had always been interested in politics, so it had been natural for Jerry to get involved. In any town there are political activists, and Jerry was one of a group which kept having meetings to protest the poor representation they felt they were getting in Washington, and finally somebody turned to him and said, "You're making such a fuss about it, why don't you get in there yourself?"

When he first told me he was going to run for Congress, I didn't know what running for Congress meant. I was very unprepared to be a political wife, but I didn't worry because I really didn't think he was going to win. At that time, only old men went to Congress. Also, I couldn't imagine this Dutch town turning out the incumbent, who was himself Dutch, who'd been in office for eight years, and who was as conservative as most of the voters in the Fifth District he represented. The incumbent, by the way, lived on Prospect, right up the street from me, so Jerry and I had to be very careful of the hours we kept; he never lingered at my apartment past midnight, for fear somebody would turn us in.

Jerry's stamina was inexhaustible; he'd been active in the Urban League Society, the Red Cross, every fund drive that asked him, and he took to campaigning like a starving man to a roast-beef dinner. At last he could put that energy to work in a race where he was the underdog, which made the challenge all the more fun.

It was wild. People started to give engagement parties for us, and we tried to make an appearance at every party. But Jerry was campaigning furiously, and I was still working—I should have quit, I don't think I was much use to Herpolsheimer's during those weeks—and every night when I finished at the store, I'd go right over to Jerry's Quonset hut headquarters and lick envelopes.

The Quonset hut had been a source of dissension. Jerry had got hold of this thing, and put it on a parking lot that belonged to a department store in town. The hut's sides were covered with Jerry Ford signs and huge pictures, and once the department store saw it they had second thoughts—there-goes-the-neighborhood, it'll-scare-away-some-of-our-customers kinds of thoughts—but Jerry wouldn't back down. He went to Julius Amberg, his boss in the law firm. Mr. Amberg also represented the department store and was, incidentally, a good Democrat.

"They want me to move my Quonset hut," Jerry said, "but I've rented the space and paid for it, and I don't intend to stir."

Mr. Amberg, that marvelous man, took Jerry's side, and convinced the store it should leave him and the hut alone. It was not that long after World War II, Jerry was a veteran, and the hut was symbolic of changes which had taken place in the world and which were taking place even in Grand Rapids. Jerry's switch from isolationism to internationalism came out of his having served in the Navy. Four years abroad had taught him that the world didn't stop at our shores. That was one of the differences between him and Barney Jonkman.

Also, Mr. Jonkman had got to the point where he was filing his mail in the wastebasket, people weren't getting answers to their letters, and even some very conservative voters felt it was time for a change.

The primary was the thing to win, because at that time Grand Rapids was a Republican town. If you won the primary, you had a pretty good chance of being elected. (It isn't that way any more.)

I recruited crowds to come down to the Quonset hut. A girl would say, "I've never been in politics," and I would say, "I don't know anything about politics either, but you can lick stamps and stuff envelopes, can't you?" I had my models working for Jerry, my dancing friends working for him; everybody I knew I had out campaigning for him. While Jerry was visiting farmers, making appearances at county fairs, shaking hands with factory workers, I was running around asking storekeepers to put up posters.

Jack Stiles had agreed to be Jerry's campaign manager, though one journalist has written, "It would have been difficult to imagine two more opposite personalities. Ford was reflective, serious, not given to easy banter, candid and direct in manner and speech. Stiles was . . . a man with a flair for phrase-making and a zest for combat of every kind."

Not that most people thought there was going to be much combat. Jerry was expected to be wiped out (the most favorable odds quoted were three to one against Ford) by Jonkman, who was going around making speeches about Communists in the State Department, and telling the voters that Michigan's famous Senator Arthur Vandenberg was soft on the Marshall Plan.

After my initial misgivings, I got carried away by the momentum of the primary battle. It was exhilarating to be in a race like that. You finally found yourself wanting him to win. (Same as when he was running for President. I'd had qualms about spending four more years in the White House. It's a tough job, seven days a week, twenty-four hours a day, but when the time came to get out and fight, I was right there on the hustings waving a Ford banner and talking my head off.)

The upshot was Jerry took the Fifth District by storm.

We had a big party the night of the primary out at Jack and Phoebe Stiles's house in North East Grand Rapids, and the party turned into a victory celebration, but if I'd been thinking that Jerry was now going to have time to confer with me about our wedding, I was soon relieved of that notion. He and Jack were already huddling, planning their strategy for beating Freddie Barr, the Democrat, who was a nice married man with something like eleven kids. Jack and Jerry were afraid that all those kids would be an asset to a Grand Rapids politician.

The signs of what my future life was going to hold were there for me to read. When I complained my brother told me I knew what I was "getting into." And Janet Ford—she's married to Jerry's brother Tom, and she was my matron of honor—had warned me. "You won't have to worry about other women," she said. "Jerry's work will be the other woman."

I didn't care. I was crazy about the man, and so were Dad and

Mom. Mother felt she could relax at last and stop worrying about what was going to happen to me. Dad Godwin gave us our wedding, and we used his name on the invitations. "Mr. and Mrs. Arthur Meigs Godwin request the honor of your presence at the marriage of their daughter." Even though I wasn't legally adopted, I wanted it that way. Then there was something Jerry wanted. Or, rather, didn't want. The R. in Gerald R. Ford stands for Rudolph, which he's so sensitive about that he wouldn't allow it on the announcements. "Okay," I said. "It isn't right, but if you feel that way, we'll just go against Emily Post."

The Ford family gave us our rehearsal dinner at the Peninsula Club, in one of the fifth-floor rooms which were rented out for private parties. Jerry got there for cocktails, but as soon as we went in to dinner he had to go off and make a speech someplace else. I sat at the head of a U-shaped table all by myself until Don Carey, the minister, took pity on me and moved up into Jerry's place. My fiancé made it back in time for dessert, and we drank wine out of a German betrothal cup. The man drinks first, then the hinged cup is turned over, and it comes up a smaller size, and the bride-to-be drinks.

The wedding was on October 15, a Friday, as I've already explained, because we had to go to the Northwestern-Michigan game on Saturday. Jerry's fraternity brothers—the duck hunters— were ushers, and his old friend Jack Beckwith was the best man.

I wore a sapphire blue satin dress, and carried red American Beauty roses. My shoes and hat matched the dress, and on my hat was a piece of lace which had come off a parasol belonging to Jerry's grandmother.

At 4 P.M., the appointed hour, I was standing in the doorway of Grace Episcopal Church, ready to start down the aisle, and growing more livid by the moment. Jerry had been out campaigning all day, and there wasn't a sign of him, when all of a sudden he came flying in. I told him later if he hadn't showed up soon, I was going to go ahead and marry Jack Beckwith.

There was a small group at the church for the ceremony, and Jerry's mother, who'd gone a bit weepy over losing her oldest son (he was the last to marry), bowed her head and saw, to her horror, under the groom's pin-striped gray trousers a pair of dusty brown shoes. He'd been out shaking hands on some farm, made it back in time to change suit and tie, but hadn't remembered to switch shoes. Mrs. Ford, who was the epitome of propriety, became so incensed she forgot her tears, and the minute we got to the country club for the reception she buttonholed poor Jerry and gave him the devil.

I look at the picture of Jerry and me coming out of the church and wonder who those young people are, he with the carnation in his buttonhole, and the breast pocket handkerchief so neatly folded to show two points, she hanging onto his arm, her heart in her eyes.

I had a whole book of wedding pictures, but it finally fell apart, and a while ago Jerry took it back to Grand Rapids and had the photographer—whose studio is still in business—make us a new one.

It's really funny to look at the faces now. There's Mary Ward, my glamorous cousin from Chicago, who showed up in a gorgeous dress and a big flowered hat, and totally upstaged me. A whirlwind of a woman with a ferocious social conscience, Mary once came by our house on her way to India to preach birth control, and I remember my stepfather laughing at her and saying he knew India, and carrying birth control to India was just a waste of money. She went anyway.

There's a picture of some guests being handed little bags of rice to throw at us, and there are lots of pictures of friends and relatives—so many of them dead now, even the ones our age. And there's one picture of a cross-eyed guy right smack in the middle of a group, and nobody's ever laid claim to him or been able to figure out who he is.

We went on our honeymoon with a chocolate cake from Jerry's Aunt Julia, a bottle of champagne from my brother Bob, and Jack Beckwith, the best man. The three of us piled into the front seat of Jack's car and he drove us to Ann Arbor. (One of Jerry's brothers brought Jerry's car down the next day because we needed it for after the game.)

In Ann Arbor, we went to the Town Club, had dinner, drank

champagne, and whooped it up until all hours, so we were still lying abed when the guests showed up next morning for a big pre-game brunch Jack Beckwith was throwing in our honor. The party was taking place in the room adjacent to ours, on the second floor of the Allenel Hotel. (You never stayed above the second floor at the Allenel Hotel because it was such a fire trap you wanted to be sure you could jump.)

People were already shoving newspaper clippings about the wedding under our door when I finally struggled up and dressed and went next door to say hello. There were old school friends of Jerry's whom I'd never met, and professors, and a bunch of Grand Rapids people who'd come out for the game, and after a couple of hours, I was feeling so exhausted I told Jerry I was going to skip the kickoff. "Leave my ticket behind," I said. "I'll lie down for a while, and if I feel better I'll come over and join you."

I lay on the bed and listened to the first quarter on the radio. Michigan was behind. For some reason I felt personally responsible. At half time, I got up, grabbed a taxicab to the stadium, and brought our guys out of their slump. We won the game. It was either me or something the coach said in the locker room at the half that did it, you can take your choice.

That night, in order to hear Tom Dewey speak (he was running for President against Harry Truman), we drove to Owosso, Michigan, where Dewey had been born. We went out to a football field and sat in the bleachers while Governor Dewey—he was then Governor of New York—went through a political harangue which at that point didn't interest me in the least. I was freezing to death, and the thing wasn't over till midnight. A political rally goes on for as long as they can make it last, as long as they can hold people, and of course my new husband and I stayed to the bitter end.

On the way to Detroit, where we had planned to spend the night, we pulled in to a truck stop, had doughnuts and coffee, and phoned our hotel and asked them to hold the room, which we never reached until 3 A.M. Next morning we walked around Detroit, and I started learning more about what it was like to be a politician's wife. Jerry went from one newsstand to another, with me three steps behind him, buying every paper in the city. He wasn't known in Detroit so he wasn't followed by any public, unless you count me.

That was Sunday. Monday we were in Ann Arbor again, because Jerry had a luncheon meeting with some Michigan faculty, and after lunch, we began the drive home to Grand Rapids. Everything's going to settle down to normal, I was telling myself. Most of the frenzy is behind us.

Yeah. Just before we hit the Grand Rapids city limits, my husband described the romantic evening he had planned for us. "I've got a very important political meeting at seven-thirty," he said. "Do you suppose you could fix me a bowl of soup and a sandwich before I leave?"

A fantasy of me in a hostess gown, soft music on the radio, icy martinis, the smell of a delicious roast filling the apartment (we'd kept my apartment, because Jerry didn't have one; he'd been living with his family) died a-borning. "Of course, dear," I said. When we got in, I opened a can of tomato soup and toasted him a cheese sandwich. That was what he got for his first dinner at home.

After I decided to do this book, I told Jerry I was going to write about that complete farce of a honeymoon, and he objected. "Aren't you going to tell the truth, that you've had about fifty honeymoons to make up for the one you didn't get?"

"Nope," I said. "I'm not."

Then he said he was going to censor the book.

Back in 1948 he went right on campaigning, and he never quit until November 1. On November 2 he won his seat in the House of Representatives.

It was exciting, as was the general election that year. Headlines in one newspaper—I think it was the *Chicago Tribune*—gave the Presidency to Tom Dewey. Harry Truman went to bed defeated, and woke up the next morning to find he'd won. There was a Democratic landslide in the Congress too; Jerry was one of the few Republicans to be elected.

We came to Washington for two years, and stayed for twenty-eight.

10

❧

WASHINGTON

After the election, we took off for Washington to find a place to live. We'd only been married a few weeks, and Senator and Mrs. Homer Ferguson lent us their apartment while we were looking. One night, we went out with friends, got back at about ten o'clock, and there was a phone call from Jerry's family; my mother was in a hospital in Florida.

Jerry got me on the next plane out of Washington, which was due to leave at one o'clock in the morning. Well, that plane went to take off and I thought it was going straight into the river. It came to a stop, and we sat and sat and sat, and finally they said for everybody to get out, the mechanics had to fix something. By that time, Jerry had left the airport. I sat there until four o'clock in the morning. My mother died at six.

When I finally staggered down the ramp in Florida at 9 A.M. my stepfather was waiting for me. "She's gone, honey," he said, and we stood there holding on to one another, numb with cold in the hot glare of the sun.

A few days before, he and my mother had gone to dinner to celebrate his birthday, and later that night my mother woke up, was violently ill, and thought she had food poisoning. An ambulance had rushed her to the hospital, where it was discovered she'd had a cerebral hemorrhage.

My stepfather said he'd written me that Mother was sick, but he'd sent the letter to Grand Rapids, and by the time it arrived Jerry and I had already left for Washington.

While my mother was in the hospital, she'd had two more attacks, and the damage was done. I tried to tell my stepfather— and myself—that she would not have wanted to live a restricted life, mentally or physically, that it was probably a blessing God had taken her. I believe there's a meaning for everyone's coming into this world, that we're put here for a purpose and when we've achieved that and it's time for us to go, the Lord takes us, and nothing can make it otherwise.

I believe it, but it's hard for the ones who are left behind. When Jerry was sworn in as a member of Congress in 1949, his parents were there, and I couldn't help thinking how proud my mother would have been, how much she would have liked to see that. She never saw any of our children either.

Jerry and I managed to acquire a one-bedroom apartment at 2500 Q Street, in Georgetown. A nice woman we knew as Miss Ida came in twice a week and took care of the cleaning and the polishing, and I spent my days on the Hill, sitting in the galleries of Congress, listening. As long as I was married to a Congressman, I figured I'd better find out the way things worked. I also used to take Jerry's constituents all over town, after they arrived in his office from Grand Rapids. I don't know how many times I went to Mount Vernon. After a while, I just drove the people out there and sat in the parking lot reading a book while they trudged through George Washington's front parlor and back bedrooms.

My brother and my sister-in-law Janet had been right about work being Jerry's mistress. Weekends, when he didn't have any staff in the office, he'd go there anyway, and I'd go too and spend the day helping with the filing. I'd putter around, do what simple jobs I could, just to be with him.

I was learning things I hadn't known before, and some of them

I'd have been happier not knowing. In politics, you need a hard shell. Someone mailed me a picture, cut from a hometown newspaper, of Jerry posing with a senior high school class. The note with it (no signature) said, "If your husband would spend more time working, and less time having his picture taken with high school classes, he'd get a lot further in Congress." That burned me up, because Jerry put in such terrible hours, and I showed him the letter and the picture.

He shrugged them off. "If you're going to let things like that bother you, you may as well give up right now."

In 1829, Davy Crockett, the famous frontiersman who thought correct spelling was "contrary to nature" and who represented Tennessee in Congress, wrote home of his impatience with Washington. "We have nothing new here and is doing but little bussiness in Corgress," he said.

Well, 120 years later, I can assure you that "Corgress" carried on plenty of "bussiness." At least my Congressman did.

When we were first in Washington, a good many social invitations came to Jerry. Just to Representative Gerald R. Ford, no Mrs. attached. He'd go tootling off for the evening, and next day I'd run into the wives of other new Congressional members, and they'd ask about it. "Where were you last night? We saw Jerry, but we didn't see you."

"I wasn't invited," I'd say.

Eventually, Representative Ford and I had a few words about the situation. It took a month or so before everybody got it straight that he was married, not a bachelor.

I behaved like a typical Congressional wife. I watched the Supreme Court in session, watched how legislation went from the point where a member of the House put a bill into the hopper until that bill got to the appropriate committee, tried to find out as much as I could about the way the government conducted its business. One of the people who most impressed me was Senator George Aiken of Vermont. I went to a committee meeting he chaired, and came away with a great feeling of confidence that the country was in good hands. (It was Senator Aiken who, almost twenty years later, fed up with the Vietnam War and its attendant miseries, suggested that the United States "simply declare victory and come home.")

I became active in the Congressional Club (which is bipartisan, and composed of Congressional wives, Cabinet wives, Supreme Court Justices' wives) and took part in many of the club's programs. On Mondays, you could learn to play bridge, or study a foreign language. On Tuesdays, we went to Red Cross, folded bandages and listened to book reviews. The first time I was supposed to give a book review, I phoned a friend back in Grand Rapids in a panic. "What's new? What should I read?" She put me onto a book called *Popcorn on the Ginza.* I got hold of it, read it, reported to the club about it, and that small act of courage—for me, it took courage— propelled me toward taking a public-speaking class.

Congressional wives came to Washington from all over the country, but the year of the Truman victory there weren't more than about seven of us Republicans elected (forgive the connubial "us") to the 81st Congress, and I made many good friendships with the Democratic wives, women like Abigail McCarthy. We were all new together. That's one of the nice things about Washington. You don't carry your politics over into your social life. Men can berate each other up one side and down the other on the floor of the House, yet you'll see them later with their arms around each other, or patting each other on the back, and the back-patter will be telling the other one, "You did a damn good job arguing that point."

The Humphreys, too, came when we did and were quickly our friends. Hubert's death is a great personal sadness, but Muriel Humphrey, who is a marvelous woman, will go on with his work, and her own work too. (Muriel has labored valiantly on behalf of retarded children. The Humphreys had a retarded grandchild, which only made them more loving to their own and other people's "special" children.)

Of course there are cliques in Washington, and every newcomer has to learn about these in his or her own way. If you were a born Washingtonian, and not just a misplaced citizen down there from the Midwest, you were called a Cave Dweller; there were so few genuine Cave Dwellers that the rest of us got invited out too, but not to the insiders' private affairs. I remember at one of our first Washington parties Lady Bird Johnson introduced us to her husband, the Senator. She called him over and said, "Lyndon, I want you to meet this young couple, they've just come to Congress." Lady Bird was that kind of really friendly, outgoing woman; she made a special effort to include us.

Until our first baby was born in March of 1950, I was pretty free-wheeling. I cooked only when there was nobody else to do it, and my meals were simple—steak, roast beef, pork chops. I was great for short cuts too: scalloped potatoes you buy in the box, frozen vegetables, ice cream, which is Jerry's favorite food anyway. (These days the closest he comes to it is ice milk; they put him on a diet in the White House and he's stuck to it. I don't eat desserts any more either.)

I guess in the beginning I wasn't crazy about President Truman, but as time goes by and you look back at Harry Truman, you realize he was a gutsy little guy. And Mrs. Truman was a lovely woman. She wasn't a public woman, but she was a lovely woman. I met her when she gave a series of teas for Congressional wives. She couldn't entertain at the White House because one day Margaret's piano had gone right through the floor, and they realized the place was falling apart; it had to be gutted and rebuilt pillar by pillar and stone by stone.

The Trumans went to live in Blair House across the street. This meant that their parties had to be kept fairly small, and Mrs. Truman's tea ladies were invited in alphabetical order, a batch at a time. I came with the F and G contingent.

It was a rainy winter's day, I was very pregnant, and if you didn't have a driver, what you did was park your car in a nearby garage and take a taxi to Blair House. There weren't facilities for all those wives to drive up in their own cars. When I went through the receiving line, I said, "Oh, Mrs. Truman, it's so nice of you to have us. I can't tell you how much I appreciate the opportunity to be here this afternoon," and she said, "Heavens, it's you who are nice to come out in such terrible weather." With that, she went straight to my heart. I had not thought any First Lady—and she was my first experience with a First Lady—could stay so humble.

(She's formidable, too. She lives in the old family house in Independence and she won't let the Secret Service in. They rent a house across the street, and they have to watch her from there. When she goes to bed, she turns the lights off downstairs, and the agents know just about how long the lights should be on upstairs, and that's how they judge that she's safely tucked in.)

Jerry and President Truman also got to be friends, although it was more a political than a personal friendship. Being a freshman Congressman, Jerry was at the bottom of the pecking order (he wasn't invited to play poker at the White House), but President Truman gradually became a hero of my husband's. Jerry really thought he was an honest, down-to-earth, good man. (Shortly after Richard Nixon's resignation, Jerry had to fly to Vladivostok, and I stayed behind and went through the big warehouse the White House maintains, filled with chairs and beds and tables and *objets d'art*, most of them donated by public-spirited citizens, to pick out furniture. I found a marvelous bust of President Truman that someone had given, and I snapped it up. That night Jerry phoned from Vladivostok, and I told him to hurry home. "You'd better come quick, honey, because Harry Truman's back in your Oval Office.")

In Washington people in government service live pretty strictly by protocol. As a bride, I bought my first book on whether to wear gloves to a tea, and whether you take off one glove when going through a receiving line (you have to take off both gloves; you should never have just one glove on), and while these things seem silly sometimes, they make your life easier. You know what's expected of you. I recently read how even minor Soviet bureaucrats are getting lectures these days on the virtues of not spearing bread with their forks, and not talking with their mouths full.

My experience in Washington came to my aid when my husband was thrust into the Presidency. In more than twenty years, if you haven't picked up a few little tips, there's an awful lot of air between your ears.

A long apprenticeship in that town—John Kennedy once caustically described Washington as a city of southern efficiency and northern charm—is useful to anyone who's moving into the White House. A new President, even one who's been a governor of his own state, comes there and discovers it's a completely different setup, a different environment, there are different rules. The news out of the Carter camp was that they were going to do away with protocol, but I think they're gradually coming around to understanding there's a reason for the forms and the ceremonies, a certain comfort in being prepared.

(Though you're sometimes caught short anyway. When Jerry was President, there was a white-tie state dinner given for the Shah and Shahbanou of Iran. White tie is terribly formal; it usually means long white kid gloves for the ladies. I had put on a long-sleeved dress, so it seemed silly to be wearing white gloves, but just in case the Empress arrived in *her* long white gloves, I pulled on some short white gloves. Jerry and I went down the steps to greet the royal couple, she stepped out of the car, and she didn't have on any gloves at all. I peeled off my mittens, shoved them at an aide, and murmured, "Please get these out of my sight.")

Because I was thirty years old and Jerry was thirty-five when we married, we were both anxious to have children right away, and after six months had passed and we hadn't gone into production, I began to look at him accusingly. We visited doctors. Jerry was fine, but I had a tipped uterus. The necessary adjustment was made, and by summer of 1949 I was pregnant.

It gets hot in the summers in Washington. And the Carlin apartments didn't allow window air-conditioners. Jerry sent me home to spend the next couple of months with my stepfather at his cottage in Whitehall on the beach beside Lake Michigan. After my mother died, Dad had begged me to stay with him for a while, but I had a tough old aunt who had pronounced the idea unthinkable. "You're married now, and your place is with your husband."

This time, my husband wasn't listening to my aunt. The doctor was concerned about the possibility of miscarriage, and we wanted to ensure the baby's safe arrival. My stepfather's beach cottage was all on one floor, so I wouldn't have to climb any stairs, and Jerry said he'd come out for long weekends whenever he could. Congress stayed in session clear into August, and Jerry was willing to sweat, but he didn't want to sweat and worry both.

While I was away, Miss Ida, our cleaning lady, came to Jerry and said she'd got a full-time job in a school. Would he mind if her daughter-in-law, Clara, came to work in her place? Jerry said no, that would be fine.

And it was fine. Clara was like an angel that came into our lives. She stayed with us for twenty years, and helped me raise the children. Jerry always claimed that if it hadn't been for her he could never have stayed in government.

I didn't return to Washington until Congress went back into session the following January, and around Christmas, even though we were home in Grand Rapids among friends and relatives, I began to get scared. Here was my husband, a man who had been single for thirty-five years. I hadn't been sure how he was going to take to having a wife, but our marriage was going beautifully. And of course we'd been elated when I became pregnant. Now, as the pregnancy went on and it got closer to the time of the birth of our first baby, the scareder I got. We'd been together nearly fifteen months, and he'd taken to marriage, but was he really going to take to being a father? I found myself thinking, Dear Lord, please help me and give me a son because I'm sure if it's a boy it'll be okay.

11

_⚬⁓⚬_

MY THREE SONS

Clara had been cleaning the apartment on Q Street one day a week, and when I knew the baby was imminent, I asked her if she would consider a regular five-day-a-week job. She said yes. Would she rather work through dinner, or come in early? She said early would be better; she had a husband.

I felt I was set then, except for the baby's name. I wanted another Gerald Ford, but Jerry was unyielding. When he had been climbing into the car to go off with his friends to college, his mother had called out, "Now be sure and write me, Junie," and all the other boys had whooped, "Junie!" and the nickname followed him through the rest of his school days. He swore he would never do that to his child. "It can be Mike, Pat, Pete, anything, just so it's not a junior." (Really, a baby named for Jerry would have been Gerald R. Ford the Third, and not a junior anyway, but I guess that didn't occur to us at the time.)

The baby hung in there. Literally. It was long overdue. I had friends who'd been pregnant, and they'd all delivered two weeks early. Not me. I was downtown shopping, in fact I was in Woodward and Lothrop getting a check cashed, when I ran into Mrs. Mark Foote, whose husband was a newspaperman. She asked when the baby was due. "Two weeks ago," I said. "Oh, my dear child," said Mrs. Foote, "why don't you go home and lie down?"

I said I was trying to walk the baby out.

"But, my dear," she said, "you might have it at any moment—"

And stop the traffic. I didn't have it at any moment. And I went right on not having it. My doctor assured me nothing was wrong. Every week I went to see him and he made an appointment for the following week, always adding, "But I'm sure you won't need to keep it." Next week there I was, and he told me the same story all over again.

On an evening when Jerry and I were supposed to go to dinner at a friend's house, the friend called me. Her child had just developed measles. "You'd better check with your doctor," she said. "He may not want you over here."

I called Dr. Chinn and told him about the dinner party and the measles.

"Wouldn't you rather just come into the hospital and have that baby?" he said.

I was floored. "Could I? Would you do it? Honest?"

He said yes. "I think you've gone too long."

I think he was just tired of seeing me in his office.

Before I went, I asked Clara to fix me a hamburger. I hadn't eaten lunch, and I figured once I was in the hospital, they wouldn't give me anything to eat, and I was hungry.

It was the biggest mistake I ever made. Because, when they got me into the hospital, they started procedures to induce labor, and having something in my stomach didn't help. Fortunately, I had a private room and bath. I ended up spending the evening in the bathroom, and I needed the sink as well as the john. It was like a violent case of *turista.*

At about eight-thirty, Dr. Chinn appeared. No labor had started. "I think I'll just have to take you downstairs to the labor room," he said. We walked out to the elevator, and the doctor told

Jerry to go home. "There's nothing you can do. I'll call you when the baby arrives." I kissed my husband goodbye, said, "See you," and went away with the doctor.

By then, I'd stopped caring whether or not it was going to be a boy. I just hoped it would be normal and have five fingers on each hand and five toes on each foot. I think most people feel that way. In the beginning, you're hoping for a blond or a girl or a violin prodigy, but when you realize your time has come, all you do is pray for a normal healthy baby. (I used to joke that all four of our kids needed glasses and had to have their teeth straightened, but I know that to have been blessed with four normal children is a kind of miracle.)

We got our boy. The date was March 14, 1950. I said it was God's will. Jerry claimed it was the genes of the father which determined the sex of a child, and took full credit.

Mike weighed seven pounds, six ounces, he was nice and fat, but his Ford grandparents, who saw him before I did, were afraid there was something terribly the matter. They'd been on their way home to Grand Rapids from Florida and stopped by Washington in time for the delivery. They went to the hospital nursery, and an attendant held Mike up and showed him to his grandmother. He had little black feet. Mrs. Ford's heart sank; she couldn't imagine what was wrong. She knew she couldn't ask me—she wanted me to believe I had a perfectly beautiful baby—but a day or so later she got up the courage to accost one of the nurses. "What," she said, "is wrong with his feet?"

"His feet?" said the nurse. "There's nothing wrong with his feet."

"They're coal black," said my mother-in-law.

The nurse laughed. "You must have seen him right after he was footprinted for his birth certificate. They ink the soles of their feet."

It's true. They ink their feet and put little tags on them, like so many Perdue chickens, because they don't want mixups among the clientele. The amazing thing is that a footprint doesn't change, even when the baby grows to be a man. It's like your fingerprints; unless you have plastic surgery, or file them off, you've got them for life.

Jerry and I were ecstatic with the newcomer. There weren't a lot of pressures on me because I had Clara, and Clara was just as crazy about the baby as we were.

Once, when Mike was six or seven months old ("just beginning to giggle and grr," according to Clara) and Clara, who used to hold long conversations with him, was chatting away, Jerry walked in. "Gurgle, gurgle," went Mike, and Clara nodded approvingly. "That's right, talk to your Dad, because some of these days he's going to be President." Since nobody but Clara, and maybe God, knew this amazing fact, I have a lot of respect for Clara's gift of prophecy.

Mike asserted himself at a tender age. For instance, he didn't like beets. I kept buying them in those little glass jars, and trying to feed them to him, but it never really went over very big. We had a struggle of wills about beets. Baby foods look different, the carrots are orange, and the beets are red, but I thought all that mush tasted the same. Mike disagreed, and eventually he made me understand his position, which was that he did not want to be served beets.

He was sitting at one of those tables on wheels, where the baby's in the center and there's a kind of counter all around him, and Clara was feeding him his lunch. Beets. She put the little spoon in the little jar, shoveled the contents into the little mouth and sat there, stirring up the beets which were left in the jar.

It was the usual caper. You think, Ah, I'll get another spoonful in, and pry the spoon between the baby's lips. Clara kept on going until the jar was pretty well empty. What she didn't know was that Mike wasn't swallowing; he was storing up beets in his cheeks the way a chipmunk stores nuts. Finally he got his whole face completely packed with beets, and he let fly with all of this fine-chopped red stuff, just blew it all over Clara's white uniform, the table, the floor. You couldn't help but laugh, it was so funny, but what a mess. It was as bad as milk. (I've wiped up more milk. A glassful drops, it splashes and splatters and flies about six feet in every direction, and you can never believe all that disaster came out of one tumbler. I don't think there's anything worse than having to clean up after a little kid.)

So far as I was concerned, that was the end of the beets. Mike had won.

We stayed at 2500 Q Street until the baby was about a year and a half old. It was hard on Clara. Every time she wanted to take Mike out, she had to go down to the carriage room, bring up the carriage, put Mike into it, get him, herself, and the carriage on the elevator. And it wasn't easy to keep him in the carriage because he climbed before he could walk. Once I took him to visit somebody and turned around, and there he was on top of the piano.

By the time he started running, we wanted a place where he could be outdoors, and be watched, and have friends to play with without having to be taken to the park, so we moved from Georgetown to Park Fairfax, across the river in Virginia. I'd had a miscarriage seven months after Mike's arrival, and we'd waited until we could find a garden apartment which wouldn't have steps. We were determined to get on with having our family.

The summer after Mike was born, Jerry and I had bought a two-family house in Grand Rapids, with the idea that we would rent the upstairs and keep the downstairs ourselves. A Congressman has to stay in close touch with his constituency or they won't re-elect him, so he knew he'd be flying back home every couple of weeks. (The way it turned out, we spent about half our time in Michigan; our first child even went to a Grand Rapids kindergarten.)

Jerry and Mike and I went home to Grand Rapids for the Christmas holidays the year before Jack came along. When we were ready to come back to Washington, Mike got sick with a bad earache. He was crying, and Jerry and I took turns walking with him, trying to quiet him, and this went on all night long. We didn't want to bother the doctor until morning.

Finally Jerry got hold of the doctor, who gave Mike some medicine and said it would be all right for me to fly with him. Jerry would pile our gear, baggage, toys into the car and drive to

Washington, and he would be at the airport to meet us when we got there. Fine. His parents saw me and the baby off. We came in late, but Jerry was waiting, and by the time we got Mike home and in bed and settled down, it was about ten o'clock. I fixed a vaporizer, filled it with hot water, scooped up some Vicks with a knife, put it into the vaporizer cup, then closed the door of the baby's room and collapsed on the living-room couch, exhausted.

"Let me fix you something to eat," Jerry said helpfully.

"All I want," I said, "is a martini and a sandwich. Give me peanut butter, anything, I don't care."

He prepared a drink, and while I was sipping it, he found the peanut butter. It was just the idea of putting something into my stomach; I didn't want to go to bed hungry. When he brought me the sandwich, I bit into it and thought it tasted sort of peculiar, but I never said a word. Just ate it. Later on it came to me. He'd picked up the knife I'd used for the Vicks, and stuck it in the peanut-butter jar, so I'd had a peanut butter and Vicks sandwich. Oh, well, I told myself, it'll probably be good for me.

Our Park Fairfax apartment was modest but pretty, and we were still living there when Jack was born. Jack was another one who just wouldn't come. Reluctant. I thought seriously of having him induced on Mike's birthday, so they'd be exactly two years apart, but I decided that would be a dirty trick; it would rob both of them of their own celebrations, so I waited until the 16th of March.

First I went to the grocery store, did my shopping, got the supplies in, phoned Clara, who'd gone home to her husband, Raymond, and said, "You'd better come back and stay with Mike." Then I picked up my bag—this time it had been packed for ten days—and went to the hospital. Jack arrived about one o'clock in the morning.

Mike and Jack. One born March 14, one born March 16, both Pisces, and as different as night and day. I've never understood it. They've been opposites all their lives. One's a minister, the other's uncertain of his religious beliefs, one's neat, the other's sloppy. You could have drawn a line down the middle of any room they shared, and one side would look like a picture out of a *Boys' Life* magazine, and the other side would look as if a bomb had gone off in a thrift shop.

Clara insists they were both perfect. "Oh, they were the nicest babies. They weren't fussy. 'Course Jack had a colic for about six weeks and he cried quite a bit."

I'll say.

Because my husband seemed to me so wonderful, I thought there was nothing better than having produced two boys for him. I was bursting with pride. And Jerry worshiped the kids. I was scared to death something would happen to one of them, and then he'd spoil the other. (Now he's ended up spoiling all four. I think that's because he spent so much time away from them—he's like my father bringing home the stuffed animals.)

The year after the Vicks sandwich, Jerry and I decided to stay in Washington for Christmas, and on New Year's Eve we got a sitter and went to a party given by some good friends. This couple's idea of greeting you at the door was to shout, "Happy New Year!" and throw confetti all over you. We were quite young then, and we came home very late, or very early, depending on how you look at it, still covered with confetti. It was stuck in our hair, our ears, our eyebrows. We fell into bed without much ado, and we'd no sooner got to sleep than we were wakened by the children. It wasn't the usual gurgling that parents, who learn to sleep with one ear open, disregard. It was real howling, and it was coming from infant Jack.

We dashed into the kids' room and found Jack's eyes glued shut. Apparently Mike had climbed out of bed, taken a bottle of Johnson's Baby Lotion and then, imitating what he'd seen Clara and me do, poured it all over poor Jack's head.

We snatched Jack from his crib, took him to the bathroom, washed his eyes and his hair, changed his diaper, got him cleaned up. He kept screaming. By now, Mike was back in bed looking like an angel—he had a *Who, me? I didn't do anything!* expression on his face—and we were frantic. The baby would not calm down.

Suddenly he dozed off, which made us more frantic. Why was he going to sleep like that? I searched the crib, found a bottle of Dr.

Somebody's teething syrup. It had a little sedative in it. The bottle was empty, and I couldn't remember how full it had been before. Maybe Mike had fed him the whole bottle and he was awash with sedative.

Jerry pulled pants on over his pajamas, I grabbed a robe, and we jumped into the car with the two children. We had to take Mike with us. Clara was gone for the weekend, and the sitter had left as soon as Jerry and I had got home.

At seven o'clock on a New Year's morning there isn't much traffic, so we were down at the emergency room of the hospital in no time at all. There were other cases there, cases who'd also drunk something they shouldn't have, but they weren't babies. I'd taken the baby-lotion and the teething-syrup bottles with me, so the doctors would know what the child might have swallowed, and they said the only thing they could do was pump out his stomach.

It takes a very few minutes to pump out the stomach of a baby, but, believe me, Jack didn't like it. He's never liked doctors since. When I've been in the hospital, he hasn't even wanted to come to see me.

The doctors found nothing. "He was probably just tired from all the excitement and wanted to go to sleep," they said. "Take him home and put him to bed."

We took him home and put him to bed. By that time, Mike was wide awake and raring to go. And then I got a look at myself in the mirror. Nightgown, slippers, and confetti in my hair. "Good lord, Jerry," I said, "what must they have thought of us at the hospital? Neglectful parents out partying while the children are left at home to drink the paint thinner. . . ."

Jerry didn't answer. Like Jack, he was already asleep again.

Mike was never a patient child. Once I got trapped in the washroom of a plane (I was the only woman aboard, and we were about to land in Pittsburgh) with both him and Jack. Mike had needed to go toidy. I'm sorry, but that's what we called it. Jack was only nine months old, so I thought I might as well change him at the same time. Locked in that tiny space, I struggled to get off the baby's snowsuit and Mike's coat and leggings, and then, the serious business over, I sank down on the john, Jack in my lap, to get him dressed again. Mike didn't want to wait for that part of the act. He started pounding on the washroom door, screaming, "Out! Out! Let me out! I have to get out of here!"

It was terrible. I was trying to hang on to one fat squirming baby and shut up his older brother, the landing gear had already dropped, and the plane was bouncing wildly. When we finally touched down and I got up and opened the door, about forty businessmen were standing in the aisle peering around one another, trying to see into the washroom, where some crazy woman had been trying to murder a cherubic little boy.

When the boys were two and four, I dressed them alike. They were so similar in appearance that I had to write their names on the backs of their baby pictures so I'd know which was which. Also, Jack was a big baby, and often people thought they were twins.

Early on, I decided I had to dispatch our older son and heir to nursery school. I'd been putting him down for naps, which he didn't care to take—he felt about naps the way he felt about beets—and one afternoon I went in and found that, while he was supposed to be napping, he had been very busy painting lipstick on all the little fox mouths and the little mink mouths of my fur scarves.

God bless nursery schools. As soon as I could, I sent Jack too, and I must say it was a joy to have half a day without two little boys running around pulling out all the pots and pans.

It was back in those days that I first met Mamie Eisenhower, not at the White House but visiting Dottie Schultz. Colonel Bob Schultz had been President Eisenhower's military aide, and stayed with him to the end. The Schultzes lived in Park Fairfax and had a little girl with whom Mike went to nursery school. (A mini-bus came around in the morning and picked up the children and brought them home at noon.)

Mamie Eisenhower and her daughter-in-law Barbara, the wife of John Eisenhower, used to come out and have tea with Dottie Schultz, but Barbara's David, who was just about Mike's age, wasn't interested in playing with the Schultz girl, so he'd hightail it right down to our apartment and get into action with Mike and Jack and their fire trucks.

Mamie was very friendly, very big on teas. At her White House socials, she always had something personal to say to each guest. I remember trying to cue her in to who I was—your name's announced, of course, but I thought the name might not mean anything—by saying, "Mrs. Eisenhower, I've met you at Dottie Schultz's," and she said, "Oh, yes, and how are your darling children?"

As it happened, my darling children were outgrowing their quarters, and I was tired of tripping over tricycles and trailer trucks. Also, I thought it would be best for Mike, now that he was reaching grammar-school age, if we settled in one place. Jerry was *not* going home to Michigan, that was obvious. He planned to stay in Congress.

By the time Jack had come along, we were already regretting that we hadn't bought a house right at the beginning, when Jerry was first elected to Congress. A house in or near Washington, I mean. But a Representative only serves a two-year term, and you don't really feel too secure until you've been through a couple of elections. After Jerry had run three times and survived, I put my foot down. "If you're going to run for Congress again, you've got to buy, rent, or build a house, that's all there is to it."

I started militating for a house in 1952, the year General Eisenhower was elected President, but we didn't get into our own place until three years later, when the boys were three and five. There was a tract of land in Alexandria, Virginia, which was going to be turned into a residential development. We bought a lot on a street called Crown View Drive. The sidewalks were still being put down, and our house, No. 514, would be the second one on the block. Then we hired a builder and began poring over blueprints.

Jerry and I had been trying without success to further enlarge our family, and had pretty well adjusted to the idea that two boys were going to be it. If I'd known we were going to have two more babies, I'd have built more bedrooms and more bathrooms. And if I'd even considered the possibility that my little boys might grow up to be six foot something apiece, I'd have asked for thicker walls and higher ceilings.

When we first moved to Alexandria, we were surrounded by

empty lots and trees and mounds of red Virginia clay, some of the things boys love best. With Mike, as a baby, Clara and I had made a mistake. We'd kept him dressed in white and pale yellow, spic and span, and the minute he got dirty, we'd rushed to change his clothes. There were times later when I thought, Really, I wish I'd let that child play in the mud more. If he happened to find any mud on his own, we grabbed him and shoved him in a tub and scrubbed him clean. It was enough to have ruined his personality.

By the time Jack was born, we were more relaxed, and Crown View Drive was the ideal place to be relaxed in. The boys could go out in cowboy hats and discover snakes and beg cookies from Harriet and Wendell Thorne, who lived right across the street from us. The Thornes' was the very first house built on Crown View Drive, and for a long time we were the only two families there.

Once our house was finished, I suddenly realized I didn't want to move all my old furniture into those brand-new rooms, so that was another crisis. Also, I'd been so involved with the completion of the interior that when I began to look around outside I wasn't satisfied with the amount of landscaping the builder had thrown in. It was nothing compared to what I wanted. I did my own garden. I shoveled every pile of dirt through a screen to cull out the crab grass, which doesn't speak highly of the dirt I had. But in Virginia if you don't have crab grass, you don't have grass. I was always afraid to kill it all off, because without the crab grass and the dandelions we would have had nothing but brown lawns.

And then I discovered that I was pregnant for the third time. Now, I thought, it would be nice to have a girl. I'd had a girl's name picked out—in the event we'd need one—from the day I got married. I wanted to call the dear little pink-wrapped bundle Sally Meigs, Sally in honor of Aunt Sally Steketee, who'd lived next door to us when I was growing up (right, she wasn't really my aunt) and Meigs for my stepfather, Arthur Meigs Godwin. A girl could take her choice, be called Sally, or Meigs, or even shorten it to Meg, if she liked.

When the dear little pink-wrapped bundle turned out to be Steve, I gave up on Sally Meigs, and presented Steven with Meigs as *his* middle name. For quite a long time he didn't have a name. He was supposed to be a girl, and I was sulking.

Steve was born on May 19, 1956, and the following summer I took the two older boys back to Michigan. As I've mentioned, our ties to our home state were many. (Jerry spent so much time flying back there that after a while he had to turn down personal appearances unless the people who invited him would at least pay his air fare. We were going broke, and we didn't even own a piece of the airline.)

So that summer, we left infant Steve with Clara—if we were gone for any extended period of time, she'd move into our house— and transported Mike and Jack to Ottawa Beach, just outside of Holland, Michigan. Jerry had to stay in Washington while Congress was in session, but we were both convinced that the two little boys would love the beach, and Jerry would try to come out for weekends whenever possible.

The boys and I settled into a cottage. And it rained. And it rained. And it rained. Every night Jerry called to say, "How is it?" and I would cry, "It's horrible! Nothing but rain!" It's grim being stuck in a cottage with a four-year-old and a six-year-old in the rain. We played every kind of game I could dream up, and sometimes, in desperation, I'd walk the kids down to the local candy store and give them money to play the pinball machine. I couldn't believe I was doing it. I didn't approve of letting them play pinball, it was like teaching them to gamble, but I'd have done almost anything to entertain them.

Then the weekend would arrive, Jerry would fly from Washington, and the sun would come out. Jerry would spend two days on the beach watching his sons splash in the water, and he'd come in to dinner shaking his head. "I don't know what you're complaining about. It's perfectly gorgeous down here."

It was heartbreaking. As soon as he flew back to Washington, the rain would come again, and he never *did* know what I was talking about. It wasn't bad enough that being locked up with two kids won't keep the mind alive, Jack managed to catch poison ivy. If he went anywhere near poison ivy, he got it. We had an old-fashioned kitchen table with a porcelain top which had come out of the attic at home, and we'd had it cut down to make a children's dining table. I'd stand Jack on that porcelain shelf and put calamine lotion all over him from his forehead to his toes. His little body was completely covered with rash, so he couldn't go in the water any more, which meant he stopped having fun at the beach. That made two of us.

I was glad to leave Ottawa Beach and go home and see Steve.

To tell the truth, I was beginning to feel the tiniest bit sorry for myself for reasons other than that it seemed always to be raining on me. Having got what I wanted—a house and children—I knew I couldn't start blaming anybody else, but, locked in, I suffered pangs of jealousy when a bunch of our friends went to Hawaii. They flew over and took a freighter back.

And I can remember standing in the kitchen of my nice new split level and thinking of all the fun the gang was having in Hawaii and how we were stuck here because we had this house to pay for and we couldn't afford trips to the Pacific.

I told myself I was more fortunate than most people, and I'd better grin and bear it—whatever "it" turned out to be—but I kept dreaming of adventures in faraway places.

A little while later, my stepfather died and left me some money. Jerry and I consulted about it. Surely, we told each other, he meant for us to pay off the house.

We didn't.

Instead, we went to Europe.

12

VACATION

Before we left on our trip, I went back to Dr. Chinn for a post-natal examination. Not that I thought there was anything wrong, just that I felt if I was going to be in Europe for several weeks I'd better make sure everything was okay.

After he finished examining me, I went back and sat down in his office. Dr. Chinn came in. "Mrs. Ford," he said, "I have a strong suspicion that you're pregnant."

"Oh, no," I said. "I'm not pregnant, Dr. Chinn. I couldn't be pregnant. I mean, I know."

I swore up and down that it was impossible, that he couldn't be right. For the first time in my life, I didn't want to have a child. And I'd been cautious.

Steven was only six months old, but Clara assured us she could handle all three boys, so Jerry and I went off to Europe laughing about Dr. Chinn's mistake.

It was November. President Eisenhower had just been re-elected, and though a lot of other Republicans hadn't done so well in various state contests that year, Jerry had been sent back to the House for the fourth time.

Jack and Phoebe Stiles came on the trip with us, for which I eventually thanked heaven, because even on vacations Jerry worked. He was a member of the Defense Appropriations Committee, so naturally he had a list of army posts in Europe he wanted to check on.

Historically speaking, it was an awful—but enthralling—time to be making that trip. It was right at the height of the Suez crisis. Planes were going over to Europe empty and coming back full of Americans fleeing Europe. Jerry, Jack, Phoebe, and I had a commercial airliner all to ourselves.

This was my first trip to Europe. I marveled. We went to Spain first, and headquartered in Madrid, staying at the old Palace Hotel, not the newer Hilton. There were gorgeous carpets in the halls, and the elevator was a sort of circular cage, and I had *turista*. Well, I thought, this food over here just doesn't agree with me, and I kept going.

We went to the jai alai games, and I was fascinated by the betting. People threw down little leather sacks filled with money, and papers with the numbers of the players they were betting on, and the bags were tossed back up with verifying slips in them, and then, if your player won, you'd go and get paid off. I loved it, and I loved the flamenco dancers in the night clubs, and I would probably have gone to the bullfights too, but the season was over. I don't believe I would have liked the bullfights, but I'd have thought it was the thing to do.

Spain was fabulous, though I had trouble adjusting to the schedule. Some of the restaurants didn't open until ten o'clock at night. We finally got so we took afternoon naps the way the Spaniards did. One night Jack Stiles took us to a marvelous little restaurant he knew of where they served suckling pig. I think that's all they served; they had an open kitchen kind of setup, very picturesque. We got in there and all I could smell was pork, and then they brought this whole little baby pig to the table. I passed. (I've heard since from a woman who had a similar experience, only worse. She was served a slice off the pig's head, and when she turned it over it still had the ear on it.)

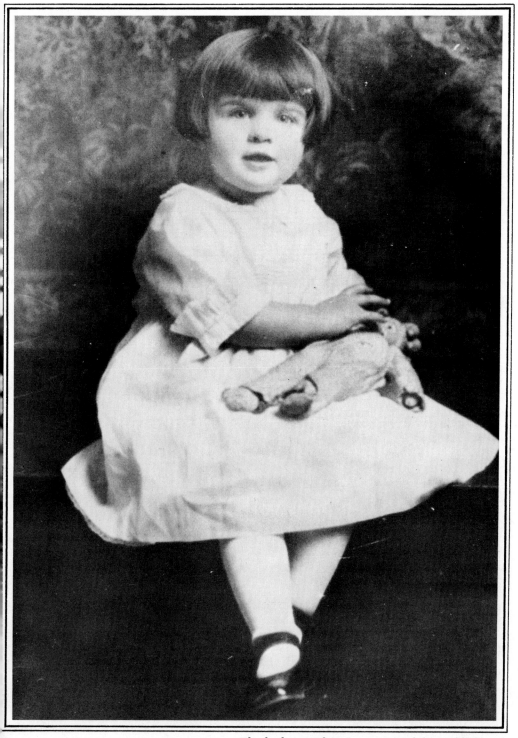

Elizabeth Ann Bloomer, age 3, with her teddy bear

Father William Stephenson Bloomer,
tintype, as a child

Mother Hortense Neahr Bloomer,
as a child

William Stephenson Bloomer, adult

Hortense Neahr Bloomer, with Betty
Ford's brothers Robert (left)
and William, Jr.

Betty (left), age 4, with her
friend Martha Rood

At Whitefish Lake in 1927;
Betty is the youngest

At an Ottawa Beach house
party with her sorority,
"The Good Cheers," 1934

Betty Bloomer at 14

Betty ("Skipper") and Mary
Snapp Clark ("Snappie"),
clowning at Bennington, 1937

Class at Bennington College
Summer School of the Dance,
with teacher Martha Hill, 1938

Betty Bloomer in 1938

William Gutaskus

Dancing in "Fantasy," Grand Rapids, 1945

Betty and Gerald Ford
leaving Grace Episcopal
Church after their wedding,
October 15, 1948

Playing with Mike in the back
yard of their Park Fairfax
home in Alexandria, summer 1952

Clara Powell, with Jack (left),
Mike and baby Steve, summer 1956

At home on Crown View Drive, with Jack, Steve, Susan and Mike, spring 1958

The family, on skis at Boyne Mountain, Michigan—their Christmas card in 1963

In the family living room, 1967

Wash-up time in the kitchen
on Crown View Drive

At Mike's graduation from
Wake Forest College, 1972

All I ate was dessert. In those days I was still eating desserts.

My *turista* continued. Never mind what Dr. Chinn had said, I knew it was *turista*. I'd never had a lot of morning sickness with my children, and anyway this was evening sickness.

My husband, who has a cast-iron stomach, ordered the specialty of the house wherever we went, and whatever it was. Fish soup, octopus, turtles, frogs' legs. He ate the food, drank the water, visited army installations, and thrived.

At one point Jerry and I separated from Phoebe and Jack for a few days and went to Majorca. That was wonderful. We drove all over the island and took a boat through caves lit by candles and hanging with great stalactites. In Majorca, too, we finally came to a restaurant where it looked as though I could have a fairly American meal, something my provincial Grand Rapids stomach would not rebel against. I ordered a steak, the waiter brought it, I took one look and said I was sorry. "I don't feel well."

After Majorca, on to Barcelona, and then Italy. We went to Herculaneum, the ancient seaside city which was buried in torrents of lava and mud, and only rediscovered in the 1700s, and where some of the houses are still being excavated. It seems to me there was a wine shop, or a brothel, some room where the guide would take only the men to show them wall paintings of an exotic nature, and Phoebe and I were left waiting outside, wild with curiosity.

We visited Naples. We went to a restaurant right on the bay, with a view straight over the water. It was a beautiful soft night, a violinist was playing his heart out for us—we kept giving him money and he kept playing—and Jack, who hadn't been sparing the wine, was making plans for the violinist's future. "I'm going to import him back to the United States." So it seemed a good idea to have oysters. Jack and I ate oysters out of the Bay of Naples. You probably shouldn't eat *anything* out of the Bay of Naples, but I think of myself as a tough old bird (or, in those days, maybe a tough *young* bird) and I wasn't afraid of a few slippery bivalves.

By the time we got to Venice I was sick again. I took to my bed. Jerry and Phoebe and Jack went to dinner at the palace of an official, and I stayed in the hotel. When I wasn't cursing oysters, I was blaming my allergies. Before I'd left home, I'd started a series of allergy shots, and I wasn't supposed to break the chain, so the doctor had sent the junk along with me, and every so often Jerry would have to find a military hospital where I could go and get my injection.

Oysters and allergy shots, that's what was knocking me out. I believed it. I wouldn't stay down. I went shopping and bought my sister-in-law Janet a handmade black wool skirt with silver threads woven through it. I started collecting *demitasse* spoons. I fed the pigeons in St. Mark's Square and was sorry. Jerry handed me a bag of grain, and the minute I opened it the pigeons were all over me like Hitchcock's *The Birds*. I dropped the bag and ran.

We took a train from Italy to Austria. As we traveled north, I began to feel better. The further I get away from the Bay of Naples, I told myself, but I *was* beginning to wonder just a little about Dr. Chinn's prognosis.

All hell broke loose that fall and winter of 1956. It wasn't just the Mideast. The Hungarian uprising had jolted Europe, and when we arrived in Vienna Hungarians were escaping, crossing the borders into Austria by any means they could. People from the American Embassy had set up a soup kitchen for refugees, and I worked there with the embassy wives, dishing up hot stew. Jerry and I had taken a car and driven down to a crossing at Andau, at the end of a very muddy old dirt road, and there was this store that had been set up where refugees got their first food after they had scrambled across a terrible swamp. We'd read in the papers how many were shot trying to cross. They came with just what they had on their backs and what they could stuff in those little string bags Europeans carry, those bags that keep expanding. They were a conglomeration of wealthy and poor, intermingled, it didn't make any difference, and they were all trying to get away from the Russian tanks and the situation in Hungary.

I couldn't speak their language, but you could tell by the strain in their faces what they'd been through.

Jerry and I went to some of the barracks where the Austrian authorities were trying to take care of the refugees. One of the sites in which people were actually being billeted was an old German encampment left over from World War II. Before the Germans had retreated in the face of the Allied advance, they'd poured cement down the toilets, so there was no working plumbing. And there were no beds. The refugees were sleeping on nothing but straw. Even the babies. I thought of my own baby safe at home, and I picked up so many of them and held them in my arms because it was cold. They didn't have heat, and they didn't have enough clothes to keep them warm.

My vacation, which had been filled with violin music and gondola rides, suddenly wasn't fun any more. I wanted all these sad, tired people to have blankets and coats, to be protected against the night and the pain of loss, and there was nothing in the world that I could do about it. Take the names of a few who hoped to come to America, promise to talk to some people in Washington about them when we got back, but that would be a drop of water in the desert. I felt useless, like a frivolous woman who's taken too much for granted.

I wanted to go home.

13

〰

IT'S A GIRL

Not that the cold war hadn't been on our minds in America too. Jerry and I almost asked for a bomb shelter when we built the house in Virginia, but in the end it didn't seem to make much sense, because if a bomb fell there would be so much fallout nobody would be saved anyway.

We'd moved out there with Mike and Jack at the peak of the East-West tensions, and everybody was discussing what to do if Washington was attacked. I had a lot of canned goods stored in the basement, and Jerry and I and the boys had an understanding about where we would meet if we got separated. Air-raid warnings were being sounded regularly, just to test the equipment, and of course we were sitting right near the Pentagon, which was the most likely enemy target because that was where the high officials congregated.

Not long afterward, the government tried decentralizing. They built the Air Force Academy out in Colorado, they dispersed some big shots to other areas, they trained people all over the country to watch for enemy planes. Grandpa Ford was involved in plane spotting out in Grand Rapids, and Jerry told me the government had troops on twenty-four-hour alert, dressed and ready to take off, able to counter-attack anything that might be coming in.

But in 1956, after weeks of racketing around Europe, all I knew was that it felt good and safe and sweet to be back in Virginia. The first thing I did when I got home was call up Dr. Chinn and make an appointment. I walked into his office with my head hanging between my knees. "I'm afraid you were right," I said. "Obviously I'm pregnant."

I was fully prepared for another boy. Grandma Ford had had four boys, so probably I would have four boys. It was my destiny. I thought it would work out okay. We had a four-bedroom house. With two boys to a bedroom, I'd still have an extra room for guests. Some of my pals were doing a bit with a pink ribbon. After a woman's baby came, she'd pass on this pink ribbon to the next friend who was expecting and who hoped for a girl. I was sent the ribbon by Kay McInerney, but I didn't set too much store by its powers, especially since Kay had just given birth to a bouncing boy.

It was funny about that last pregnancy. I got through it so well, when I'd had to be so careful with all the others. I'd been ricocheting through Europe, taking no special care, but Susan was tougher than nails.

Still, like her brothers before her, she was in no hurry to come into this world.

I remember the fourth of July, 1957, two days before she was born. The Harold Hearnlys, who had a big old farmhouse up on a hill, used to invite everybody for blocks around (everybody from what we called "the Clover") to their place for the annual celebration. When we first lived on Crown View Drive, everyone knew everyone else, and the grownups chipped in for community fireworks, so the children wouldn't be setting off cherry bombs and damaging eyes and fingers.

We'd all pack fried chicken and picnic suppers, go up to the Hearnlys', and spread our feasts on the ground. Sometimes you'd double up with a family next door, say, "I'll fix the chicken if you do the potato salad." We wouldn't let the children handle anything but sparklers—even sparklers could be dangerous if kids threw them—but the men would set off the Roman candles and the big stuff.

That fourth of July I was so pregnant I refused to go to the Hearnlys'. I wasn't going to parade around in that condition; I looked like a tugboat. Steve was just a baby, but I fixed Jerry and the two older boys their picnic supper, and the three of them carried it away. After I'd tucked Steve into bed, I went out and sat on the grass in the dusk, and waited for the fireworks to begin.

It was already hot summer in Washington. The fourth of July was humid, the fifth of July was humid, and I woke up at dawn on the sixth of July, swollen and sweaty, and I thought, I cannot stand another day of this, and I started to cry. I cried so hard I went into labor.

Fortunately, Jerry was there. It was a Saturday, and he was taking the boys to a baseball game. It was Mickey Mantle they were going to see. The Yankees were playing Washington, and Mickey Mantle was Mike's and Jack's idol. They collected baseball cards, they traded baseball cards, they spent their allowances on square sheets of bubble gum which were packed flat against these cards printed with color photographs of baseball players. The idea was to keep trading until you got a complete set.

We rushed to the hospital, not because the birth was so imminent but because the ballgame started at one o'clock. Jerry drove like the devil, had me admitted, then rushed back to pick up the boys.

I don't remember who won the game, I really wasn't much interested, but I do recall a conversation about it with Dr. Chinn. "Where's your husband?" he asked, and I said, "He's taken the boys to the baseball game," and he said, "Oh, where are they sitting? I'm watching it on TV." Great, I thought. Here I am having pains every two minutes, and you're watching the baseball game on TV.

Susan was very cooperative. She was born in the seventh inning stretch, so we didn't disturb anybody.

When they told me I had a girl, I was dumbfounded. They held her up and showed her to me, and I still couldn't believe it.

Everything worked out perfectly. After the game, Jerry took

the boys home, turned them over to Clara, and came back to the hospital. By that time, I was in my room sitting up, supposedly conscious. Of course you can never really remember anything afterwards, but I was so smug about having a girl, I thought I had accomplished the impossible. "There goes the guest room," Jerry said, teasing, but we both felt very happy.

Clara claims Jerry phoned to tell her the baby had been born but never said a word about its sex. "I didn't know until the next morning," she insists. "Then Mr. Ford says, 'We have a girl.' "

At night we always kept our babies with us until they were old enough to lift their heads. I was worried about their spitting up and choking; I wanted them right where I could hear them for the first three or four weeks.

We had a bassinet which had belonged to Jerry when he was a baby. We still have it, and I hope our grandchildren will sleep in it. It's a typical old wicker bassinet that you dress up with ruffles and ribbons. It sits up high on wheels, but you can lift the basket part off, and it has a little half hood. I always did it up in fresh lace and net for each new baby.

Faced with the problem of rearing and educating four children, Jerry and I began to talk about money. He'd been in Congress almost ten years, and while Congressmen don't starve, they don't wind up with solid gold bathroom fixtures either. Not if they're honest, they don't. It seems to me that when we went to Congress the pay was only $15,000 a year. I had enough clothes to last me for years, because all the time I'd been working at Herpolsheimer's I bought and bought and charged and charged—a fashion coordinator had to be well dressed, didn't she?—and the store gave me a discount. Every week, as soon as I got my paycheck, I went right upstairs and handed it back to the accounting department. (My mother had been helping me stay out of hock, too.)

In Washington I learned to balance a budget. Jerry just gave me the checkbooks. We had joint accounts in a bank back home in Michigan and in the Sergeant at Arms Bank, which is right there in the Capitol. A Congressman's pay goes in and, if he wants, his deductions are made automatically—taxes, Blue Cross, money toward a pension, things like that. We used the Congressional Club for entertaining, and Jerry joined Burning Tree, which was important to him because so many members of Congress belonged. (It's a male chauvinist club; they don't allow women.)

We'd been managing. But now we discussed the possibility of his going back to practicing law. He wasn't too old, and his law-school friends who'd gone into private practice were raking it in. Our discussions came to nothing. Jerry didn't want to leave government; he loved it. And we didn't want to send our kids to fancy private prep schools anyhow; we wanted them to grow up going to public schools just as we had done in the Midwest.

I often think how lost I would have been if I'd sent my children away to school. Especially in later years, when Jerry was so busy traveling, the children were my whole life. They brought laughter into the house. In England, people pack tads off when they're seven years old, and after that they never see them again except on vacations. Our gang was brought up differently. As soon as one was able to toddle around and carry a dish of nuts, we'd have him in at the beginning of a social evening to meet our friends. And, if the dish of nuts spilled, it wasn't a big deal.

But I had to learn that. A teenager would have been looser; coming to motherhood after thirty, I had a hard time not getting upset over every scratch that appeared on the furniture. And with four kids you can forget about order; you just have to hope you don't crack your ankles stumbling over three bags of marbles and a Tinker Toy.

Recently, someone asked Susan what her first memories of me were and she said, "Funny, when I think of Mother, I remember her clothes, the blue linen suits and the yellow linen suits, and her trying to get dressed in the morning, but having Steve and me screaming at her ankles to do this or that. We used to play sick, so that Mother would stay home with us and not go to luncheons. I remember her in the garden too, always working on the garden."

I wasn't much crazier about the luncheons than Susan was, but I had accepted my position as the wife of a member of Congress and I did take on increasing responsibilities. At one time, I was program chairman for the Congressional Club—we put on cultural programs without any budget by begging and borrowing from museums and friends—and as Jerry's seniority grew, so did the social demands on me.

But both of us felt my main obligation was to the kids. Despite the fact that we had Clara, I wanted to rear my own children. I was always there at three-thirty when the older ones came home from school, and in the days when we still had infants I was a pretty average mother. If I had a quiet hour, I dived into a historical novel. I loved any novel that had a bit of honest-to-goodness history in it, and though most of my hours weren't so quiet, that was fine too. After all, I was lucky enough to have these four children, and they were terribly interesting. At least to me.

I was a den mother.

I was a Sunday-school teacher.

I was an interior decorator and a peacemaker and a zoo keeper.

We raised every kind of animal in the world. Including an alligator which was sent to us when it was a baby. It grew so large the boys had to build a box for it out in the backyard. It was a nasty thing; they had to put on their boxing gloves when they went to feed it, and they had to catch live things for it to eat. Jack always wondered what happened to that alligator. Because, when the fall came, I started thinking about their bringing the alligator into the recreation room, or the laundry room, to get bigger and bigger all through the winter. It was already about four feet long, and if Jack or Mike ever took it out, they had to put a rope around its neck, and the instant it got free, it took after them. So I just decided to let nature take its course.

One night there was a frost, and next morning Jack went to check the alligator, and came back looking puzzled. "He's not moving," he said.

I felt guilty. "Do you suppose it was so cold last night that he got pneumonia and died?"

Jack nodded soberly. "I think that must have been it. I should have protected him."

Clara helped dig the grave in the backyard, and the horrid pet was buried with all due ceremony, a cross planted over its head.

We had gerbils. We had rabbits. We had praying mantises which would only eat live flies, so you couldn't just swat their dinner and bring the bodies in on a tray; you had to go after the flies with butterfly nets. We had chickens. We had turtles. Susan had a bird. She had it for years, until she went away to camp. Then she wished it on Clara. That bird was so noisy nobody wanted to keep it; it would sing at all hours of the night.

For a time Jack was into, as they say, fish. He took the birthday money various aunts and uncles had sent him, and we drove to the pet store and loaded up the station wagon with a tank and a filter and a heater and a thermometer and nets. By the time the passion had waned, he'd expanded to three tanks, and we'd gone through guppies and fighting fish and black mollies and those exotic ones that I would buy and they'd get eaten up by a member of some uglier but tougher breed. I'd come into the room in time to see the tail of a rare fish disappearing between the lips of a cannibal who was swimming around with a satisfied look on his face because he'd just had a twenty-dollar dinner.

The boys built a shack in our backyard out of wood they picked up around the neighborhood. By then, a lot more homes were going up on the nearby lots, carpenters were sawing off and throwing away scrap lumber, and Mr. Beech, who owned the whole development, was very nice about children taking these odds and ends.

Jerry helped out with anything that had to be bought, like the roof, and the families of the other neighborhood boys were more than willing to put in a few dollars too. As long as the shack was in our yard, not theirs. It didn't bother me. We didn't have a swimming pool yet, so the yard was mostly used for baseball (I allowed one broken window per child, and after that I held them accountable for replacing the glass), and the shack was a terrific addition. It had windows for which I made curtains, and the boys enjoyed it for years. When they finally outgrew it, they tore it down and it provided us with a lot of firewood, so it was useful to the end.

Mike and Jack shared the largest bedroom in the house, Susan got the next largest (because I'd been told that girls needed more room than boys did), Steve got the smallest, and Jerry and I took the one that was left. Without a guest room, we couldn't have overnight visitors, and that was nice too. When you have four youngsters, you don't need overnight visitors; you just don't want to see any more faces in the morning.

As soon as my boys were old enough to be Cub Scouts, I became den mother to a pack of ten little guys who were working on their merit badges. I put in three years' hard time. The children met once a week at our house, and I had to plan projects for them. When the weather was good, I'd take them outside for games. They didn't understand how I could turn cartwheels when they weren't able to, so I got a modicum of respect for this minor talent. On rainy days, we tiled ashtrays, made leather belts that said MOM on them, and did messy things with milk cartons and flour and water.

Sunday school was even harder. I wasn't a great teacher, but I felt I owed it to the church to teach Sunday school. How could I just drop off my own kids and go blithely on to church without contributing? Well, the worst student I ever had was a minister's young son. He never would mind me. One day I told him he had to sit there and draw a picture, and he hauled off and hit me in the face.

"Okay," I said. "If that makes you feel good, you go right ahead and hit me again."

So he hit me again.

"I still want you to draw a picture like the other children are doing," I said.

He lifted his tiny fist one more time, and I lost my temper and gave him a good wallop on his bottom. He probably figured he could do whatever he wanted to do in church; it belonged to his father.

Walloping him was an admission of defeat for me. I had a theory about kids that you mustn't ever let them bring you down to their level, get you to arguing back and forth with them. If you find yourself getting terribly mad, then they've won.

Our children weren't spanked. Once in a while, I'd snatch off a slipper or a moccasin and give one of them a whack on the behind. Those darn blue jeans were so hard that, if you used your bare hand, you felt as though you'd broken it; it was literally a case of its hurting you more than it did them. But it was smacking a puppy on the nose with a newspaper, nothing more serious. No kid of ours was ever taken out to the woodshed and belted.

Still, I could be firm. Many times the children came to me and put up a big show about "Everybody else's mother is letting *them* do it," and I'd say, "I don't care whether everybody else's mother is letting them do it, *you're* not doing it," and they'd stomp away, their faces screwed up, but underneath they were grateful that I'd made the decision. Besides which, when I talked to the other mothers I'd discover their kids had been playing the same game. "Mrs. Ford is gonna let Mike and Jack jump out of a plane without a parachute, and they don't even have to eat their breakfast first. . . ."

When Jerry was home, he was completely devoted to the children. Once they started playing Little League football, I'd take the boys out to the field, but Jerry always showed up there as soon as he could get away from work. (And later, when they were playing high school football, he'd mark the home games on a calendar, and turn down speaking engagements that came up at the same time.)

He was never around on our anniversary. Mid-October found him back in Grand Rapids campaigning. But always, when he came in off the road, he'd try to make it up to me. "Why don't I take you out to dinner?" he'd say, and I'd know he was just being sweet; he'd been out to dinner every night. What he really wanted was to be able to eat with the children and be a daddy, so I'd say no. "We'll go some other time."

Despite Jerry's tough work schedule while our children were little, I had a good life. Other Congressional wives and I belonged to a country club in Virginia where members of Congress could belong simply by paying dues, without having to put up the sizable initiation fee, and we brought our kids there to swim and to take tennis lessons, and we tried to learn golf—I was a hacker—and it was all extremely pleasant.

You turn around, and ten years are gone. Mike was born in 1950, and in 1960 John F. Kennedy beat Richard Nixon for the Presidency. I look at pictures of Julie Nixon and David Eisenhower as tykes and can't believe they grew up and got married. One's grandfather was President, one's father was Vice President, so they were thrown together constantly, and in almost every snapshot they're making ferocious faces at one another.

The Eisenhower White House had been managed very efficiently, in a very military way, which was only natural. The Eisenhower Congressional parties were tremendous affairs, and formal. But what stands out most in my memory about Mamie and Ike is their affection for each other. Again, I document my observation with photographs. So many pictures of them look unposed, as if they'd been caught in the act of touching. I can't help thinking that book by the woman who claimed to be his girlfriend was a fraud. In May of 1977, the widowed Mamie, then eighty years old, gave a commencement address at Eisenhower College in Seneca Falls, New York. She talked about her husband's "wonderful hands." Every knuckle, she said, "was broken from football or whatever, but I always felt in all the years we were married that I could grab onto them when I felt sick or worried, and nothing was ever going to happen to me."

It isn't a bad testimonial to a marriage.

In 1960 the Eisenhowers went home to Gettysburg, the Kennedys moved to 1600 Pennsylvania Avenue, Gerald R. Ford began his seventh term in Congress and, for the first time in ages, I didn't have a baby any more. Susan was almost three years old, and the part of my life that had been measured out in Pablum spoons was over.

14

END OF INNOCENCE

Under the Eisenhowers, Jerry and I hadn't visited the White House very often. The fact is that the party in power doesn't do as much entertaining of its own people as they do of the opposite party; it's the opposition you have to convince on legislation.

The Kennedy White House was much more sophisticated, more European, than the Eisenhower White House had been. Mrs. Kennedy didn't have many friends among the Senate wives, at least not that I knew of; but the Kennedys had their own private parties that went on until all hours.

At most official functions, the Kennedys did away with the receiving line; they just circulated, and everybody liked that except for a few people who felt they didn't have a chance to meet or speak to them. When Jerry was President, we sometimes did the same thing, mingled with the crowd. If there was a special cocktail party before a dinner, an aide would tell everybody to please "stand wherever you are, and Mrs. Ford will be brought around and introduced to you." It's an ideal setup. You're the one who's doing the walking, and the person who is escorting you is careful not to let you spend too much time with anyone, just a few words and you move on to the next group.

Jackie Kennedy did a terrific job of decorating the White House. The Eisenhowers had pretty much left everything as they'd found it, but Mrs. Kennedy hired a French decorator. She went on TV and gave the whole country that tour of the refurbished State floor, but I thought some of the changes she made upstairs were equally marvelous. For instance, she furnished the Yellow Oval Room with yellow silk sofas and chairs which had great big overstuffed down cushions, and then the family used the room for informal gatherings. If you were invited to eat in the private dining quarters, you'd gather first in front of a fire in that beautiful yellow salon and sink into those soft cushions to have a drink before dinner.

(Clem Conger, who was later brought in as curator by Mrs. Nixon, claimed Mrs. Kennedy had done everything wrong, and took away a lot of the French touches. The Yellow Oval Room was changed again; stiff chairs were brought in, all arms and legs; they were more "authentic," but so uncomfortable I used to call that chamber the standing room.)

One of Mrs. Kennedy's most famous parties was given at Mount Vernon, soon after she came back from her triumphant visit to Paris. If you recall, President Kennedy said the French had been more interested in seeing his wife than they were in seeing him. He was a smart politician, both he and she were good with languages, and he always greeted crowds in their native tongues, which added considerably to his popularity. (Jerry and I aren't great language students; it's just not our cup of tea. For us, greetings in foreign languages always had to be written out phonetically if they were going to come out sounding half right.)

We were not in the Kennedys' inner circle, but we *were* invited to that Mount Vernon party for Pakistan's President Ayub Khan. In his book, *Upstairs at the White House*, Chief Usher J. B. West wrote about the planning. Mrs. Kennedy had insisted on rehearsing every detail that went into the evening: "We made a number of trips down the Potomac on the Presidential yacht, *Honey Fitz*—Mrs. Kennedy standing at the bow like Cleopatra on the Nile—to perfect the timing of transporting over 150 workers . . . the National Symphony Orchestra, the Marine Honor Guard, the Army Fife and Drum Corps, the Air Force Strolling Strings, not to mention 132 guests, to the home of the first President where dinner was served by candlelight on the front lawn overlooking the river."

The party was to be taken up the Potomac in four boats, the Presidential yacht and three others that belonged to the Navy. We all met at dockside and were piped aboard. The women had been told to wear short dinner dresses, because we'd be getting on and off these boats, and then Mrs. Kennedy turned up in a long dress. I gave her the benefit of the doubt. I figured she must suddenly have realized that the wives of the heads of state and other visiting dignitaries might be in native costume, and she'd better sport a long skirt to make them feel more at ease. I was a bit miffed because I'd had to go out and shop. I didn't even own a short evening dress— short evening dresses weren't fashionable then—but I got a black chiffon that was pretty. I think Susan still has it.

All the elements were with Mrs. Kennedy that night. The air was warm and balmy, the guests' mood festive. There was live music aboard each yacht, and even though it was a short run along the river to Mount Vernon, drinks and hors d'oeuvres were provided on deck. At the boat landing, cars were waiting to drive us up the hill to the mansion.

To this day, I don't know how Mrs. Kennedy ever got the ladies of the Mount Vernon Association to let her give a dinner there. They're a very elite, very closed society; in order to belong, your heritage probably has to go back to George Washington, or one of those soldiers who was in that boat with him when he crossed the Delaware.

I'd been to Mount Vernon countless times, but this was different. We came in the back door, filed straight through the house and out onto the front portico, the one with all the pillars you see in the paintings and photographs, and tall, handsome mahogany-colored gentlemen in white gloves and tailcoats served us mint juleps. It was unbelievable. It took you back in time. You could just imagine what it would have been like on a southern plantation long ago.

Some of the guests had belted a few quick ones on the trip down, thinking there wouldn't be any alcohol at Mount Vernon, so they were surprised and pleased to have these frosty juleps put into their hands the minute they came through the doorway. Jackie (I ought to say Mrs. Kennedy; I'm not on first-name terms with her, not to her face) had arranged for dinner to be served in a tent.

We left the portico and walked down into the tent, which looked more like a lovely open garden living room, its poles done up in great floral wreaths. Attached to the roof were rolled-up clear plastic sides which could have been dropped in case of rain, but the night continued gorgeous.

My dinner partner came and found me and seated me (I've been to parties where you had to wander around wondering where your dinner partner was), and of course the food, which had been brought down from the White House by truck, was superb. Even as Jerry and I had been dressing to go, we could hear the sirens screeching on those military trucks, but we hadn't known they were headed for Mount Vernon loaded with our dinner.

A bandshell had been set up in another part of the grounds, the trees were lighted from below, and after dinner chairs were set out on the lawns, so you could sit and watch the river and listen to the orchestra. Again, the handsome waiters with their spotless gloves moved among the guests and offered champagne.

During dinner, Vice President and Mrs. Johnson had asked us to go back on their boat, and we'd said yes. Next thing we knew, we got a message that President and Mrs. Kennedy wanted us to go back on *their* boat. Of course they outranked the Johnsons, so it was the *Honey Fitz* for us. I have no idea why we were so sought after, but I had a ball, and danced all the way home.

That was a very dancy administration (Hubert Humphrey was a great dancer, so was Lyndon Johnson, though he was so tall and held you so tight you felt sort of squashed) and a very stylish administration. Mrs. Kennedy had such marvelous taste that all women in Washington, all the women across the country, copied her. We wore the same things she wore, the little pillbox on the head, the sleeveless shift. It was epidemic, that wardrobe.

Despite his being a member of the "loyal opposition," Jerry sometimes sided with President Kennedy on political matters. In

1961, when so many Republican Senators and Congressmen were denouncing the President for the fiasco of the Bay of Pigs, Jerry wasn't among them. "Ford was aware that the recruiting, training and planning for the [Cuban] invasion had begun within the CIA during the Eisenhower administration," Jerald terHorst has written. "Ford felt he could not in good conscience attack Kennedy for the failures of a covert scheme to depose Castro that had been inherited from his Republican predecessor."

Jerry also supported President Kennedy when he asked Congress to vote more money for foreign aid, and won a citation which said Gerald Ford was "nonpartisan where the defense posture of the nation is concerned."

Two years later, on Friday, November 22, 1963, John Kennedy was assassinated in Dallas. The news was crushing. It was inconceivable to every one of us that this could happen in our country, to our President.

On one level, I couldn't believe that he was really killed, that this was not some sort of dream. We seemed to move through a haze of pomp. On Saturday, Jerry and I called at the White House, met with the Kennedy family, knelt to pray beside the President's casket in the East Room.

On Sunday, we went to the Capitol and paid respects again, after the President's body was brought to the Rotunda to lie in state. I remember the sound of the muffled drums, and the seven white horses leading the caisson, and how quiet the crowds were along Pennsylvania Avenue. People waited, six, eight hours, to file into the Rotunda to view the flag-draped coffin and the guard of honor, who stood like carved statues.

There weren't many tears, faces were blank. I think most people must have been like me, too deep in shock to cry.

On Monday, November 25, President Kennedy was laid to rest in the National Cemetery at Arlington. The funeral cortege had moved from the Capitol to St. Matthew's Cathedral, stopping at the White House long enough for the Kennedy family and President Johnson and Chief Justice Warren and various visiting dignitaries, including three reigning monarchs, to get out of their cars and walk behind the caisson the rest of the way to the church. Mrs. Kennedy wanted this—all these heads of state walking down the street with tall buildings on either side of them—and the Secret Service was absolutely petrified.

Jerry went to the mass at the church. He was there after the ceremony when John Kennedy, Jr., who had turned three that morning, saluted as his father's casket was carried down the cathedral steps.

I hadn't gone to the church. I knew if you weren't a top official you couldn't possibly attend services and still get out to Arlington, so I chose to go to the cemetery with two other Congressional wives who were my close friends. Mrs. John Byrnes, Mrs. Walter Norblad, and I went down to Capitol Hill and caught a bus. Arrangements had been made to transport Congressional people back and forth.

The roads through Arlington Cemetery are winding and not very wide, and when we got near the place where the President was to be buried, my friends and I decided to stand away from the site, up on a rise where we wouldn't be in the way. We waited for a long time on the wet, cold ground, the damp penetrating right through our boots, and finally we saw the funeral cortege coming over Arlington Memorial Bridge across the Potomac. There were hundreds of cars, traveling very slowly, and all their lights were on.

In the cemetery, the first car pulled up beside the grave site, and let Mrs. Kennedy out, and then her car stayed there, and all the other cars began to pull up behind hers one by one, and since none of the cars in front moved out, you had the Queen of Greece, the Crown Prince of Japan, the King of Belgium, and dozens of others left way down a hill.

Suddenly, Mrs. Byrnes and Mrs. Norblad and I, who had thought we were totally off the beaten track, were caught in the middle of a mob of world leaders. We were standing there, and up over the hill came Charles de Gaulle of France and Haile Selassie of Ethiopia, De Gaulle as tall as Selassie was short, both in their medals. How Haile Selassie could walk with all those medals I don't know. This whole group came pouring over the slope, behind us, in front of us—we were like a tree, the three of us. It was such a shock to see them erupting all around, and there was no way for us to move; we just had to stay quiet, and stay back.

The coffin was brought in to the wail of bagpipes, and fifty jet planes, one for each state of the Republic, flew in formation overhead. Then Air Force One flew over alone, and dipped its wings, and Cardinal Cushing said a prayer, and there was a twenty-one gun salute, and a bugler played "Taps," and the flag which had covered the President ever since he'd come back from Dallas was folded and given to Mrs. Kennedy. She bent to light the eternal flame, and then she and Bobby Kennedy left. The family and dignitaries followed.

It was clear that our buses wouldn't be going for some time because the cemetery had first to be cleared of notables. I waited until the crowd had thinned out, and I went down to the grave site. When I got there, there wasn't another soul around except for one man. I was standing looking at the casket and the little basket of flowers that the Kennedy children had left beside it, and this man pressed a button, and with that, the casket was automatically lowered into the ground. And then I knew that he was really dead.

Up until that moment, it had been a nightmare; now it was real, and I started to shake. I turned around and walked back and joined the rest of the people who were climbing onto the bus.

15

THE CHILDREN
ARE GROWING...

The White House was still in mourning for President Kennedy when the Johnsons moved in, but after a few days President Johnson couldn't stand the dolefulness around him, and Lady Bird phoned me to say they were having some friends in for dinner on a Saturday night, and they wanted us to come.

The gathering took place in the family quarters, and we were the only Republicans invited. Lyndon and Jerry had worked together so much, ironing out kinks in legislation, compromising here, there, and everywhere, and Lyndon always kidded Jerry: "You're a great man, but you belong to the wrong party."

There weren't more than fourteen of us; the table in the private dining room doesn't seat more than fourteen. Among the guests were Judge Homer Thornberry and his wife, and Hale and Lindy Boggs. (Hale, a Democrat from Louisiana, later died in a plane crash, and Lindy ran for his House seat, was elected, and proved to be a fine Representative. She's a brilliant woman; I think she could do even greater things.)

At the end of the dinner, someone toasted the new President. The country had survived a hideous wound; the government was going forward. Then came other toasts, wishing the President success in his foreign policy, success with the Congress, I don't remember what all.

We were on our feet when the last toast came. "President Johnson, may he be returned to the White House in the next election." I didn't know what to do. A good Republican could hardly drink to that. I stood with my glass in my hand and thought, I just won't take a sip and I hope nobody notices. I guess Jerry did the same thing. All those Democrats; I felt like a thief among them.

Both Hale Boggs and Jerry were appointed by President Johnson to serve on the Warren Commission to investigate President Kennedy's assassination, and Jerry attended meetings religiously, trying to digest hours of testimony and stacks of research produced by the commission's lawyers. He and Earl Warren even went down to talk to Jack Ruby, and later, Jerry and Jack Stiles wrote a book called *Portrait of the Assassin*. It didn't sell very well.

I would imagine that Jerry knows as much as anybody in the country about that assassination, yet people who have no facts whatsoever are always coming around and saying Oswald never shot Kennedy at all, or it was a conspiracy.

There are a lot of kooks in this world, kooks who want to dig up something that will make a big splash in the papers, kooks who will commit violence to get publicity for themselves or their ideas. The authorities try to know who they are, and keep an eye on them, but in a democracy you can't put them all in jail just because the President's coming to some city.

Often I've been asked how I feel about gun control, particularly since my husband was shot at twice within a period of seventeen days in 1975. Well, we never kept a gun in our house until Steve started hunting, and then of course his was a shotgun, and it was locked up in a cabinet in the laundry room downstairs. I believe handguns and Saturday-night specials that are bought over the counter should be registered, but I'm not sure gun traffic *could* be controlled; there would still be bootlegging, just the way there had been bootlegging of booze.

Jerry and I thought a gun was too dangerous to have around little children. Many of the nights while we were living in that garden apartment in Park Fairfax, and Jerry was away, and it was hot, and there was no air-conditioning, I would leave the front door open, with just the screen door locked; but the only weapon I kept beside my bed was a heavy leaded-glass ashtray. Also, I'd put Mike's tricycle in front of the screen door. Anybody came in the screen door, they'd fall over the tricycle, and I'd have a straight shot with the ashtray.

Our house kind of grew along with the children. In Alexandria there was a shop called Market Square which stocked lamps and samples of fabrics, and while they weren't a big enough operation to have staff decorators, they'd discuss colors and prints and upholsterers with you. I didn't furnish the place elaborately; it was more important to have it comfortable and easy to care for, and I didn't want a crisis every time the kids brought their friends home. I used sand-colored carpeting throughout, and draperies of rosy beige linen, and the rest of my color scheme was basically blue and green and white. We had rules: if a child wanted cookies and milk or a Coke after school, he or she was expected to eat and drink in the kitchen or the recreation room. Down next to the recreation room, there was a whole wall of hooks where children could hang sweaters, raincoats, jackets. Those tennis shoes that have ridges on the bottoms—mud gets picked up between the ridges, dries and drops off, so you have a floor covered with little cakes of mud—weren't welcome in the living room either.

Besides Market Square, there was another shop I adored in Alexandria. It was run by a woman named Frankie Welch, who bought and sold dresses in a price range I could afford as the wife of a member of Congress. Frankie and I got to be good friends. She knew my taste, and sometimes when she went to New York to the market she'd bring back something she knew I'd like, but always with the assurance that I didn't have to buy it.

Once she came into her shop, caught me parading around in a dress I thought was really pretty, and hooted. "Take that off. You don't want that, Betty; it was designed for Hubert Humphrey's campaign workers." Sure enough, the decorative stripes down the sides, and the white band across the waist, formed a very nice capital H. Frankie's shop is in a famous old house. George Washington visited there, though I'm not sure he ever slept over.

George Washington spent a lot of time in Alexandria, and not too much in Washington. After all, Mount Vernon was in Virginia, and the White House hadn't been built yet. Once a great port city, Alexandria still has old warehouses there on the river. Dockside, the area is called. To this day, shipping news is posted up on big boards—when the boats are coming in, where they're coming from, what they're carrying. Cargo arriving at Dockside is sold to shoppers for less than you would pay in stores because you don't go through a middleman; you're buying right from the importer.

Alexandria protects its beauty with all kinds of restrictions. You can't put up a gas station or a shoe store which isn't in the Federal style, and you can find cobbled streets and old homes with signs above the front doors saying the original owner had been a volunteer for the fire department or a member of the constabulary.

Though the truth is, throughout my years in Alexandria, I didn't spend nearly as much time visiting historical sites as I did visiting emergency rooms.

If you have four children, you spend a lot of your waking hours in hospitals. When the children get old enough to stop drinking teething syrup, they start breaking bones, and unless you've been through it, you have no idea how many bones there are in the human body.

Sometimes it isn't even bones. Mike fell out of a wagon when he was a little boy, and put his teeth through his lip, and he had to be taken down to the hospital and sewed up. Steve got his fingers smashed on what had started out to be a festive Sunday. All six of us were going to Family Day at the Congressional Country Club. There were going to be games for the little ones, and gifts of baseball bats for the older boys, and balloons and clowns and a barbecue at night. I'd cleaned up Steve and Susan, put him in his little plaid jacket, her in her little white pinafore, and sent them outside, so Jerry and I could get dressed in peace.

All the children were running around like wild Indians, and Jerry yelled that they should calm down and get into the car. Susan hopped in the back, slammed her door shut, and never noticed that Steve's fingers had been curled around the door frame.

I took one look at that hand and knew this child wasn't going to a picnic; he was going to the emergency room. Jerry and I took him, leaving the older boys and Susan at home. While we were gone, the phone rang. It was the White House calling for Congressman Ford.

"He's gone to the hospital," said Jack.

President Johnson came on the line. "What do you mean, he's gone to the hospital? What's wrong with him?"

"Nothing," said Jack. "It's my little brother's fingers—"

Lyndon wanted to know which hospital.

The mashed hand was being X-rayed when the next call came from the President. He'd rung up the hospital to find out how Steve was doing. President Johnson was that way; you couldn't go anyplace without his tracking you down. It was one of the Fords' more interesting trips to an emergency room. Not all of them were honored by a call from the President of the United States.

Some of them weren't even honored by Jerry's and my presence. Every so often, we used to sneak off to White Sulphur Springs, to the Greenbrier Hotel, for a weekend together, and we left the children with sitters. (I think one of the reasons Clara and I got along so well, and never had an argument, was I usually didn't ask her to babysit. When five-thirty came, she was free to go home to her husband and her friends, except for those times when Jerry and I had to be away for more than a couple of days, and then she was perfectly happy to stay at our house. She and the kids would get on the bed in the master bedroom and watch television, and there'd be a fight about which one was going to spend the night with her. Sometimes she'd wind up trying to sleep with all four of them curled around her like a litter of kittens.)

Lee Mason, a teenager who lived across the street, was my favorite sitter, partly because her mother was always home, so if there was a crisis, Mrs. Mason could come over. And once we'd built our swimming pool there were plenty of crises. It was very pretty; we'd transformed the backyard into a patio and swimming pool area, plus my garden, and it was completely enclosed by antique brick walls covered with shrubbery, which made it private. But it tempted children to all kinds of mad games. The first time Jerry and I came home from the Greenbrier, Susan was in bandages. She'd fallen into the pool and cut her chin. The next time, the children were fine but the sitter was gone. "Where's Lee?" I said.

"Down at the emergency room," said Mike airily.

Playing tag around the pool, Lee had tried to jump from one corner to another, and taken all the skin off both her shins when she missed.

We also had some animal problems. Susan yearned for a kitten but I had an allergy to cats. Until she fell in love with a horse. We gave her horseback-riding lessons, and one day she came home from the stables and said there was a horse she'd like to buy. I saw the horse. Not only was it an old horse, it was a sick horse. Susan wanted to nurse it back to health; she was afraid it was going to die. And of course it *was* going to die, and I thought I'd be happier if it went to its reward straight from the stables, rather than from our front yard. We compromised. "Susan," I said, "why don't we settle for a cat? I think I've outgrown my allergy."

Before she got the cat, my daughter kept a snake in a hatbox under her bed. None of us knew about this until the morning we noticed Susan prowling up and down the halls searching for something. She'd given up and gone to school when I overheard a conversation between Clara and a woman named Alice, who came in to do the heavy cleaning. "Clara," Alice was saying, "do we have a snake?" "A snake?" said Clara. "Heavens, no."

"Well," said Alice, "there's one upstairs in Mrs. Ford's bathroom."

Sure enough, there was a black snake slithering up the Venetian blind. Clara and Alice trapped it. One of them raised the blind, the other held a box underneath, the snake slipped down into the box, and they took it out to the garage and put it in an empty fish tank.

When Susan came home, she was relieved. "I looked all morning," she said, "and I couldn't find it."

The boys claim I gave Susan special treatment. I didn't, but Grandma Ford did. She had raised four sons, and she was tired of zipping up corduroy pants, so a girl was bound to get individual attention from Jerry's mother. Grandma Ford even made a Christmas stocking for Susan's Shirley Temple doll.

Every time a new baby came along, Grandma Ford made a new Christmas stocking. They were unusually pretty, decorated with teddy bears and sleds and sequins and stars. The only trouble was, she never remembered how large she'd made the one before, and with little children that's murder. You'd get an earful of "Your stocking's bigger than mine!" and the Christmas spirit went right out the window. Clara settled the matter by taking the biggest stocking, then sewing pieces of white felt onto all the others so they'd be exactly the same size. Shirley Temple's stocking was powder blue with white trimming. Even the dogs had stockings.

Grandma Ford's dressmaker made clothes for Susan and copied those clothes, detail by detail, for her Shirley Temple doll. When Susan put on her blue coat and hat, Shirley was dressed the same way. Susan still has a wardrobe trunk with hangers full of that doll's costumes.

On Christmas Eve we always left out crackers and milk for Santa Claus because he'd be hungry by the time he reached our house. The milk and crackers would be gone in the morning, only a few crumbs left on the plate. We tried to keep the children believing in Santa Claus as long as possible.

When they got older, and I grew tired of filling all those family stockings, plus the dogs' stockings and the dolls' stockings, I retired. "Look," I said, "I'm going to put everybody's name on a slip of paper in a basket, and if you pull out your own name you put the slip back and pick another. Otherwise it's up to you to fill the stocking of the person whose name you draw."

They went crazy. Somebody put the Playboy Calendar in Jerry's stocking, and the year we discovered Steve had started smoking, somebody stuffed a small emergency tank of oxygen into his stocking, We padded the spaces around the presents with the usual oranges and nuts and candy canes. (I was so glad that cellophane had come along, because in *my* childhood those sticky crumbly canes were a mess.)

Steve and Susan have always been particularly close, but all the boys gave their sister a hard time. She used to come down to breakfast dressed for school. The night before she would have laid out her clothes carefully, dress, shoes, the right-color ankle socks to match the outfit, and she'd get to the table and they'd start. "Ow! It hurts my eyes!" "Boy, what an ugly skirt." "You're not going to wear *that*, are you?"

She looked darling, but they never quit criticizing. Which didn't mean they'd let an outsider do the same. It was okay for them to pick on her, but a stranger had better not try it.

Steve has always been the charmer of the family. From the time he was four years old, when we'd go to visit Grandma Ford, he'd act as her escort. He'd meet her friends, take their arms, open doors for them. He knows how to turn it on and off, and he knew from a tender age. He could do it with teachers, storekeepers, neighbors. All the elderly ladies used to compliment me about what a treasure Steven was, and I'd chuckle to myself and think, "If you only knew how you're being taken." At home, he'd get cross and willful the same as any other child. His magic didn't work on me. He tried, but I always said, "How much do you want now?" or "Save it for Grandma."

Steve's charm still abounds and has brought him show-business offers. But his theatrical career died a-borning. The first script he was offered was the movie version of *Grease*, which would have required him to dance. One day of rehearsal and he quit. He had two left feet and he knew it, so it was a nice clean break.

I'm such a ham I have to say I was disappointed that he didn't want to be a star, but I respect his decision. Mike wrote a letter telling him to be true to himself, and the letter meant a lot to Steve; he doesn't really like or understand Hollywood people; what he really likes and understands is horses.

Steve has bounced in and out of schools like a ping-pong ball (my two older children are educated, my two younger ones are dropouts) but Steve is talking now about going back again. Only this time he wants to go someplace where, when he's not in class, he can work on a ranch.

You start to notice the differences between your children when they get closer to adolescence. Even Mike and Jack seemed more alike than different to me until they were ten and twelve years old. Sometimes we celebrated their birthdays together, but each had his own cake—one always wanted chocolate, one always wanted a white cake—and his own friends to the party.

Every child is unique. If Steve was famous for his ability to con, Susan was equally famous for her lack of this gift. She's totally up front, so she's had to learn everything the hard way.

She spent four summers at a camp in Michigan. It was a good camp and she liked it, but there wasn't much horseback riding available and horses were her passion. Because of this, I investigated what was supposed to be a very fine riding camp in Pennsylvania. The place *did* have good horses, so the next year, Susan was sent there. As it turned out, campers were permitted to ride only one hour a day, and my daughter loathed everything else about that institution.

"It was an *etiquette* camp," Susan says. "You could not go from bed to bathroom with no shoes on; you could not chew gum out of the cabin. Every time you did anything, you were breaking a point. Your captain would come around at night and say, 'Did you break today?' and you had to be honest and say, 'Yes, I broke twice, I chewed gum, and I got out of bed after "Taps," ' or whatever it was. I hated that camp so much I went out and rolled in a patch of poison ivy so I'd have to be shipped home. They didn't ship me home, I just spent the rest of the summer scratching. They almost put me in the hospital because it started to go down my throat; they were afraid if it got any worse I'd suffocate myself."

Unhappy about the demerits piling up against her, Susan asked to be taken off her team. "I didn't want them to lose because of me."

I think all my children are bright, each in his own fashion. Mike, the tidy one who's gone into the ministry, did fine in school and never went through a frivolous period. Jack, who is in my mind the best read and most intellectual of our children, has been the last to find himself. And he's looked in some funny places, having tried the big-city jet set, rock music, night-life bit, running around with people like Bianca Jagger. Jack's the son with whom I've crossed swords most often. There were times when he—as a child— wouldn't talk to me, wouldn't answer me, because he knew that got under my skin.

Years ago, he said, "Well, *I'm* not the golden boy, *Mike* is, so don't expect too much of me." He obviously thought we cared more about Mike because we'd been stricter with Mike. You're always more relaxed with the second child. But Jack seemed to feel every other child was more special to us than he was. Mike was the oldest, so he was special. Susan was the only girl, so she was special. Steven could charm the stars out of the sky, so he was special. And poor Jack was filled with resentments.

"Sometimes you end up loving the most difficult child more than the others," Grandma Ford told me. "You spend so much more time trying to help work out their problems, you're so much more involved with them." Jack and I can have bitter arguments, but we always resolve them. My husband says we're too much alike, and that makes me mad, but I think I understand Jack better than Jerry does.

Because he seemed so much brighter than his marks indicated, we had him tested when he was in fifth grade, and he turned out to have a terrifically high I.Q., but he was always reading *Time* or *Newsweek* or *Sports Illustrated* when he should have been cracking his school books.

Jack's the one who goes away now and doesn't get in touch for a month, and forgets to call his father on his birthday. He'd never admit it, but he'd be hurt if we forgot *his* birthday, because he's always been remembered. For so long, I worried about him because he was ambitious and dissatisfied with himself, and it made him miserable. He was jealous of Steve. He couldn't figure out why his younger brother, who had little drive and no discernible theatrical ability, was being offered parts. "Steve doesn't know how to act," Jack would say bitterly, and I'd try to smooth it away. "I guess he doesn't have to act; he just has to play himself."

Jack's complicated, and he can be impossible to live with. He runs from any display of emotion, but underneath it all there's a great deal of affection in him.

Though once he got so angry it practically caused a disintegration of our household. It was on a Thanksgiving. Clara had prepared food the day before, so all I'd have to do was put a turkey in the oven. Cooking wasn't the problem; deciding when to have dinner was. The football games started about ten o'clock Thanksgiving morning and they went on and on and on. I think we finally discovered there would be a lull between 5 and 6 P.M., when we might get everybody to the table.

Thanksgiving Eve, Jack, who had new contact lenses, couldn't find his lens case when he was getting ready for bed. He took a couple of paper cups—I kept a paper cup dispenser in the children's bathroom so they wouldn't be passing germs back and forth—marked an L for left eye on one, and an R for right eye on the other, put water in them, and dropped his contact lenses into the water.

Next morning, Jerry was being a good soul and helping me because Clara wasn't there. Jack was out of bed, I don't know where; maybe he'd gone down to breakfast, but Jerry was straightening up the boys' room. And he took these two paper cups with water in them and threw the contents down the sink.

When it came time to watch the first football game, Jack went to look for his lenses. Gone. Oh gruesome circumstance. No matter how close he sat to the television set, Jack couldn't see anything. We phoned the eye doctor, who was at home watching the game too, and he was a real good sport. "Meet me at my office at the half," he said. "Maybe I've got something there that's close enough to his prescription so he can wear them until I can get new ones made."

I can't remember why Jack didn't even have a pair of glasses around. He must have broken them or lost them, but he was absolutely furious.

I felt sorry for Jerry, but I also thought he should have known those cups were sitting there for some reason. The eye doctor saved the day. He fitted Jack with something he could see out of, the games went on, tempers cooled down, and during the break we had Thanksgiving dinner.

Every Christmas vacation, we tried to go skiing. When Mike and Jack were seven and five, we took them to Michigan, leaving baby Steve home with Clara. As soon as Steve was five, we said he was big enough to come too, and of course we could hardly go off and leave four-year-old Susan, so she got started even earlier than the rest of them. She's a very good skier.

They're all good skiers. Their father is too, though he takes a lot of razzing from them. He came home a year or so ago with an award that named him "America's Number One Skier," and the children kidded the life out of him. "It should say, 'For His Age,'" one suggested. The kidding doesn't bother their old man. He skis with Henri Petty and Pepi Gramshammer, who used to be famous racers, and they claim they can't keep up with him, he goes so fast. And they're younger men than he is.

(Jerry's awards often amuse us. He was given a physical fitness trophy, a sculpture of a weight lifter, so heavy it takes a weight lifter to move it.)

We switched from skiing in Michigan because the children were dying to go West. First we tried Sun Valley, Jerry's old hangout, and the next year we had to skip because Jack had broken his collarbone playing football. There was no way the doctor would let him ski, even in a neck brace, and we felt it would be too cruel to make him come along and watch. Later, we went to Utah, skied at Alta, where they have marvelous deep powder, and finally we went to Vail, fell in love with it, and have been going ever since.

We always traveled as a crowd, hired a ski instructor, and that way were taken straight to the head of the line waiting for the lift. (Nobody expects you to pay an instructor for standing in line for forty-five minutes, so it's a terrific, if somewhat immoral, solution to the problem.)

We also went as a crowd to more serious affairs. As soon as they were old enough, we took Mike and Jack to the Republican National Conventions. From the time we first came to Washington, the only convention Jerry and I missed was Eisenhower's second. (That was such a cut-and-dried thing, and we'd been to San Francisco before, so we sat it out on Ottawa Beach in Michigan and watched Ike on TV at night.) Twice, Jerry was permanent chairman of a convention, which meant he had to be there all the time, and

Mike and Jack became platform pages, and carried messages to people seated on the platform.

There was one convention that scared the living daylights out of me. I think it was in 1960. We were flying to Chicago and Jerry turned to me and said, "There may be some people to meet us when we get off the plane."

"Who?" I said. "Why?"

"I've been chosen as Michigan's favorite son," he said. "There's going to be a band and a motorcade—"

"You go ahead without me," I said. "I'm not getting off the plane."

He told me not to be silly, and of course I got off the plane. When we walked into the Congress Hotel, there were great big pictures of Jerry around the lobby, and streamers and banners and people wearing blue-and-gold Ford buttons. It was really strange. The Wisconsin Republicans were running our friend John Byrnes as *their* favorite son, and there were rumors everywhere that Richard Nixon, if he won the Presidential nomination, was going to choose Jerry as a running mate.

We sat up until four o'clock in the morning waiting to hear, and then Nixon picked Henry Cabot Lodge instead, and asked Jerry to make the seconding speech on Lodge's behalf.

I think if Nixon had picked Jerry he might have beaten Kennedy, but I'm not unbiased. (Clara's even worse than I am. She's still convinced Jerry won the last election, and she'll say so to anybody who'll listen. I just agree. "Right, Clara, right, he'll always be *our* President.")

In 1964, after the Goldwater-Miller convention, Jerry and I had made plans to spend some vacation time with all four children. The month was August, and we'd rented a cottage at Bethany Beach in Delaware for a couple of weeks.

Two days before we were supposed to leave, I woke in the night with a terrible pain in my neck. The pain was shooting down my left arm, and that scared me. I couldn't sleep. I didn't want to disturb Jerry, so I went downstairs, and he found me there on the couch the next morning.

He drove me over to National Orthopedic Hospital, and they put me to bed and into traction.

I urged Jerry to go on, take the kids to the beach. He stayed away a week, then left the children with the mother of one of Mike's friends and came back to see how I was doing.

I was doing lousy. They had me strung up to various devices and they were giving me gold shots. My problem had been diagnosed as a pinched nerve.

How had I got it? Nobody knew. I blamed it on my having reached across a four-foot-wide counter in my kitchen to try to raise a window, but there's no way of proving that. The first time the hospital attendants took me for therapy, I cried from the pain. I couldn't lie down as they wanted me to and they had to work on my back while I sat on a chair and leaned forward across the treatment table.

When I came home from the hospital, I was still holding my left arm across my chest, and I was all crouched over; I could have played *The Hunchback of Notre Dame.*

Jerry had a traction setup installed at home, and I spent another couple of weeks in bed.

The day I got up, I glanced at myself in the full-length mirror in our bedroom, and I thought, My lord, here I am, forty-six, and I look like an old woman of ninety. A crippled old woman.

I made up my mind I wasn't going to go on that way.

16

*

... BUT I GET THE GROWING PAINS

I started working on exercises to get myself back in an upright position, and to relax my arm, so it would hang by my side again and I wouldn't have to support it.

Being home with the family made it nicer for me, and Clara was there to fix meals and supervise the kids.

I continued my therapy, going to the National Orthopedic Hospital at least three times a week for hot packs and massage that loosened my muscles. I got so I could drive a car again, do the shopping, take over more of my duties as wife and mother. But, from that time to this, I've never been really free of the problem because I developed arthritis, and the combination of pinched nerve and spinal arthritis is really unpleasant. You don't have your arm in a sling, or your leg in a cast, you're not on crutches, and you try to appear as normal as possible, but you can't always fool people. A friend takes you by the hand, says, "How do you feel?" and you say, "Fine, I'm fine," but the friend can see by your eyes that you're hurting.

In 1964 I was hurting, but I couldn't let that be the end of the line for me. I had a long way to go, four strapping children only half raised, a great responsibility.

How great I hadn't a notion until Jerry became Minority Leader of the House of Representatives on January 4, 1965. (Many people wonder why he never ran for the Senate, or the Governorship of Michigan, but he loved the House dearly. His sole ambition from the day he went there until the day he was plucked out and named Vice President was to become Speaker of the House.)

The preceding November, President Johnson had been sent back to the White House (my abstaining from the toast to his victory hadn't mattered a bit) and the Democrats had kept control of Congress, so there wasn't going to be a Republican Speaker of the House, and up until a few days before Christmas, Jerry hadn't made up his mind about running for Minority Leader.

I remember sitting in the living room with him and our two older boys, discussing the pros and cons of Jerry's going into battle against Charlie Halleck, who'd been Minority Leader for quite a while. (There was a group of Republicans, always referred to as the Young Turks, who wanted Charlie deposed.) Jack, at twelve, had the confidence of a seasoned political observer. "Why don't you try, Dad?" he said. "I know you can make it."

Jerry tried. And he made it.

Charlie Halleck had a lot of political IOUs out, and he called them in; many of Jerry's close friends had to vote for Charlie. Jerry won anyway. "By an overwhelming majority of seven votes," he says. "But I wasn't going to ask for a recount."

The Congress got a new Minority Leader, and I lost a husband. There followed a long stretch of time when Jerry was away from home 258 days a year. I had to bring four kids up by myself. I couldn't say, "Wait till your father comes home"; their father wasn't going to come home for maybe a week.

Sometimes he'd fly back to Washington and head right for his office, and we wouldn't even get to see him. He'd phone me, tell me what he needed, I'd pack a suitcase with clean clothes, and Frazier, his driver—as Minority Leader, he had a driver—would bring his dirty clothes out to the house, pick up the clean ones, and Jerry would be off again that afternoon at four o'clock. He could make a dinner meeting in someplace like Denver, or maybe California. He might miss the dinner, but he'd be there for the speech.

I remember one week when I prayed the entire time. I really was afraid Jerry would collapse. He started by going to California after the Monday session in the House, showed up back in Congress for the Tuesday session, flew to Maine right afterward. For five straight nights he was in different parts of the country, yet he never missed a day on the floor of the House. I figured if he lived through that week he'd live through anything.

Why did he let himself be booked so heavily? You'd have to ask him. (I've asked him many times. Even since we've been out of the White House, I've asked him.) Have a few lines from the *New York Times* of December 21, 1977, after Jerry had been back to Washington for a four-day visit:

> He conferred Sunday with Israeli Prime Minister Begin about Middle East peace moves. He met with a bipartisan group supporting ratification of the Panama Canal treaties. He lectured before a group of business leaders, attended a symposium on famine prevention, conferred with Arthur F. Burns, Chairman of the Federal Reserve Board, met with members of his old Cabinet, was briefed on Salt II negotiations by Henry Kissinger, his Secretary of State, and Paul H. Nitze, Secretary of Defense.

I should have known he was not a man who could ever retire. I look at a June schedule and say, "Well, I guess I'll see you in July." He's lecturing, teaching, speaking, he's golfing, he's helping somebody raise funds. It's just his personality.

I still had the neck pain. I went from doctor to doctor. A neurosurgeon signed me into George Washington Hospital for ten days and gave me more tests. They tried putting my head in a machine which lifts your neck and releases it. I couldn't stand that machine. I couldn't dance any more, either, and dance had been my purest pleasure all my life. After Mike was born, I'd gone right back, taken classes organized by Francesca Lodge, in Georgetown. Later, in Alexandria, I went to a class given by a woman named Hedi Polk. Basically, she was trying to help young mothers regain their figures, but for me it was just fun.

That fun was over now.

Also, since Jerry had become an important Republican, I had

taken it upon myself to shake up the Republican wives. I thought the Democratic wives were more effective. "If anybody asks you to do anything, say yes," I advised my peers. "Get off your duffs. It's always the Democratic wives who model in the fashion shows for Multiple Sclerosis or the Heart Fund."

I coerced a lot of women who'd never done any modeling in their lives into chasing up and down runways for charity, and they got so they liked it.

Nobody made me take on these jobs; I was convinced it was my duty.

My duty to my children obsessed me even more. When Mike and Jack got to high school, it was at a time of heavy drug use, and we had PTA meetings where experts came in and told us what drugs looked like, and how we could identify the smell of grass if our kids were smoking it.

Congressional wives have the same problems other wives have. Some Congressional wives drink, plenty of Congressional wives divorce. I was amused by the stories that the Carters were going to try to wipe out divorce in Washington. I don't know how you're going to wipe out divorce. The loneliness, the being left to yourself at night, is what makes marriages crack, makes liquor more attractive, but who am I to criticize? During the time when Jerry was gone so much I developed a problem, and I quit drinking entirely for a couple of years. (I have now quit drinking again. For clarification of this subject, see the last chapter of this book.)

In 1962 Grandpa Ford died, and my sister-in-law Janet and I went to take care of Grandma Ford until she recovered from pneumonia. She'd wake in terrible sweats, and we'd have to get her up and change her dripping nightgown and her bed. I stayed in the guest room, but Janet went right into Grandpa Ford's room and slept in his bed. "It has to be done sooner or later," she said.

Dear, smart, funny Janet; she was the one who'd have cared for our children if anything had happened to Jerry and me. She's an interior decorator who got into the field through inadvertence. Her husband, Tom, worked for the Ford family's paint and varnish company, and Janet started helping out on commercial jobs, advising clients not only about paint but about how to fix their offices more attractively. She redid her own place every season—she'd change the furniture around, put things away, get other things out; you never knew when you walked into her house what was going to be where. She did the same when she came to *our* house, rearranged every object it was possible to move. I finally learned not to say a word; I'd wait until she left, and then put it all back the way I liked it.

Janet is the sister I never had, and my best friend.

I kept up other friendships with people back home in Michigan, but once in a while I came a cropper. Jack and Phoebe Stiles got a divorce, and I was right in the middle of it. Three times Phoebe moved out, and three times I advised reconciliation. Finally I got a letter telling me not to interfere any more, Phoebe had made up her mind, and she didn't need help from me. I kept that letter a long time. I didn't know how to respond to it. It was almost as if she were shutting off our relationship. She wasn't, actually, but she was sick and tired of having me talk her into going back to Jack. The problem was always some other woman, and Phoebe wasn't going to share her husband with another woman.

Please mind your own business. In pen and ink.

Poor Phoebe, I thought. She's in trouble.

I didn't realize that I myself was in trouble. It appeared to me I was doing okay, except for the neck pain.

Now it all seems obvious. I was resentful of Jerry's being gone so much; I was feeling terribly neglected. But I didn't let myself know these things. Sometimes a true word might be spoken in jest— one night I rolled over in bed, saw Jerry beside me, and said, "What are *you* doing here?"—but mostly I bottled up my misery.

And one day the bottle broke.

I've asked Susan to tape what she remembers about what happened. This is her testimony:

I'll never forget it. I was eight years old. And Daddy was on the Sequoia *with President Johnson, and Mother was in her room crying and very upset about something, and I ran and called Clara, and Clara came (she'd been across the street) and settled*

Mother down and got hold of Daddy and he came home, and while he was in seeing her and the doctor, Clara pulled Steve and me outside. She said that Mother was very sick, and she had to go to a psychiatrist. At eight years of age, you can't handle that. I thought, Well, my mother's a lunatic, I'm highly embarrassed. I didn't know what I was supposed to do, where I was supposed to go. I was scared that Mother might fall apart in front of my friends.

It must have been hard on Susan. It was fairly hard on me. The collapse had been a long time building. I'd felt as though I were doing everything for everyone else, and I was not getting any attention at all. I was so hurt that I'd think, I'm going to get in the car, and I'm going to drive to the beach, and nobody's going to know where I am. I wanted them to worry about me. I wanted them to recognize me. I wanted them to say, "Well, my gosh, Mother is gone, what are we going to do?"

I started seeing a psychiatrist twice a week. He was a sounding board. I could tell him all the problems I couldn't talk to anybody else about. My back hurts, there's dope in the schools, Jerry's away. It siphoned off the pressures. I could talk out my feelings of frustration. Up until then, I'd thought I should be strong enough to shoulder my own burdens, not carry them to somebody else. I wasn't a woman who could run to her husband with "The cook has quit" when he came home tired and hoping for some tranquillity.

Jerry was great. He would have agreed to anything that would help me. He went to the psychiatrist himself. The doctor wanted to see us together, but I said no. I don't know why. Anyway, the psychiatrist talked to Jerry a couple of times, just to discuss my situation.

I made good progress. The doctor taught me that I had to take time out to do some things for myself. He told me I had to believe that I was important, and that if I went to pieces I wouldn't be of much value to Jerry or the children. "Sometimes you have to say to yourself, 'Look, Betty, this is your day. You just go and do what you please,' " he said.

I've often said I'd lost my feeling of self-worth, and that's what sent me for help. I think a lot of women go through this. Their husbands have fascinating jobs, their children start to turn into independent people, and the women begin to feel useless, empty. After I went into therapy, Jerry and I talked it over, and we came to the conclusion that my mental state had a lot to do with my physical illness. Sometimes the body makes you pay for what the head is struggling with.

I don't believe in spilling your guts all over the place, but I no longer believe in suffering in silence over something that's really bothering you. I think you have to get it out and on the table and discuss it, no matter what it is.

After a while, even Susan stopped being ashamed of her loony mother:

It took me about a year and a half to realize the psychiatrist was doing her good, that it was the right thing for her. She started talking to me about the sessions. It was up to her to make me understand because I guess she did know I was somewhat afraid of her.

Only last year Susan told me that she too had resented Jerry's being gone so much, which surprised me because she'd never really known anything different. I was aware that she'd been jealous of Jerry's closeness with the boys, but that was inevitable. Jerry was athletic, the boys were athletic, and as soon as he came home for a couple of days, they'd all be out throwing balls, and Susan couldn't compete. "I tried to get some attention for myself," she says, "but it didn't work. I did not have a chance against three big brothers."

Ironically, she dates her own feelings of tenderness for Jerry from a time when he made a remark which might have enraged a different child. The schools were giving out prizes called Presidential Awards to kids who could run the six-hundred-yard dash in so many seconds, and throw softballs harder and faster than other kids. One of Susan's friends came home with a Presidential Award, and Susan didn't. She just couldn't throw a softball. I got rather upset—I may already have been closer to the thin edge than any of us guessed at the time—and I said, "Where's your award? Why didn't you get one?"

Jerry, who happened to be there, interfered. "Leave her alone," he said. "She's only a girl." From that day forward, Susan gave him her unqualified adoration. Figure it out if you can.

Jerry is sometimes criticized for calling me "Mother" by people who say, "She's not your mother," but I find it endearing. It comes of having so many children around, and explaining, "Mother and I think this," or "Mother and I are going to do that." I'd sign "Mom" on an anniversary card or a birthday card to Jerry, or even on a note. Often, he'd get home from a trip in the middle of the night, and he always tried not to wake me, so I'd leave a message—"Hope you had a good trip, I love you—Mom"—on his pillow when I went to bed.

But where he was concerned, I had an inner clock. If his plane was due in at National Airport at four o'clock in the morning, I woke up at four o'clock in the morning to will that plane down. He could be home from the airport in twenty minutes, and I would lie there totally alert until I heard the downstairs door open. I knew he'd be exhausted, wouldn't want to talk, but I'd listen for that door and the sound of his suitcases being put down—they were always left in the hall—and his footsteps starting up the stairs, and then I'd roll over and go back to sleep. By the time he picked the note off his pillow, I'd be dead to the world again.

A while back, an interviewer asked Jerry how he thought his constant traveling had affected our lives.

"It put a strain on the marriage," Jerry said. "I called every night unless, through some unusual circumstance, a phone wasn't available, but I was all over the country, and sometimes overseas, and with four active children, Betty had a tough obligation. They were all doing their thing, and although they grew up to be nice kids, they had their problems, and she had to be not only the mother but the father. Then, when I was home I wanted to make everything smooth and nice, which made it more difficult for her because I would never be the one to reprimand them. Even before I was Minority Leader, in election years I'd go to Michigan after Congress adjourned, be away for three weeks, come home for the weekend, go back to Michigan and my constituents for another three weeks.

"We always tried to take family vacations at Christmas and in the summer, and those were wonderful times. Still it was ten and a half to eleven months a year I was gone. But the kids weathered it. And the marriage weathered it."

With a little help from a psychiatrist. Dr. William Menninger has said, "Mental health problems do not affect three or four out of every five persons but one out of one." After I became First Lady, I went before a national meeting of psychiatrists and said I'd had psychiatric care, and that I thought it was just as important to take care of your mind as it was to take care of your body. I got a standing ovation. Because so many people think it's shameful to confess that they can't make it alone, that it's an admission of something terribly wrong with them. There was nothing terribly wrong with me. I just wasn't the Bionic Woman, and the minute I stopped thinking I had to be, a weight fell from my shoulders.

17

LOVE AND DEATH

"The kids weathered it," Jerry said. Amen. It's always been my feeling that God lends you your children until they're about eighteen years old. If you haven't made your points with them by then, I think it's too late. You want to set their feet in the right direction, help them develop into good citizens and decent human beings, and some of what you have to do is easy, and some of it is very hard.

You can teach table manners, but how do you deal with the big questions, like death?

"No kid ever has death really explained to them," Susan says, adding that the topic was "somewhat hush-hush in our family."

I'm sure she's right. You try to shield your children from pain, and there's no way to accomplish that.

When Grandpa Ford died, Susan was so young the death didn't mean a lot to her, but she was ten when Walter Norblad, her godfather, died. "It was my first experience of going to a funeral home and seeing a dead body," she remembers. Not long afterward, we lost Grandma Ford.

Grandma Ford had been a dervish. She whirled from one thing

to another; she had to be busy in order to be happy. She'd said she was going to die with her boots on, and she did. She died in church. One of our cousins who was ushering got her out and to the hospital. She had suffered her third—and fatal—heart attack. Going through her belongings later, we found her calendar for the next month. It was completely filled. She drove, she swam, she was never home for any meal but breakfast, and Jerry's just like her. I'm sure he'll go just like her.

Susan had been fond of her grandmother, but her chief memory of that funeral is "seeing my father cry, which just ripped me apart." Then, when Susan was twelve, my brother Bob died unexpectedly, of a stroke, and that was another blow. "Oh, I loved him, he was super," Susan says. "All of us kids were in love with him. We always stopped to see him on our way to or from camp, stopped at his house or Aunt Janet's; we knew we'd have a good time both places."

To be remembered with joy has to be a kind of immortality.

If Susan is correct, and I treated death in a sort of "hush-hush" fashion, I certainly attempted to speak out loud and clear on the subject of sex, usually to a child who was horrified. I was always telling the boys they must be gentlemen, but my real weapon was car keys. (They all got cars as soon as they turned sixteen.) If a boy came home in the middle of the night, and I could tell by the way he was tiptoeing and how guilty he looked that he'd been drinking beer and wooing some girl in a secluded parking lot, I'd just say, "Okay, hand over the car keys."

We set curfews. And child who came in late had the time subtracted from his next weekend.

Susan insists that I sat her up on the kitchen counter in Alexandria and gave her a book which explained about love and the relationship of a man and a woman when she was still so small that I could pick her up and sit her there.

"I was fascinated," she says, "but I still don't understand relationships between men and women. That book didn't say what pains in the neck men are, that's the problem."

Once the kids started going on dates, I used to envision all those teenagers trying to kiss with the braces on their teeth. I mean, if a boy and a girl ever got their braces hooked, it would be like cars locking bumpers; you'd have to call the AAA to free them.

I said our youngsters got cars when they reached sixteen. In the sixties, that meant only Mike and Jack. (Steve didn't turn sixteen until 1972, at which time he broke out in a yellow Jeep.) They didn't drive old heaps—Jerry and I were too concerned about safety—but they worked to earn part of the cost of their wheels. Jerry would always match every dollar the children earned, and put in a bank, with another dollar, an incentive to make them think about saving rather than spending. He's been a generous father. When Steve wants a horse, or Susan wants a condominium, or Mike and Gayle need the down payment on a house, Daddy's there to help. Mother too, if the truth be told. I used to say Susan would hit me for fifteen, twenty bucks just to window shop.

Our children have had all kinds of jobs. As a teenager, Jack worked his way across the Atlantic on a freighter, loading and unloading cargo. He was well paid, but he didn't see much of Europe, unless you count the docks.

As for Steve, he worked in Alaska. That adventure began in August of the year he was twelve, in 1968. Jerry was going to Alaska on a political campaign, to help one of his GOP colleagues, and he wanted me to come. I took a look at his itinerary, puddle jumping from one place to another in a little plane, and it didn't appeal to me. So he took Steve.

They were gone one week, but while they were up there, Steve met some people who ran a summer camp for hunters. These people had youngsters about Steve's age, and for the next two summers Steve went back there. He'd fly to the closest airport and pick up a bush pilot plane which would set him down as close as it could to the camp area. The nearest town was just a crossroads in the wilderness, with a bank, a saloon, and a grocery store, like a western movie. Indians came to town every Saturday night, a lot of people got drunk, and once in a while somebody was knifed. The hunting lodge was comfortable, but sixty miles from a telephone.

Steve learned to shoot and he learned to shoe horses. He was kicked a couple of times, but he finally learned right. The family who owned the camp would book a group of hunters—ten doctors, say—for a few days. The group would set out on horseback into the mountains, looking for caribou and those great big gorgeous mountain goats with the curled horns. The goats live so high in the hills you have to go way up past timberline to find them, but they're considered fabulous trophies.

Steve and the camp owners' kids would go on ahead and build shelters for the hunters to stay the night, and the summer he was thirteen, Steve shot a white-neck caribou. It weighed 550 pounds, the second-largest shot that year. We hung the magnificent head over the big fieldstone fireplace in our condominium in Vail.

We've had a lot of laughs in front of that fireplace, and some pretty good family arguments too. The Christmas Jack was sixteen was a case in point. He was getting phone calls from friends, and he wanted to fly home to Alexandria for a New Year's party.

I talked to Jerry privately: "Tell him no."

Jerry disagreed. "He's old enough and wise enough to make the right decision." By the right decision, my husband meant *his* decision, and I knew perfectly well that Jack was pulling in another direction.

Had I been handling the situation, I'd have said, "Dismiss it from your mind, Jack, you're not going home." I didn't want him alone in the house in Alexandria, and I didn't see the point of bringing everyone to Vail for a few days of skiing—we used to ski through New Year's Day, then leave immediately afterward to get back in time for school—only to have Jack waste a couple of those precious days.

But Jerry was in charge. "I'm going to leave it up to you, Jack, to do what you think is right," Jerry said.

What Jack thought was right was to catch the 3 A.M. bus from Vail to Denver, get a plane in Denver, and go home. Mike, however, had placed a great number of tin cans along the route to the front door so Jack was thwarted in his attempt to make a silent departure. And there we all were, roused up in the middle of the night. Jerry had been so sure Jack would behave in a "mature" fashion, but a sixteen-year-old doesn't care about maturity; he was off on a lark, he was headed for a party.

After a good deal more argument, Jerry said Jack could not go. I thought that was bad too. It didn't seem fair to change the rules after the game had started. Make your own decision. No, that's the wrong decision.

Finally, I stepped in. "The two of you quit this. Jack, you're not going, and Jerry, you're coming back to bed."

Jack moped for a couple of days, but he got over it.

All of our children except Susan went to public high school. When she was twelve years old, Susan started at Holton Arms, in Bethesda, Maryland. She boarded there during the week and came home weekends. She thought it was a good idea. "I was at that age where mothers and daughters don't get along well anyway," she says. "You'd do anything to make your mother mad."

As it turned out, Holton Arms was tougher than Mother. "We had to stand up when a teacher came into the room; I wasn't used to it."

But that was fine too. I hadn't ever asked my children to bow, curtsy, do a lot of no-sirring and yes-ma'aming of people, but I didn't mind their finding out that the world makes demands of you which your doting parents do not.

Various people have described Jack and Susan (never Mike or Steve) as rude and arrogant. I think that only started after Jerry became Vice President. At that time, Jack and Susan didn't always handle the limelight particularly well. Mike and Steve simply avoided it. Jack and Susan flirted with it, alternately fascinated and repelled. They were resentful of being on display, of the intrusion on their privacy, so to prove themselves independent and above it all, even though they knew better, they were occasionally a bit obnoxious.

Back in the sixties, though, before we were famous, we were one big scrappy family. When we all got together at the dinner table, it was like a debating society. And there was plenty to debate, with riots in the cities, riots on the campuses, Kent State, a third party growing up around George Wallace, the country divided against itself. Mike, only ten years old when the decade began, was a man before it ended; and although he respected his father's rights to his views, he was fiercely opposed to the war in Vietnam.

On March 31, 1968, President Johnson, hobbled by losses in Asia and dissension at home, announced that he would not run again, and the following August, at the Republican National Convention in Miami Beach, Richard Nixon was nominated as the GOP's candidate for President. He chose Spiro Agnew to be his running mate. People ask me why, as if I knew the answer. Only God knows the answer, and He won't tell. When Agnew's name was announced, we all looked at one another and said, "Agnew? Agnew who?"

The Democrats lived a horror story at their convention in Chicago. Police beat up protesters, protesters dropped bags of garbage out of hotel windows on innocent passersby. It was awful. We didn't have anything like that in Miami, but I do remember anti-war demonstrators lying in the street, body to body, outside the convention hall, and our having to walk over them to get in or out.

As always, Jerry was dreaming of a Republican landslide which would make him at long last Speaker of the House, but even after Nixon had defeated Humphrey for the Presidency, that dream was not realized. The Democrats retained control of both House and Senate.

My husband, still Minority Leader, began his eleventh term in Congress.

Our oldest son turned eighteen and went off to Wake Forest College in North Carolina, where, dove or not, he joined the ROTC.

We all hoped Richard Nixon might find the answer to our national "crisis of the spirit" which he talked about in his First Inaugural Address.

18

THE OTHER WOMAN

Whenever anyone in the Ford family suffered a crisis of spirit, he or she tended to turn to Clara Powell. I've joked that I stayed home (most of the times) when Jerry went back to Michigan to campaign because I didn't want my children to think that Clara was their mother.

But in a way she was their mother. In a way she was my mother. Even now, at an age when she might be taking it easy, she spends her days ministering to her own mother, who's old and blind.

Clara Boswell was born in Arlington, Virginia. She'd have liked to be a nurse. "But I didn't get the opportunity. My mother and dad was separated when I was young, and my grandmother raised me. When she passed, I came to live with my mother. I went to high school to the third year, then I went to work. When I was seventeen, I got married to Raymond Powell. I really didn't have a chance to nurse, but I've been nursin' ever since."

Clara tended our children as though they were her own. Even though she had to leave us in 1970—"My dad got sick, and I couldn't see him be put in a home, so I just went to take care of him"—the kids would still go visit her two and three times a week.

It was only a ten-minute drive from our house in Alexandria to Clara's dad's place. "Susan used to come up and we used to sew," Clara remembers. "We did a lot of sewing for her one summer." Clara also taught Susan to cook.

When Jerry became Vice President, Clara was there with us, and when he made his first address to Congress as President, she was there, and whenever she came to the White House for dinner, he would always say that particular dinner couldn't compare to Clara's pot roast.

It tickled Clara. "He used to tell 'em down at the White House, anybody come in, he'd say, 'I've had pot roasts, but they don't taste like Clara's.' "

She was with us in the family quarters on that last election night, and she stayed until 3:15 A.M., which was when Jerry went to bed.

Last year Clara crocheted an afghan for each of the Ford children—they chose the colors they wanted—and she's still feeding them. One or another is always calling up and asking if he can come for a meal.

She keeps every memento they ever sent her. There in an album is the prayer from Mike, dated Easter, 1973 ("He wrote it himself," she says proudly), along with the note Steve mailed last Mother's Day, thanking her for the afghan ("I sleep with it all the time. We love you, Babe"), and the card from Susan which says, "To Clara, my second mother," and quotes from Carl Sandburg: "There is a place where love begins, and a place where love ends, and love asks nothing."

One Virginia family quit coming to our church, Immanuel-on-the-Hill, because Clara—who's black—was there with us for Susan's christening (the boys had all been christened in Grand Rapids), but most of the other church members said, "Well, *they* certainly are stuffy," and nobody took it too big one way or another. Actually, Clara was often the most decorative member of our gang, a handsome woman who dressed for an occasion. I think of her in a long powder-blue gown at Mike and Gayle's wedding; she looked like a million bucks.

We always said Jack was her favorite Ford, but Clara denies it. "Jack was a little different in some ways, and to me he's always been an ideal boy, but Mike was darling too. Grandma Ford brought him in when they came home from the hospital and handed him to me and says, 'Here's your baby.' "

Clara the archivist. She keeps pictures of the dogs we used to have ("This is Sugar, this is the second Sugar") and pictures of Crown View Drive, and a picture of me holding the newborn Mike and looking terribly pleased with myself, and numberless snapshots of little crewcut boys—I'd forgotten how we used to practically shave their heads—running, jumping, grinning for the camera.

Clara suffered over Jack's grades, and he wrote her from college: "I know there were a lot of times when you felt like giving up on me, but you never did. . . . I think it is finally paying off, all the encouragement and help both you and Raymond gave me."

The night before Mike left to get married, Clara came back to Crown View Drive "to carry their wedding gift," and Mike, who'd just had a tooth pulled, was upstairs asleep. Clara set down the beautiful silver tea service she'd brought him and Gayle, and went to his room. She patted him on the cheek, and he opened his eyes. "Ah," he said, "it does me good to wake up and see you; it makes the hurt go away."

Having started working at fifteen ("You wasn't making much at that time, but what you made went a long ways"), Clara'd had her share of employers who weren't winners, yet she never knocked anybody. "I've worked for people there would be unkind things I could say about them" is as mean a remark as you're apt to hear from her.

She and I used to laugh about everything and nothing. One day, I'd put on a record I loved, Fred Waring's group singing "Get Out on Your Knees and Pray," and I was down on my knees, literally, scrubbing the family–TV-room floor in time to the music, and Clara was down on *her* knees scrubbing the hall a few feet away, and we were both singing along with Fred's chorus at the top of our voices, and pushing our brushes, and suddenly we both started to laugh; we laughed until we were weak and flailing around in the soap suds.

When she wasn't working for money, Clara was still working. "My grandmother had a stroke, and I taken care of her for years, and then after I got married Raymond's father had a stroke, so I looked after him to help out Raymond's mother."

If a child of ours had a sore throat, a broken bone, a pip of any sort, it didn't faze Clara. "Whenever they taken sick, I was never frightened because I had been around so much sickness. Jack broke his collarbone playing football, and they carried him to the hospital, and I was the only one at the house when the hospital phoned. Jack had been askin' for Clara, Clara, Clara, and when I came in the emergency room, the coach said, 'There's no point of us stayin', Clara's here.' "

Clara's house is full of homemade presents, and presents saved up for out of allowances that started at a dollar a week. She has a papier mâché candle holder Susan put together in kindergarten; she has a little Christmas tree pin Steve bought, and a rhinestone locket in the shape of a heart from Mike.

She knows our good traits and our bad. She teases me about my lust for clothes, and the night my entire wardrobe hit the floor with a crash. Jerry and I were away, and the children were sleeping. "All of a sudden, I heard this big thump," Clara says, "and I was scared. I thought, oh my lord, is somebody out in the backyard tryin' to break in? So I got up, and here was this rack that ran the whole length of the bedroom, and it had fallen clear off the wall because there were so many clothes on it."

Because we didn't like fancy dishes, Clara thought we were easy to cook for. "I'd make the kids jello or instant pudding," she says, "or I would bake a pie or a cake whenever I felt like it. We had one dessert made of angel-food cake, and then you used this chocolate and whipped cream, put it together, put it in the freezer, took it out later. Good, but awful rich. Used to make it way ahead of time to serve at parties."

The parties weren't the same after Clara left. She tended her dad for five years, and then she had not quite a year of freedom before she had to start taking care of her mother, who is senile and sleeps most of the day. Watching over her is nevertheless full-time duty. "She doesn't realize she's blind," Clara says. "She just wants somebody there for attention. Even the radio's no good. Sort of confuses her. If she hears about a fire or something, she thinks it's here, and this gets on her mind, and you can't get it off."

Raymond, who used to be a cement worker (he set forms), is retired, and he tends his garden, growing kale, string beans, corn, okra, peppers. "He's a wonderful person," Clara says. "I can remember him sayin' to me—this was after his mother passed—'Do all you can for your mother.' I'm so grateful. I don't know whether it's something back in his mind that he didn't do that he's giving me the opportunity to do, but as far as me bein' over there takin' care of her, he's never complained one time."

Clara's never complained one time either. Not about the years of shuttling children back and forth to the orthodontist, nor about the tons of dirty laundry to be fed into machines and fetched out again, nor about the endless bowls of boiled potatoes to be mashed with milk and salt and pepper and butter, nor the piles of dishes and pots to be scrubbed, nor the thousand minor wounds which required patching up with Band-aids and with hugs.

Denied a higher education, and therefore the career she would have been well suited for, she never wasted a single minute feeling sorry for herself.

"When you sit back and think about it, it's been an adorable life all the way through," she says.

Beautiful Clara. She was our bright particular star.

19

⁓

1968-1972: WE EAT SEA SLUGS, AND PLAN OUR FUTURE

Jerry and I thought President Nixon was doing a good job his first term in office. So far as the war in Vietnam was concerned, I was more of a hawk than my children. I remember when Goldwater ran, everybody kept saying he was dangerous because he would shoot from the hip, and Johnson wasn't going to do any of those things Goldwater suggested. The minute Johnson was elected, he turned right around and did them all. It's like the crack I've heard attributed to William Buckley. Buckley said something along the lines of "I was told if I voted for Senator Goldwater there would be an escalation of the war. Well, I did, and there was."

Long before such action was authorized, I was for bombing the harbor at Haiphong. Goods were piling up on the docks, and I thought if we gave ships twenty-four hours' warning so they could clear out, and then bombed the port, we'd get a quicker end to the war. Most mothers of sons wanted that war to be over.

Even though I believe all citizens—and that includes females— should give two years of service to their country, I was very relieved when Mike and Jack drew high draft numbers. (We were just lucky. By the time Steve was old enough, the government was no longer drafting.) Mike was talking about maybe becoming a lawyer (he hadn't yet settled on the ministry) but no one could imagine his going to war; he couldn't kill anyone, no enemy, nobody.

There was a lot of talk about flying saucers in those days, and I was convinced there were such things. Jerry used to laugh at me because every time there'd be a flying-saucer story in the paper I'd rip the article out and save it to show him. "That was probably a meteorite," he'd say, but I wasn't satisfied.

In 1969, Betty Vanik, the wife of Congressman Charlie Vanik, a Democrat from Ohio, and I took a man from Westinghouse to lunch and talked him into backing a series of half-hour television shows dealing with the three branches of our government. The man from Westinghouse said it was the most expensive lunch he'd ever had.

Forty half-hour programs resulted, and I don't know whether people learned anything about government, but I learned a bit about television. I was told that the shows had to be keyed to a ninth-grade level in order for people to understand what they were seeing. I still think viewers are smarter than that.

Nineteen sixty-nine was also the year in which a poll conducted by the American Institute of Public Opinion showed that Richard Nixon was the most admired man in America. He won three times as many votes as Billy Graham, who placed second. The voters' third choice was Spiro Agnew, who, according to the *New York Times Encyclopedic Almanac* "has the distinction of ranking higher than any other incumbent Vice President in the history of the list."

In 1971, the People's Republic of China was admitted to the UN, and in the winter of 1972, an election year, President and Mrs. Nixon made a trip to that country. The leaders of the Senate, Hugh Scott and Mike Mansfield, followed, and then in June the House leadership, Hale Boggs and Jerry Ford, and their wives and staffs got to go.

It was fascinating. The Chinese are likely to feed you anything—it's quite an experience, trying to choke down sea slugs—but visiting China was much more cheerful than visiting Russia. I'm sure there was just as much surveillance, but it wasn't so obvious; you felt more at ease.

We went up north to Old Manchuria, where there had been no Caucasians for twenty-four years, and the people were enthralled by us. Children would see our cars, and they'd come running from the rice paddies at full tilt.

The Chinese children seemed happy, but very controlled. You'd hear this martial music, and here would come these darling little youngsters marching two by two off to school.

I visited a rice commune run by a woman, and I went into a store which was mainly stocked with the colorful plastic sandals the children wear, and bought a turquoise-blue Thermos-type bottle with a painting of a panda on it. (Chinese vacuum bottles are terrific; one filled with very hot water would be put in your room at night, and the water would stay hot forever. Or till morning, anyway.)

The Chinese in the North are much larger than the Chinese in the South, and the cooking in the South is much hotter, with more spices, more seasonings. At breakfast I stuck to American food. I could face sea slugs at night, but not first thing in the morning. The Chinese drink orange soda pop—warm orange soda pop, which they call orange juice—or beer. They also have a very good red wine. Strong. It'll clean your rusted pipes, but I noticed the women didn't empty their glasses.

One of the most extraordinary things Jerry and I witnessed was an operation performed without anesthesia; they used acupuncture instead. The patient was a pretty young girl with a large ovarian tumor. She was lying flat on the table, and we were in a gallery above her looking down through a glass dome. She would look up and smile at us, and we would smile back at her and wave and make gestures of encouragement. She sipped tea and orange juice all through the operation, and there was a little machine between her ankles, which kept the needles (placed in her ankles) vibrating.

It seemed to me as though they sewed up seven layers of skin to get her back together again, but there was very little blood. I hadn't been sure I'd be able to watch, but it was so amazing I got through it. What surprised me most were the cameramen: they were scrubbed and in surgical gowns and masks, right in the room taking pictures while the operation was going on.

(After Jerry became President, we went again to China and took Susan. It meant she'd miss some school, but her teachers agreed that she should seize the opportunity. It wasn't until this second visit that we met Chairman Mao, and when Susan came in, the old Chairman's eyes lit up. The sight of a young blonde delighted him, there was no doubt about it.)

When we came home from our first China trip, in 1972, Jerry went into the hospital for a knee operation; he had trouble from an old football injury. Then he threw himself into campaigning for President Nixon's re-election.

In June of 1972 the news of a Watergate break-in had hit the papers, but it seemed like such an inept effort at God knows what by God knows whom that it didn't affect the voters. Nixon beat McGovern in forty-nine states—it was a true landslide—and still Congress remained in Democratic hands. Jerry began to face the fact that he was probably never going to be Speaker of the House.

He promised me he would retire at the end of President Nixon's second term, but he said he felt he ought to continue as Minority Leader until then. I agreed to that. We'd already been thinking about Florida as a possible retirement place, weighing the virtues of the East Coast against the virtues of the West Coast. We wanted to be close to the children, so they could visit often, but we didn't know in which directions the children would choose to roam.

Mike and Jack were already gone from home, Jack to Utah State University, where he was majoring in forestry, Mike to Massachusetts, where he was studying for the ministry. After his graduation from Wake Forest, Mike, who'd been preparing for the law, had decided to take some time off and find out what he really wanted to do. He got a job with his fraternity, a job which gave him the opportunity to travel out of Evanston, Illinois, where Sigma Chi had its main office. He'd go on the road for three weeks at a time, visit different chapters of the fraternity, come back to Evanston, and spend a week making his reports.

He worked for six months, then enrolled in divinity school. He chose Gordon Conwell Theological Seminary in South Hamilton, Massachusetts. Jerry and I thought that was fine. We believed in independence. Just because his father was a lawyer didn't mean Mike should be a lawyer.

In any case, Jerry and I decided, no matter where we retired to, we'd keep our house in Alexandria.

Then Spiro Agnew upset our applecart.

20

VEEP

In June of 1973, Spiro Agnew's troubles with the Maryland U.S. Attorney's office made headlines; the Vice President was being investigated in connection with kickbacks he had allegedly taken from contractors while he had been Governor of Maryland. And that was only the beginning. The Justice Department was said to have a forty-page document chronicling evidence against Agnew.

Republicans, already—and increasingly—embarrassed by Watergate, now were faced with rumors of illicit payoffs being made right in the Vice Presidential office.

All through that summer, Agnew proclaimed his innocence, and I for one believed him. I mean, I thought you'd have to be off your rocker to accept bribes in that position.

Then in October Agnew resigned. He was allowed to plead no contest to a single charge of income-tax evasion, in return for a suspended sentence. The price was his stepping down from the Vice Presidency.

(Living in Palm Springs now, I often think about the mystery of Spiro Agnew. He's a great friend of Frank Sinatra's, and we see

Frank and Barbara at parties here. They've been very nice to us and we like them very much. I suspect they didn't vote for Jerry in the 1976 primary, but we're all part of this very small desert community, and our social life is constantly overlapping. I would rather be pleasant and ignore past wounds. I'm not inclined to carry a chip on my shoulder.)

Anyhow, on the afternoon of October 10, 1973, Jerry got a note from Spiro Agnew saying he'd quit out of "deep concern for the country."

Jerry still didn't have a clue that this would affect his own future. Because he was planning for his retirement, the Agnew problem, and even the growing mess of Watergate, found him, as one journalist put it, "more the dismayed partisan observer than a personally interested principal."

Susan bet me five dollars that the President would choose Jerry to replace Agnew, and I lost the bet. "Your father is much too valuable in the House, getting legislation through," I said. "The President would never take him out."

I've heard since that President Nixon really wanted John Connally for his Vice President, but he couldn't take a chance on naming anybody who would have trouble getting Congressional approval. He needed a Mister Clean. Especially since the 25th Amendment to the Constitution said that Congress had to confirm his choice. (Connally had been in trouble over that milk business, and even though he adamantly maintained his innocence and was later cleared, he might have run into difficulty with the House and Senate.)

It seemed to me there was an ample field of material from which to choose a good Vice President. Jerry too was so sure Susan's intuition was laughable that he tried to discourage David Kennerly, who was working for *Time* magazine, from coming around. Kennerly had been out photographing possible Vice Presidential candidates—he was always thinking ahead—and when he got in touch with Jerry, Jerry told him to save his film. "It's not going to be me," he said. "You can take my picture if you want, but you're just wasting your time."

David paid no attention, so he had *Time*'s cover shot ready to go when Jerry was nominated. (David tells people he likes me because the first time he came to Crown View Drive, he was hung over, which I'd realized from the incoherence of his speech when he phoned to say he'd be late; and I greeted him at the door with a cold beer and said, "Here, I think you're going to need this," and invited him to breakfast.)

There were other signs besides Kennerly's attentions that should have warned me, but we'd done our sitting-up-until-four-in-the-morning number in 1960 and the President had come up with Henry Cabot Lodge; and since then, we'd been impervious to rumor. Impervious, or unconscious. Because in the two days between Agnew's resignation and the President's announcing Agnew's replacement, our phone never stopped ringing. A reporter would call up and say, "Has your husband told you to get your hair done?" and I'd say no. "I just had it done yesterday, and if you think my husband's worried about my hair, you have a wrong idea of my husband."

Or one would call and ask, "Has your husband told you to go out and get a new dress?" to which I could answer quite honestly, "That's the last thing he'd tell me."

Mike even phoned from Boston to say he'd heard on the radio that his father might be nominated. I assured him the story was farfetched, not to worry.

President Nixon had said he was going to announce the name of his nominee on the night of October 12, so that night, when Jerry came home for dinner, I was rustling steaks, something simple that I could throw on the table, in order for him to be able to eat quickly and get back to the White House for the big disclosure.

We were eating when the phone rang. It was the private phone, the unlisted one which had no extensions, and which we didn't let the children use. (Susan and Steve kept the other phone so busy nobody could ever get through to us.) Susan leaped to answer, convinced it would be the President. It was the President. Jerry went to the phone. "I've got good news," President Nixon said, "but I want Betty to hear it too."

"Well, I'm sorry, Mr. President," Jerry said, "but you'll have to call back on the other phone. There's no extension on this one."

President Nixon called back and told us both that he'd picked Jerry to be his Vice President. I didn't know whether to say thank you or not.

My lord. I was wearing slacks and a blouse, and Susan was already up in my closet trying to figure out what I could change to. We had to go to the White House immediately; the whole ceremony was going to be on TV at nine o'clock. I was starting to quake, but Susan kept her head and went on thumbing through my wardrobe. "It can't be a print, and it can't be black, and it should be a pretty color. . . ."

She narrowed it down to one green dress, and that was what I wore.

When I got to the White House, they sneaked me in the side gate and took me to Rose Mary Woods's office, where I watched the beginnings of the proceedings on television. I was terribly nervous because I knew that before the President named his choice I was going to have to make a mad dash over to the East Room.

The moment came, I made the dash, and was shoved through the door of the East Room and told to go down and sit with Mrs. Nixon. I crept down to the front row, where Pat and Julie and Tricia and it seems to me both of the girls' husbands were sitting, and there was no empty seat. "Pat," I whispered, "they told me to come sit with you," and she said, "Oh, yes, of course, I'll move over," and Pat and I shared one chair.

I was scared to death. President Nixon was talking about the person he was nominating, how many years he'd served in Congress, and the applause was already beginning because the members of Congress knew exactly whom he was talking about, and Jerry was very well liked. I still couldn't believe it.

Jerry got up and took the accolades, the ovation, and then they asked me to come up, and afterward there was a receiving line, and everybody came through and shook our hands.

In the midst of the congratulations, I heard Jerry explaining to the President that on the following morning he (Jerry) was supposed to fly to Michigan for Red Flannel Day. Cedar Springs, in our Congressional district, is the red flannel capital of the United States. Of the world, as far as that's concerned; that's its claim to distinction. And Red Flannel Day is a big celebration, everybody has to wear red, and there's a Red Flannel queen, and a band. "That's okay," President Nixon said, "it's perfectly all right, you go ahead. I'll see that you have a plane."

It was sure going to be a big Red Flannel Day in Cedar Springs; they hadn't expected to have the Vice President Designate at the festivities.

After a while, the President and Mrs. Nixon disappeared, and we were left there. John McCormack, the Speaker of the House, who was such a dear, was pumping Jerry's arm, and later Jerry met in the Red Room with the entire Cabinet.

I still didn't know what had hit us, but I was excited, and so were the children. We didn't have a chance to think about what it really meant. We knew, of course, that Jerry would have to be checked out by the Senate Committee on Rules and the House Committee on the Judiciary, and that those hearings couldn't even start until hundreds of FBI people went out and got all the information about him from kindergarten on up.

But the Republicans were sure Jerry could get through those hearings; there had never been a trace of scandal about him. Two months later he was confirmed and sworn in as Vice President before a joint session of Congress. I wore a bright orange wool crepe dress and a broad smile.

If I had known what was coming, I think I probably would have sat right down and cried.

At Gerald Ford's swearing-in as Vice President, December 6, 1973 (from the left, Chief Justice Warren Burger, Speaker of the House Carl Albert, Mrs. Ford, President Pro Tem of the Senate James Eastland, Vice President Ford, and President Nixon)

Susan photographing Steve and her parents in the back yard at Crown View Drive, February 1974

Gerald Ford is sworn in as President by Chief Justice Burger
as Mrs. Ford watches the ceremony in the East Room
of the White House, August 9, 1974

President and Mrs. Ford pack mementos in their Alexandria home
as they prepare to move into the White House

Mrs. Ford congratulates Mrs. Nelson Rockefeller after her husband has been sworn in as Vice President on the floor of the House, below

King Hussein and Queen Alia of Jordan, arriving at the North Portico of the White House for the first State Dinner given by President and Mrs. Ford, August 17, 1974

Mike and Gayle Ford in the Presidential Suite of the National
Naval Medical Center in Bethesda, on the eve of Betty Ford's
surgery for breast cancer

The President and Mrs. Ford walk back to her hospital
suite after he has caught the football she tossed him,
one week after her operation

Fred Ward, Black Star

The welcome home from the hospital. The Fords are greeted by
Susan, Liberty, the retriever, and Janet Ford, the President's
sister-in-law

White House photo by Karl Schumacher

Mrs. Ford holds her first press conference in the East Room
of the White House

From the Family Quarters of the White House,
Mrs. Ford looks out over the West Wing to get a
glimpse of her husband when he leaves for the
Oval Office

Catching up on paperwork in the
Family Quarters study on the
second floor (September 1974)

Mrs. Ford works in her White House
study area (January 1975)

Mrs. Ford leads the audience in silent prayer for Dr. Maurice
S. Sage, president of the Jewish National Fund of America,
after he collapsed with a fatal heart attack during a gala dinner
of the Fund in New York on June 22, 1976. Secret Service
men in the background tried futilely to revive Rabbi Sage

Liberty's pups have their first outing on the
South Grounds of the White House

Family horseplay
at Camp David

Mrs. Ford coaches a tag football game between
the Secret Service Presidential Detail and
the First Family Detail, Vail, summer 1976

21

MEET THE PRESS

Crown View Drive was invaded by the press. Hordes of press. You couldn't move without bumping into a reporter; you couldn't go out your front door.

Pete and Louise Abbruzzese, who lived across the street, were heroic. The news people were all over the Abbruzzeses' lawn (the Secret Service wouldn't let them on *our* property), and Pete and Louise opened up their garage so the reporters could come in out of the rain. They let them use their phone (one made a call to Singapore), their TV, their bathrooms. At six o'clock Louise would appear with a pitcher of martinis, and all day long she supplied glasses of water. The press had taken over the Abbruzzeses' garage, and the Secret Service had taken over our garage for what is called a command post. The Vice Presidential limousine and the follow-up car were stationed in our driveway, so the only place we could park the family automobiles was in the street.

Meanwhile, we were posing for pictures until the children said they wouldn't sit still for any more. A famous photographer came down from New York to shoot the family around the breakfast table, but it took him so long to get his camera set up that Jack (who must have flown home from Utah to offer moral support; I really can't remember) just put down his napkin and left.

The person who stayed coolest was Matthew Abbruzzese, who was about six years of age and unimpressed by our new celebrity. To this day, if he sees a picture of Jerry in a magazine, he says, "There's my old next-door neighbor."

Later on, their uninvited guests came back and gave the Abbruzzeses a party. It was a kind of block party, marvelous and informal. The reporters and photographers invited the neighbors; they brought in lemonade for the children, and a keg of beer, and hotdogs and hamburgers and corn on the cob, and then they cleaned out the garage. They planted a tree too. They'd asked Louise what kind of tree she'd like, and Louise deferred to me. "You're the one who's going to have to look across the street and see it."

I chose a red maple. When it was planted, that tree was practically bald, and the reporters had tied ribbons and clippings all over it so it would look as though it had leaves.

Jerry's Vice Presidency must have been one of the shortest on record—from December to August—but those eight months were incredibly busy for both of us.

Before he'd got this new job, I'd been planning to work at a hospital three days a week, because I needed to feel I was doing something for someone else. I could have kept busy going to luncheons; you can always find a friend who wants to go out to lunch, but that was boring to me. All my life I've had to have a project.

Suddenly I had more projects than I could handle.

As soon as the announcement of Jerry's nomination came, friends showed up on our doorstep offering to help in any way they could. Nancy Howe, who had been in charge of book sales at the White House—various souvenir books are available to tourists who go through—worked with me for several weeks, and finally I hired her as a secretary.

We made plans for moving to Admiralty House. When Hubert Humphrey was Vice President, Congress had bought a piece of property which was well protected, very private, with the idea of building a Vice Presidential residence on it. Then they found the house they were talking about was going to cost three million dollars, and they wouldn't spend the money. Admiralty House (which had been used by the Chief of Naval Operations at the Naval Observatory) was already standing, and now Congress had decided to make *that* into a Vice President's house, and appropriated limited funds for the transition from the Navy.

(I never got to live there; Happy Rockefeller took over. I think Congress was lucky that Nelson became Vice President because he put so much of his money into that old place. The government repaired the leaks and the wiring, but Nelson and Happy fixed it up.)

I started facing up to all those interviews my husband had told me I had to give because I couldn't go back on my word. Even with the ground rules set by my team, it was terrifying. I agreed to do a show with Barbara Walters on the understanding that I didn't want to talk about anything political. After we got through the amenities—"Good morning, Barbara, how are you?" "Mrs. Ford, wife of the new Vice President," and so forth—my eyes focused on Barbara sitting there with a pad on her lap, and the pad had her questions written on it. I felt as if she were holding a stick of dynamite, waiting for me to light it. If she looks down while I'm talking, I thought, I'll panic.

The very first question she came out with was how I felt about the Supreme Court's ruling on abortion. I said I agreed with the Supreme Court's ruling, that it was time to bring abortion out of the backwoods and put it in the hospitals where it belonged.

The mail which came to me after that show was angry, at least for a while, but my reputation for candor was established.

Dick Cavett traveled to Crown View Drive to capture the Fords on television, and I wasn't crazy about that experience either. It was a mild day, and Cavett's crew moved the furniture out of our living room onto the patio. (They left a couple of chairs and a table in one corner.) I didn't mind too much about the furniture because it wasn't raining, until I looked out of an upstairs window and realized they'd parked my upholstered pieces right under a tree where every bird in town congregated. I got hold of Nancy Howe. "Get down there as fast as you can and tell them to get that stuff covered so the birds don't decorate it," I said. "Pronto." It was a case of Whoops! quick, before a bird flies over.

After the crew dragged the furniture out, they brought three tremendous studio-type pieces of equipment—a camera and I don't know what else—into our little house. Jerry and Dick Cavett and Steve and Susan and I huddled into that one underfurnished corner, and all I can remember is Cavett sitting in one of the chairs with Steve standing next to him, and Cavett looking up and saying, "Do you think I could learn to ski?" and the look of disgust that crossed Steve's face. It was as if he wanted to answer, "Dummy, anybody can learn to ski," and was controlling himself with difficulty. Hours later, it was over. I was never so glad to see a bunch of people get out in my life.

Change was the order of every day. I wasn't a House of Representatives wife any more; now I was a Senate wife. Being married to the Vice President automatically makes a woman president of the Red Cross Senate Wives. Judy Agnew, a very nice lady, was unceremoniously relieved of the position, and Mrs. Eastland, Senator Eastland's wife, acted as president pro tem until I could take over. I ran around getting a Red Cross uniform marked to reflect my new position, and making a new sign. We wore signs (hanging from strings around our necks) giving our names and our states. They were kind of like bumper stickers.

The Red Cross Senate Wives, yours truly presiding, gave one luncheon at which Pat Nixon was guest of honor, and of course she sat on my right. People had already started those marches in front of the White House with picket signs, and I'd seen one on TV which said, "Pick out your curtains, Betty."

I was afraid maybe Pat had seen it too, so I mentioned to her that I was embarrassed by some of the placards. "Oh," she said, "I never watch the news." I thought about that at the time of the David Frost–Richard Nixon shows; I hoped she hadn't watched.

I'm often asked how I felt about Jerry's being "a heartbeat

away from the Presidency" during those days when President Nixon's woes were increasing, but I have to say again that—White House pickets notwithstanding—the prospect of anything happening to the President didn't seem real to me. Call me stupid; I had my hands full trying to figure out how to be Mrs. Vice President.

Old habits had to be changed. We stayed in our condominium in the Lodge at Vail during Christmas vacation of 1973, and it was devilish. For the command post to operate, there had to be a truck parked down below our windows, and there were agents sitting at a table outside our front door, and other people who had apartments in the Lodge weren't allowed to come up the outside stairs. (Ever since then, we've rented, from a friend named Dick Bass, a larger house in Vail. We've also tried to buy the Basshaus, but Dick won't sell.)

At that time, it was only Jerry who was being protected; he was covered around the clock, but the children and I came and went as we pleased. Shortly thereafter, Susan's freedom was also abruptly curtailed.

It started back in Virginia, on a Friday. Susan and some of her friends traveled to and from Holton Arms by car. We parents took turns; one of us would pick the girls up on a Friday night, bring them home for the weekend, and another of us would drive them back to school on Monday morning.

This particular Friday, the Secret Service phoned me. "Don't let Susan out this weekend; she's not to leave the house," the man said. Jerry was in Denver, and I didn't know what was going on, but I kept Susan home and let her have house guests and parties all weekend. By Monday, Secret Service protection had been arranged for her, and I was told what had happened. A small fanatic group called the Symbionese Liberation Army (SLA) had threatened Susan's life. I was very frightened. The authorities had turned up an SLA list with three names on it. One of the people, a school superintendent, had already been shot and killed, the second person was Patty Hearst, who'd been kidnapped, and Susan, because she was the daughter of the new Vice President, was the third.

It drove her wild being tailed all the time, and it bothered the people at Holton Arms, having agents all over the premises, but I have to say I was grateful.

Particularly since the murders of figures in the public eye showed no signs of abating. In June of 1974, Martin Luther King, Jr.'s mother was shot while she was sitting playing the organ in the Ebenezer Baptist Church in Atlanta. Jerry had gone to Maine to meet President Nixon, who was coming home from Moscow. Nobody from the administration was planning to attend Mrs. King's funeral, so I took it upon myself. I checked with Jerry first, and he said sure. "Go on down, somebody ought to be there."

When I got to the Kings' house in Atlanta, I was told old Daddy King wanted to see me. He was dressing for the funeral, and somebody took me up to his room. He had his pants and shirt on, but his suspenders were hanging down, and he hadn't put on his stiff collar yet. He took me in his arms and hugged me, and he cried. He was broken up; he'd been through so much.

Together we went downstairs and got into our cars and joined the procession that took us to the church for the service. I can remember only two white people in the church—one was Jimmy Carter and the other was me—but I must be wrong about this; there were probably some white civil-rights workers there also.

I came home thinking about one more senseless death, but was jolted out of sadness by good news. Our oldest son, Mike, and his girl, Gayle Brumbaugh, had decided to get married. They had met several years earlier at Wake Forest College, but while Mike was doing his first year at Gordon Conwell, Gayle had taken off for Switzerland. She went to study with Dr. Francis Schaeffer at L'Abri. All kinds of people go to study with Dr. Schaeffer—addicts trying to work their way out of drug problems, Buddhists wanting to learn about Christianity, seekers after a deeper understanding of the Bible.

Gayle came back to the United States that Christmas when Jerry was Vice President, and spent part of the holidays with us at Vail. But she and Mike had been separated so much I began to be afraid Mike would miss the boat with her. And where was he going to find another girl as interested in religion as he was? A boy who's headed for the ministry can't join up with a go-go dancer. Gayle even looked like a Ford. (In pictures of the family, people often don't know for sure which is Susan and which is Gayle.)

Mike had insisted he wasn't going to marry until he was through school and could support a wife. I took him aside and had a talk with him. I told him girls sometimes grew impatient. I told him I didn't think it was necessary for him to be graduated before he married. He listened, and he didn't say much.

Months afterward, back in Washington, I was dressing to go out to dinner when Mike and Gayle came waltzing into my bedroom, beaming. "We've got something to tell you," says Mike, and Gayle brings her left hand up under my nose and shows me an engagement ring. He'd got her a nice diamond, not big but respectable. I'm sure they shopped around for it; if I know them, they went to a discount store. I wanted to turn cartwheels, but I didn't have time. I had this reputation for lateness, which, as the wife of the Vice President, I could no longer afford.

Next day, I gave Gayle my turquoise cross (I have several Zuñi pieces made by the same Indian artist) because I didn't want to buy her an engagement present; I wanted to feel I was parting with something that was precious to me. Then we discussed wedding dates. So many of their friends were getting married that spring and summer, there were only a couple of days that would work out for Mike and Gayle. They liked August 10. I said they shouldn't wait until August. "You might as well get married in July and enjoy the summer, before you have to go back to school."

Thank goodness my reasoning appealed to them. The way it turned out, Jerry was sworn in as President on August 9. Somebody up there has been looking after me for years.

Okay, they said, July 5. Oh dear, I thought, there goes Susan's birthday again. Something fateful always seemed to happen around July 6 to prevent Susan from having the spotlight on her alone. (Although her eighteenth birthday was later celebrated in great style at the White House.)

There was a rush for the wedding pictures, the invitations. All kinds of lists had to be made and checked and misplaced and found again. Gayle's parents lived in Catonsville, Maryland, so that's where the wedding was. We practically rented a whole motel, we had so many friends come out from Grand Rapids.

The children were married by an Episcopal minister—they wrote their own vows—and Gayle's sorority sisters were her attendants. Jerry was Mike's best man, and Mike's fraternity brothers were ushers.

At the reception afterward, the boys from the fraternity held lighted candles and sang "The Sweetheart of Sigma Chi." They all looked so young and shiny and confident that it was very moving.

One month and four days later, Jerry became President of the United States.

22

ORDERLY TRANSFER

Jerry *had* to become President. He was Vice President. He had no choice. And I had such belief in my husband I never doubted he could do it. He is an honest man. (In his first State of the Union speech, he came out and said, "The state of the union is not very good," even though that wasn't what people wanted to hear.)

But I wasn't sure what kind of First Lady I would be. There was a good deal of whooping and hollering right at the beginning because I'd said Jerry and I were *not* going to have separate bedrooms at the White House, and that we were going to take our own bed with us. It really wasn't one bed, it was twin beds which swung out from a single headboard. It's funny the fuss that was made about that. Even now, after all these years of married life, I like the idea of sleeping with my husband next to me. When we go to motels, and they've got a nightstand between us, we move it and put the beds together. (We can't share a double bed, because when he rolls over, everything goes with him; I'd never have a blanket.)

Well, people started saying I was disgraceful and immoral. I didn't care. I wanted to be a good First Lady, I was perfectly willing to be educated about the duties of a First Lady, but I didn't believe I had to do every single thing some previous President's wife had done. I figured, Okay, I'll move to the White House, do the best I can, and if they don't like it, they can kick me out, but they can't make me be somebody I'm not. Who "they" were, I wasn't sure, but I was feeling slightly defensive.

In Chapter 1, I dealt briefly with August 9, 1974. Sometimes it seems like ten years ago, sometimes like ten hours. What happened to Jerry will be studied for a long time to come. He was an accidental Vice President, and an accidental President, and in both jobs he replaced disgraced leaders. That sequence of events would never happen again.

Susan says she was scared. "Really, really scared. I was afraid of what was going to happen to our family, afraid Daddy's being President would tear us apart. I knew it was a privilege for him to have this position, but the boys were all dispersed—even Steve was about to leave—and I'd be the only kid left home, and I knew I would have to be very very cautious because anything I did in the White House could reflect on my parents."

We were all conflicted. I think my husband believed President Nixon had been shanghaied into a terrible position by Haldeman, Ehrlichman, and Dean. I think my children believed their father would make a very good President, but they also felt bad because they realized President Nixon had to be a sick man.

On the day Jerry took the oath, I didn't say much. It was advice I'd got from my Living Bible. Every morning, I study a verse out of a pamphlet called *Forward Day by Day*, and that morning's recommended verse had read, "I will keep a muzzle on my mouth."

Ordinarily, I'm hard to muzzle, but on August 9, if you'd asked me my name, I'd have been stuck for an answer.

Jerry told Julie and David Eisenhower, who had been left to pack the Nixons' effects, to take their time getting out of the White House, that we were in no hurry to move in. (Julie and David started right to work, and they got all the Nixons' belongings ready to move in just ten days; I'll never know how. They must have labored morning, noon, and night. The Nixon girls are strong. Once, hearing Tricia speak, I was amazed at the steel of her. Little tiny girl, little tiny voice, but she carried out the task she set herself. And to me Julie was even more appealing. People liked her sticking up for her father right to the end. She's a fighter. I saw her on a television show saying *The Final Days* was a cruel book, and when the moderator asked her if she thought the book had precipitated her mother's stroke, Julie nodded firmly. "I think it did," she said.)

After the formalities of the swearing-in were over, Jerry met the press, was briefed by Henry Kissinger, who'd agreed to stay on as Secretary of State, and talked to four old friends—Don Rumsfeld, William Scranton, John Marsh, Rogers Morton—whom he'd persuaded to help him with the transition. He worked until about 7 P.M. and then drove home to Virginia. The news people were out in the street when his car turned into our driveway, and all our neighbors were there too, cheering, and I kept thinking, What a strange twelve hours. I'd been moved in so many different ways. The morning had begun with tears, lives being broken, people being broken, and now there was laughter, and everybody from Crown View Drive was in our kitchen eating ham and salad and lasagna and wishing us well and toasting the new President, and Jerry was in his shirtsleeves, pouring champagne.

After everyone else had left, David Kennerly stayed on. David had turned into a kind of member of the family. He wasn't much older than our children, and I think Jerry missed having the boys around. David could always make him laugh.

(Once Jerry had been designated Vice President, the Fords became David's assignment for *Time* magazine. He'd taken pictures of Jack out in Utah, Mike up in Massachusetts, Steven and Susan in Washington, but mostly he'd stuck like glue to Jerry, who was flying all over, doing what Vice Presidents do, which is make political speeches. David tells about a trip to Oregon. In order to see Jack, Jerry had stopped off at Utah State. "He was out at the college, shaking hands with everybody," David recalls, "and he shook hands with this guy who had a beard, and went right on down the line, and the bearded guy smiled. It was Jack." Our son had grown such a crop of whiskers his father didn't recognize him. David admired Jerry's lack of pomposity. "When he was Vice

President, he'd get back on the plane, and the press people would kid him about how long he'd talked. We'd have heard the same speech for about the fiftieth time, and as soon as he came up the ramp, we'd all make these loud snoring noises. But he could take it.")

Now, with the party over, and the neighbors gone, Jerry and David sat talking. David said he wanted to work in the White House. "I think it would be an important thing to do, to have a documentary day-by-day record of the Presidency. It could have historical value. And you're good with photographers; you don't pay any attention."

At eleven o'clock we wanted to see the news, and the downstairs TV was broken, so we went up to our bedroom. David and Jerry sat on chairs, I perched on the edge of the bed, and Susan came in, and we all watched Jerry Ford making his Inaugural Address. "I am acutely aware that you have not elected me as your President by your ballots," he said, "so I ask you to confirm me as your President with your prayers."

After the news, David got up to leave. He hugged me and he shook hands with Jerry. He told me later he remembered Jerry's grabbing his hands and saying, "You know, you're really a good friend of ours." "And I felt very emotional because I was thinking, like, he's the top man in the world!"

I know what David meant. That night I lay in the dark and stared at the ceiling. "My God," I thought, "what a job I have to do."

23

THREE WEEKS IN AUGUST

I think putting down the details of one's daily life and expecting other people to pore over them with fascination is not only arrogant but boring. Still, in case a woman who's reading my book plans to marry a President of the United States, this might be as good a place as any to show what can happen to her—and him—during the course of less than a month. So here's an abbreviated diary of some of the events between August 9 and August 31, 1974, along with my comments about same.

Before the diary starts, let me explain that most of the Ford children, intent on their own lives, took off soon after the swearing-in. Mike and Gayle went back to Massachusetts; Jack returned to Yellowstone Park and his summer stint as a ranger. Steve didn't stay behind long enough to move his clothes to the White House. He'd been accepted by Duke University, but decided he'd rather put in a year as a wrangler on a ranch, and he headed West, hoping to reach the Snake River before Evel Knievel tried to jump it. Susan would be the only child of ours to live in the White House for any length of time, although Jack did come back there after he finished college.

August 9. Oath of Office. Enough said.

August 10. At 7 A.M., the President of the United States, in baby-blue short pajamas, appears on his doorstep looking for the morning paper, then goes back inside to fix his orange juice and English muffin. Before leaving for his office, he signs autographs on his lawn.

At 10 A.M., an aide from the White House phones the wife of the President of the United States in Alexandria, and says, "What are you going to do about the state dinner?"

"What state dinner?" I say.

"King Hussein is coming," says the aide. "On the 16th."

I am staggered. I don't know a thing about this. If anybody has made any plans for King Hussein's visit, they've been kept a deep, dark secret from me.

I pitch in and do the best I can. Fortunately, Jerry and I have entertained the King at the State Department during Jerry's Vice Presidency. (I've been coming up through the ranks, so it isn't like being thrown into the front lines straight from Grand Rapids.) Besides, the White House is filled with people who can do anything— cook, bake, serve, design and hand-letter place cards, arrange flowers, choose music. All you have to do is know what you want and ask for it. I also get my friend Peggy Stanton, wife of Bill Stanton, a member of Congress, to help me. Peggy's clever, and we fall to work making up a guest list. I remember King Hussein is very charming, but I've never met the Queen.

August 11. Sunday. We go to church at Immanuel-on-the-Hill in Alexandria, where we've been going for twenty-some years. There aren't going to be any more private services in the East Room for a select few.

August 12. Jerry addresses the Congress, and tells legislators he doesn't want a honeymoon with them. "I want a good marriage.... My office door has always been open and that is how it is going to be at the White House."

He and I have been talking about an open, friendly White House, and not just for Congress, either. The White House isn't private property; it belongs to the citizens of the United States, and the people who live in it sometimes forget that.

August 13. Susan and I are invited to tour the White House with the head usher, Rex Scouten; the curator, Clement Conger; and Mrs. Nixon's social secretary, Lucy Winchester. Object: So we can tell them where we want things. In the second-floor family quarters, a bedroom right across the hall from the room which will be Jerry's and mine is suggested for Susan. The expression on her face is priceless. "I don't," she says, "like pink." At this point, I decide she'll be happier up on the third floor, and I'm right. (She eventually takes over a bedroom and bath and sitting room that Julie and David Eisenhower used when they visited, and has it all repainted. (She wants yellow, and she gets yellow—and when she asks for a brass bed, she gets a brass bed so beautiful you've never seen the likes of it. A benefactor provides it. On loan. When we leave the White House, Susan makes sure the bed goes back where it came from; she can't bear the idea of anyone else's sleeping on it.)

My daughter and I sit in a pleasant air-conditioned room sipping iced tea and chatting with the staff, and it's only when we get up to leave that I discover the press have been waiting outside for an hour.

Ghastly. There's a great crowd of reporters standing around a microphone in this awful heat. One poor woman who's fainted has to be taken into Dr. William Lukash's office. It makes me feel like Marie Antoinette. I am really provoked. Why hasn't anyone told me the reporters are out there? I could have gone and talked to them and *then* come back and had my tea. I think the episode puts me in a bad light with the press just at the time I am most anxious to make a good impression, and it certainly puts the White House staff in a bad light with me.

August 16. Jerry and I make it from Alexandria in time to welcome our guests, but if it weren't for my records, I couldn't tell you much about that night. The King and Queen aren't staying at the White House because their *hosts* aren't yet staying at the White House, so they've been put up right across the street at Blair House. Usually the Blair House staff and the White House staff work together to time out the arrivals of dignitaries. The President and his wife are supposed to be standing at the head of the steps, the entire press corps down in a press area below, and the driveway lined with military men in dress uniforms when the visitors drive up and are ushered out of their car.

There it all is in the scrapbook, His Majesty Hussein I of the Hashemite Kingdom of Jordan, and Her Majesty Queen Alia. We dine on cold salmon, roast beef, artichoke salad, Brie, and mousse, and there's dancing. (Months afterward, Queen Alia told me she'd been worried about whether or not I was going to make it through that evening. Poor beautiful Queen, she later died in an air crash.)

August 17. Susan goes off to the beach for a week and leaves me with her cat, Shan, and mixed emotions.

August 19. Jerry and I fly to Chicago, where Jerry tells the Veterans of Foreign Wars he wants to work out an amnesty program for Vietnam draft dodgers. He thinks fellows in Canada who want to come back could put in time working for a hospital or some other worthwhile project to make up for having deserted. The idea is not very popular with the veterans. The veterans are bitter about deserters, think they shouldn't be allowed back, or if they do come back, they ought to be put in jail. Jerry has known this audience would be tough. "It would have been a little cowardice, I think, if I'd picked an audience that was ecstatic," he says. "You can't talk about healing unless you're going to use it in the broadest context."

We fly back from Chicago on Air Force One, and when we get to Andrews Air Force Base, a helicopter picks us up and takes us directly to the White House. It's the first time, and it's a very strange feeling.

That morning, our house in Alexandria had been left in utter chaos, crates and cartons everywhere, chunks of our lives uprooted and labeled for storage. It'd been a very traumatic experience for me. That night we come back to new living quarters in perfect order, our clothes, our knickknacks, everything just where I've said we'll want it.

Our bed and bedding and pillows are in the First Lady's Bedroom, and the room usually referred to as the President's Bedroom has been made into a private sitting room for us. There are Jerry's favorite blue leather chair and footstool, and his exercise bike, and all his pipes and his pipe rack, and our old television set. The pictures of the children—from babyhood through Mike's and Gayle's wedding—are hanging on the walls. So Jerry and I will have one room in that great big White House that isn't all stuffed with important furniture. Besides, at the end of the day, no matter how marvelous the help is, I'm going to want a place to escape to, a corner I can crawl into, someplace where I can shut a door. I am not going to want to sit out in some dumb hall.

Susan's cat, Shan, ensconces herself in the bathroom.

That night Jerry and I get into bed, and Jerry looks

around and laughs. "It's the best public housing I've ever seen," he says.

August 20. Jerry nominates Nelson Rockefeller to be his Vice President. Nelson is there for the announcement, but Happy can't get down from their summer place in Bar Harbor, Maine.

August 21. I go to Rex Scouten and say the White House employees don't like me. "I feel terribly uncomfortable here when I speak to one of the guards or the White House police; they never answer me, just sort of back off." Next thing I know, Rex has given the command that the staff are to return my greetings. Sort of funny, to be ordered to say good morning. But they had to be ordered not to speak in the first place. The Nixons preferred more formality, and the staff, trained to be as silent and invisible as possible, didn't know how to act with us. After a little while, everyone relaxes, and when we're at dinner—at least during strictly family meals—Jerry and the butler compare golf scores.

August 22. Jerry signs a proclamation of women's equality. (This is different from his signing, in the following January, an executive order establishing a National Commission on the Observance of International Women's Year, 1975, about which more later.)

Happy Rockefeller comes to lunch with me in the solarium on the third floor of the White House. She's shy, says she doesn't really know Washington, she knows New York, knows what it is to be the wife of the Governor, but being wife of the Vice President is going to be an entirely different matter. I try to reassure her that it won't be all that bad, that I'll help her in any way I can. I like both Rockefellers, there's nothing pretentious about either one of them, they're old shoe.

August 24. Ron Nessen gives a party for the press who've traveled with Jerry on his trips as Vice President. The reporters kid about the Vice Presidential plane, say it's an old crate that can't fly as fast as a bird, but when somebody writes this in a newspaper, the military get all upset. (I notice later, when Rockefeller comes in, he uses his own plane.)

August 25. Susan home from beach. Her cat has become my great friend. If I get on the bed to take a nap, Shan's right there with me. She's been permitted to wander freely through our quarters. Now she's banished. "Okay, Susan," I say, "I've had her for several days. You take her on upstairs to your room." The End. After that, Shan never speaks to me again. If I put out my hand to pet her, she scoots like a flying tiger down the whole length of the White House, and no matter how I try to coax or feed her, nothing works. (Susan loses Shan, finally. That cat just walks out on her. Typical Siamese.)

August 26. Exact dates are hazy in my mind, but I think this is the beginning of the week when some of the Ford mouths come unmuzzled. From way out West, Jack announces to a newspaperman that his mother will be upset if his father changes his mind and runs for President in 1976.

Jerry says he wishes reporters had asked *him* about Jack's remark. "I'd have told them, 'Jack and I have a grand rapport, and perfect understanding, and I'm going to look after his mother (my wife) and the White House, and he's going to look after the bears and tourists in Yellowstone.' "

From Boston, another ice breaker. Mike says that Richard Nixon owes the public "a total confession" of his part in Watergate. Again Jerry receives the news calmly. "All my children have spoken for themselves since they first learned to speak," he says, "and not always with my advance approval. I expect that to continue."

August 27. I give yet another interview to a women's magazine. Later I tell writer Myra MacPherson that I've been asked everything except how often I sleep with my husband. "And if they'd asked me that, I would have told them." "What would you have said?" asks Myra. "As often as possible!" I say.

August 30. I meet with Nancy Hanks, chairman of the National Endowment for the Arts. As First Lady, I intend to help promote the arts wherever and however I can.

August 31. Jerry and Susan and I go to Camp David (which was called Shangri-La until Dwight Eisenhower renamed it for his grandson) on top of the Catoctin Mountains. Camp David is the best thing about the White House. Except you gain too much weight up there, because the staff is so glad to have you come that they prepare all these delicious meals. We take paperwork with us. Part of Camp David is a U.S. Navy installation (a commanding officer lives there with his family) and the other part is the Presidential retreat, a large complex of cabins. Aspen, the largest cabin, with its own private dining room and kitchen and two stewards and a cook, is used by the President. The newest cabin, called Laurel, has a conference room and a big dining room, and guests from other cabins—unless they're invited to eat with the President at Aspen—take their meals at Laurel.

The air, the trees, the sky—it's paradise, that place. If I get to return to this world, I'd like to come back to Camp David.

Although I've mentioned Jerry in the foregoing pages, most of what he was busy with during these same three weeks in August was weightier stuff than I plan to go into here. I'll just say that he got General Motors to back down on a price increase for their 1975 cars, he assured the Russian Ambassador that he was as committed to détente as his predecessor had been, he convinced labor leader George Meany to support a Cost of Living Council, he spoke to mayors, governors, and the British Prime Minister, he spent hours with Henry Kissinger when the Cyprus crisis erupted, and more hours studying about the old enmity between Greece and Turkey. He also tried to eradicate more recent enmities which had been festering between the White House and certain reporters, and the White House and certain liberal Senators, and the White House and certain former members of John Kennedy's Cabinet. All this before September came around.

You've heard of a month in the country? August, 1974, wasn't it.

24

~

THE WHITE HOUSE

Before going further into my life in high places, it might be useful to set up what the people in television call an establishing shot. (If a scene is going to be played in a particular room, a camera pulls back and shoots that whole room so the viewer can become familiar with the positioning of the furniture, the fireplace, the doors, the windows.)

To begin with, the White House is a house, not a castle, nothing like Franco's palace in Spain, where we once sat down to dinner and counted twenty-eight candelabra along the length of the table.

When we moved in, Jerry told the staff he didn't want the core, the central part of the house, to be called the Mansion any more; he wanted it referred to as the Residence. (He wasn't great on "Hail to the Chief," either. He realized we had to be announced, but that was about all he thought necessary. "Hail to the Chief" embarrassed him.)

The White House is the oldest federal building in Washington. The cornerstone was laid in 1792, and Mrs. John Adams, wife of the first President ever to live there, hung her washing in the East Room. Even more exotically, Thomas Jefferson kept bears in a cage on the grounds.

After the British burned out some of the rooms in the War of 1812 (the limestone walls stood), James Hoban, the original architect, rebuilt, eventually adding east and west terraces and south and north porticos. John Quincy Adams gardened out back; an elm tree Adams planted is now more than eighty feet tall and still growing. James Polk had the new-fangled gas lights installed; Franklin Pierce was the first President to enjoy the luxury of central heating.

In Lincoln's day, there were problems with sewage and rats in the basement; in Theodore Roosevelt's day, there were problems with space. T. R. said several rooms on the family floor which had been used for official business were now needed for living space, and ordered a new West Wing constructed. That's how the Oval Office was born.

In 1948, Harry Truman added a balcony to the south portico, only to discover, as I've mentioned before, that the whole house was falling down. Again it was rebuilt. Now more than a million tourists go through its public rooms every year.

After Jerry came to the White House, people said it was like opening the windows and letting the fresh air blow through. I think that even the help, many of whom had loved the Nixons, were relieved to have that terrible period over.

Help. There's a lot of it. The household staff doesn't change, no matter who's in office, and you can get spoiled by them. It's very easy, living in the White House. People feed you and take care of your laundry and wash the windows and tidy the tennis court. Barbers and hairdressers and masseurs and tailors will come to you; there is a doctor in residence, and a nurse, and you have your own movie theatre and bowling alley and kennels for your dogs.

A President can travel by helicopter from his backyard—that is, the south lawn—to Air Force One, a plane which is equipped with a phone that can call anywhere in the world, a color television set, and two kitchens. (There's a second Air Force One plane, an older one, which had been divided; I never could understand it. The

First Lady was left to sit by herself in her own little bedroom. Jerry and I had that wall taken out, so the President's cabin and the First Lady's became one large compartment. Whenever anyone came in to talk to him about business, I would just make myself disappear.)

President Nixon had traveled with his compartment door shut; Jerry usually kept his open, to the point where it troubled certain of the staff who felt he should stand—or at least sit—a bit more on ceremony. Lee Simmons, who was a steward on Air Force One, and who works for us now, would shake his head as David Kennerly, wearing jeans and plaid shirt, came barging into the Presidential cabin. "The President could be sitting there with Henry Kissinger or some other important person," Lee says disapprovingly, "and if it was the cocktail hour, and Kennerly saw the President having a martini, he'd say, 'I guess I'd like one of those too.' "

Some reporters get to travel on the Presidential plane. They have a pool, and the winners draw Air Force One, while the losers take the press plane. The press plane leaves ahead of Air Force One, so all the photographers can be on the ground to get pictures when Air Force One comes in. Reporters and photographers who travel with a President pay first-class fare, plus a dollar. Their publications pick up the tab. The doctor flies on Air Force One, the nurse on the press plane.

Sometimes the secretaries who work at the White House put on more airs than a President and his wife do. You find snobbery among them, a feeling that a person working in the West Wing, which is the President's domain, is superior to a person working in the East Wing for the First Lady.

The East Wing dates from 1942. According to J. B. West, in *Upstairs at the White House*, "Immediately after Pearl Harbor, Army engineers came in with plans to build a bomb shelter. To disguise this secret project, there was much to-do about the need for extra Presidential office space, and the President requested a Congressional appropriation to build the East Wing. The White House police force, which had been increased, moved into the basement of the East Wing, and military aides, Secret Service and social offices occupied the two floors above." (It turned out that

Franklin Roosevelt hated the bomb shelter and tried to avoid going down there during air-raid drills.)

Mr. West writes that there had always been traffic on the ground floor of the White House between the two wings until Mamie Eisenhower came along. " 'You are *not* to use the Mansion as a passageway,' she informed both the President's staff and the social staff. 'Please walk outside the House when going from one wing to another.' "

There were rooms I liked in the White House and rooms I didn't like, but I wasn't about to start redecorating. Besides, by the time I got there the State floor had already been beautifully restored; it was full of magnificent antiques and paintings.

Let me see if I can explain a bit more about the actual physical layout of the house.

Ground floor. The Ground floor has several official rooms, including the Map Room. The oval-shaped room on the Ground floor (there is an oval-shaped room on every floor, one directly above the other, naturally) is called the Diplomatic Entrance. Most visitors come into the White House through this south hall.

First (or State) floor. The oval-shaped room on the State floor is the Blue Room. When you go to an event on the State floor, you walk up the great staircase from the Ground floor and are met at the top and led into the Blue Room (which is used for formal receptions) or the East Room (which is like a grand ballroom) or the Green Room or the Red Room or the State Dining Room. If you don't feel like walking up the great staircase, you can take an elevator.

Second (or family) floor. The Yellow Oval Room opens off the Center Hall here. The rooms where we lived were off the West Hall. I know I said I didn't want to sit out in some dumb hall of an evening, but I have to admit that the West Sitting Hall is beautiful. Pretty flowered slipcovers on the chairs and sofas, wonderful Chinese lamps, yellow walls. Not cozy, though, since it's just a clump of furniture at one end of the long corridor which runs the length of the Mansion. Excuse me, Residence. On one side of the West Sitting Hall were our bedroom, sitting room, and dressing room, and across the way, two other bedrooms (which the Nixons and the Johnsons had used when their girls were young), and a kitchen and a family dining room. I *did* have the wallpaper removed from that dining room. Mrs. Kennedy had found the nineteenth-century paper hanging in an old house in Maryland, managed to have it removed and rehung as part of her restoration project. It was a valuable historical document, I'm sure, showing a lot of Revolutionary War scenes, but I couldn't stand to look at soldiers fainting and dying while I was eating my soup. I read in the *New York Times* that Pat Nixon hadn't liked it either, but she "had endured it." From our living quarters, I could look down and see the lights shining in the Oval Office over in the West Wing when Jerry worked late.

The Lincoln Bedroom, the Queen's Room, and the Treaty Room are at the eastern end of the second floor. The Treaty Room is gorgeous, one of my favorites, the walls done in deep billiard-green velour, and five different queens have slept in the Queen's Room. This floor isn't opened to the public, but I used to let special groups—children's tours, tours for the blind—go through the Lincoln Bedroom, the Treaty Room, and the Yellow Oval Room, because they're so filled with history.

Clem Conger and I had an altercation about the bed in the Queen's Room. Before Jerry came into office, Mr. Conger had bought a whole set of furniture with which to redo the Queen's Room. The orders had already been given, couldn't be stopped, with specially woven this, specially draped that. But I balked at his changing the fourposter.

"The new bed is a fourposter too," he said. "And it's more beautiful than the bed that's there now. It's in Charleston, waiting for us to move it in."

I said no. "You do not move it in because it's not the bed that five queens have slept in."

We had the same kind of disagreement about a mirror over the mantel. The mirror had been given to the White House by Princess Elizabeth, now Queen of England, and I didn't think it should be replaced, even by a more splendid mirror.

Mr. Conger's taste was impeccable, but he was more in tune with Pat Nixon than with me. I've already described his—and Mrs. Nixon's—changing the Yellow Oval Room from Mrs. Kennedy's comfortable down sofas to the stark, stiff, formal furniture, all stripes and arms and legs. The maids could tell you how many legs—something like 127—because they had to dust them. There was a ceramic bowl on a stand in the Yellow Oval Room, a bowl held up by two small Greek goddesses, and one of the goddesses had her hands out. Every time I went through, I used to put a cigarette between her fingers. The help dutifully removed this evidence of my disrespect, but I always tried again.

Everything correct in the Conger-Nixon Yellow Oval Room, but nothing welcoming. It made me gladder than ever I'd turned the so-called President's Bedroom into a hideaway. After dinner, when Jerry was home and we were alone, we'd get up from the table and go straight in there. He'd work and I'd watch television. He has a fantastic ability to study, look up once in a while, see what Kojak is doing, then go back to his papers. The sound doesn't disturb him at all; he's like those children who can study with rock music blaring.

Third (top) floor. The Billiard Room is here, and extra bed-rooms, and the solarium, which has been used for many things. Harry Truman held his poker parties in it, the Kennedys turned it into a schoolroom for Caroline, the Johnsons did it over as a teenagers' hangout, complete with soda fountain. It's the nicest room in the house, bright, informal, sunny, with windows all around. I used to have people to lunch there, and sometimes Jerry did too. It was done in green and yellow, and I brought in a big ceramic elephant. I'd given it to Jerry for his birthday one year, and he'd kept it out on the patio on Crown View Drive, but we took it with us to the White House. I hope somebody remembered to pack our elephant when we were leaving. They must have; they wouldn't have left an elephant for a Democrat. (I won't find out till all our belongings finally come out of storage.)

A lot of courting has gone on in the solarium. On the third floor, you're free of your Secret Service agents, as you are any time you get into the White House living quarters—and a President's children seem to head there as if directed by radar.

Trying to shake the Secret Service is a game to young people. On the *Merv Griffin Show*, Jack once said he'd been tempted to play around, fool his agents, "but after a while you realize they're just trying to do a job, and you can jeopardize that job by running out on them. It's easier to develop a relationship with them, tell them exactly what you're going to do so they can kind of lay back and not have to sit right on your tail."

A President and his whole family are protected around the clock. (Even from crank mail. When you're President, the mail is processed by Secret Service before it comes to you.) Each member of a President's family has a detail of agents. There were four in my detail, and a President has many more. These agents are rotated every six months, so you don't get too personally attached to them. You get attached anyway. You meet their families, their relatives are waiting at the plane when you come home from a trip, there's no way to keep it totally impersonal. I suppose the idea is that if a man relaxes he's not so alert, but I've always thought they could protect you better when they were really familiar with your habits, knew you'd be more apt to run up the stairs, say, than take an elevator.

I always missed my agents when they left.

Secret Service people go through regular training school in Washington. One of my first detail leaders, Dick Hartwig, is teaching there now. The Secret Service knows exactly where everyone in a President's family is at every moment. When you move from one place to another, the change is registered on a computer. There are boxes with little display screens all over the White House, and each person the Secret Service protects is assigned a number. When we lived in the White House, for instance, you might have seen a box that looked like this:

1: Oval Office
2: Out locally
3: Bethesda, Maryland

4: Lolo, Montana
5: Logan, Utah
6: Essex, Mass

This would have meant Jerry was working, I was in Washington but not in the White House, Susan was at school (Holton Arms), Steve was on a ranch in Montana, Jack was at Utah State, and Mike was at the seminary. We had code names, as well as numbers. Our code names all started with the letter P. Mine was Pinafore.

Agents and the people they protect work as a group. They are always with you. If you're in a restaurant, they're eating at the next table. If you have a doctor's appointment, your agents whisk you past the receptionist and into the inner sanctum before anybody sitting outside reading a magazine realizes what's happened. If a bellboy comes to pick up your suitcases, an agent precedes him into the room and follows him out again. When you go to the lavatory on an airplane, an agent is standing right by the door. I remember once a plane was about to land, and it was getting very rough as we went down. Frank Domenico, one of my agents, was yelling through the door, "Sit down, Mrs. Ford, please sit down," and I had to yell back, "I *am* sitting down."

A President and his wife are guarded by the Secret Service for the rest of their lives, and even today, when I go down a public hall, the agents don't allow anyone else in that hall. They particularly dislike hotel corridors, where a door can open and a stranger suddenly appear. I've seen someone start to come out of a hotel room, and an agent will go right up, pull the door shut again, and say, "Sorry, you'll have to stay in there and wait." Because they can't control who's in every room in every hotel. There are always cleaning people around too, which makes the Secret Service nervous. In a hotel lobby, it's not so obvious that agents are lurking because they can fade into the scenery better than they can in a corridor.

When a President goes to dinner at a public place, the Secret Service have to check that place before he's allowed to enter, and that includes checking the kitchen too. One agent has to carry the tommygun or the machine gun or whatever it is. It's bulky, it's in a case, but it's ready for use, and whichever agent gets stuck with it doesn't particularly enjoy lugging it around.

One of our agents swears—though the story's so good I'm afraid it's apocryphal—that on a day when Jerry was due at a hotel banquet the following incident really took place.

The agent with the gun was poking around in the hotel kitchen. In spite of the fact that it was very hot, he'd decided to keep his topcoat on to conceal this piece of artillery. Still, there was a strange bulge under his coat, and as he ambled through the kitchen, trying to appear casual, various cooks and dishwashers and busboys stared at him. (The Secret Service doesn't announce that it's the Secret Service, except to the management.)

"Just go ahead and do what you're doing, don't let me disturb you," the agent said.

Finally one brave woman accosted him. "You've got something sticking out of your coat."

"It's nothing, nothing at all," said the agent.

"But," said the woman, persisting, "I can *see* it sticking out."

"Oh," said the agent, "that's just a great big wrench."

Recognition dawned in the woman's eyes. "My God," she said, "you must be one of those White House plumbers!"

25

NEW TROUBLES: SOME BIGGER THAN OTHERS

Occasionally, I've seen myself described as a kind of dumpy middle-class square, a moralistic, narrow-minded woman who suddenly flowered and grew willowy in the sunshine of the White House.

Bunk. I *was* dumpier, but I still believe in God and country, I'm still against the exploitation of children—and other forms of pornography—and while I hope I never get too old to learn and grow, I think it wasn't so much that the White House altered me in any essential way as that I found the resources with which to respond to a series of challenges. You never know what you can do until you have to do it.

In the beginning, it was like going to a party you're terrified of, and finding out to your amazement that you're having a good time. But there were huge adjustments for all of us, and Susan's problems surfaced first. She made me a fierce speech. "Mom, there is no way in the world you're going to take my blue jeans away from me."

I said, "Fine, dear," and she looked surprised. In many ways, Susan was the most reasonable of our children. She had come to me and Jerry when she was sixteen and asked for permission to smoke (the boys had all done it behind our backs and got in trouble) and we said she could smoke in front of us, but we'd appreciate her avoiding it in public places, Mrs. Onassis style.

"I agree," she said. "I understand."

Susan was afraid of losing friends through moving to the White House. (Friends aren't any more important than breath or blood to a high school senior.) Sure enough, one day some of her pals came to the gate and couldn't get in. After that, we persuaded the guards to call the house and check before turning citizens away.

Nancy Howe, who had become important to me as all-round assistant, was another thorn in Susan's side. "She always had an excuse why I couldn't go in and see you," Susan says. "She interfered with our relationship."

I loved Susan, but I was dependent on Nancy, and looking back I can see that I may have been somewhat insensitive to the jealousies and insecurities of my adolescent daughter.

Partly because I was so busy trying to shape myself up, both physically and mentally. A President's wife is involved in making appearances at elaborate breakfasts, lunches, teas, dinners, and if you don't want to start buying your clothes from a blimp maker, you learn to push your food around the plate a lot. Also, for the first time in my life—this had begun when I was the Vice President's wife—I had to be on time. No waiting, no delays. Even a "drop-by," which can mean showing up at a function where you don't even sit down, is timed to the second (1:02, arrive in hotel lobby, take elevator to mezzanine, get off, turn left to Grand Ballroom. 1:05, talk to audience. 1:10, leave Grand Ballroom, etc.).

Jerry's administration had begun with a flood of good will and good wishes from all kinds of people who liked his decency, his friendliness, his accessibility, his ability to laugh at himself.

Then, on September 8, 1974, less than one month after he became President, he pardoned Richard Nixon. In the end, wrote Hugh Sidey, in *Portrait of a President*, although the process of pardon was complicated, "it rested upon the simple convictions of a plain person that the nation needed to put Watergate behind it and that a sick and burdened man needed now to be left alone."

It was the plain truth, but the public didn't buy it. Jerry's popularity in the Gallup poll, which had been up at seventy-one percent, plummeted twenty-two points almost overnight. The very next day after the pardon, he went to Pittsburgh to address an urban-affairs convention, and he was booed by citizens who thought he'd made a deal. His press secretary, Jerald terHorst, quit his job over the pardon, historians complained that they would never now be able "to get the facts," politicians talked of a double standard, reporters who had been finding Jerry admirable couldn't wait to tell of their disenchantment.

Jerry was unresentful. He hadn't asked for advice from anyone. He'd thought about the possibility of a trial for a former President—could it be a fair trial? Wouldn't it last for months?—and then he'd followed his own instincts, and while he was sorry so many people were so furious, he was willing to take the consequences of his act. "I think it was the right thing to do," he said then, and he's never changed his mind, though we both believe the pardon, more than anything else, cost him the 1976 election.

I'm not going to talk a lot about the pardon. It was hard to do, it wasn't popular, and it hurt Jerry a lot. But I think it had to be done. When Jerry took over the country, there was a sense of morass, of instability, and as far as I'm concerned, he turned that around.

I felt bad for my husband, but we both knew we had to keep on going. I plunged into preparations for a state dinner for Prime Minister and Mrs. Rabin of Israel, and another for President and Mrs. Leone of the Italian Republic (trying to do my bit toward keeping costs down by suggesting to the chef that he prepare duckling or other fowl for some of these affairs). I sat for a portrait for *Vogue*, I flew to a meeting of the National Federation of Republican Women, I opened a Greek festival, I gave an interview to the *New York Times Magazine*. And then, eighteen days after the Nixon pardon, my doctors discovered that I had cancer.

26

CANCER

The way it began, Nancy Howe was going for a routine checkup at the National Naval Medical Center in Bethesda, Maryland, and she said it would make sense for me to come along since I was about due for my six-month gynecological examination.

It was a pretty day, a Thursday, and as Nancy and I were driven along the tree-lined George Washington Memorial Highway, we talked about trivia, nothing very significant, and when I walked into the examining room of the hospital, I had no sense of foreboding whatever.

A doctor checked my breasts, said, "Just a minute," went away and came back with Dr. William Fouty, the chief of surgery. Dr. Fouty checked my breasts too.

I still didn't think much about it. Doctors had been checking portions of my anatomy for so long—ever since the pinched nerve, really—that I could take quite a bit of poking and prodding and hearing murmurs of "Mmm," and go right on wondering when I was going to be able to attack the huge pile of mail which was waiting on my desk.

Back at the White House, I was given a message. Dr. Lukash

would like to see me in his office on the ground floor that evening at seven o'clock.

I went down at seven, and Dr. Lukash had brought in a specialist, Dr. Richard Thistlethwaite of the George Washington University Medical School, to examine my breasts—by now I was getting suspicious—and when I came out of the dressing room again, Jerry was waiting. Dr. Lukash had said he wanted to talk to him, so Jerry had come straight from the Oval Office.

Dr. Lukash told us the doctors at Bethesda had found a lump in my right breast, and wanted to operate immediately. "Well, they can't operate immediately," I said. "I have a full day tomorrow."

It's funny the way you try to cling to the known, the normal, the routine in the face of news which shakes you.

The doctor said "immediately" was figurative; the hospital couldn't schedule my surgery until Saturday morning anyway. "The operating rooms are all booked up for tomorrow. But you'll go in tomorrow night."

Jerry and I took the elevator upstairs, and when Susan came in for dinner, we could tell she'd been crying. She'd heard about the trouble before I had. The way she remembers it, she'd stopped by Dr. Lukash's office that afternoon. "I had a cold and I went in to get a pill, and he pulled me in and sat me down, and I thought, 'What have I done wrong now?' He told me, 'Your mother has a lump in her breast, there's a good chance it's cancer, and she doesn't know, so hush, hush, don't say anything to anybody.' I called the twins [Susan's girlfriends, the Golubin twins] and got terribly upset over the phone. Nobody can do anything for you except just kind of hear you out."

After dinner, the three of us discussed how we would manage. I wanted to go through my Friday activities without making any kind of announcement. Jerry agreed.

Friday morning we went to ground-breaking ceremonies— Jerry presided—at the Lyndon Johnson Memorial Grove, a park in Virginia, and I invited Lady Bird and the girls and their husbands to come for tea at the White House later that afternoon. (In between, I made a speech at a luncheon for the Salvation Army.)

Still, nobody knew I was headed for the hospital. My bag was packed, and it was just a question of getting me out to Bethesda before the White House made the announcement. It came on the six o'clock news that I was going in for the operation.

The car pulled up in front of Bethesda at 5:55 P.M., and I remember saying to Nancy Howe and Rick Sardo, Jerry's Marine Corps aide, "Well, I wonder how Louise is doing."

At the moment we were arriving, Louise Abbruzzese was inside the very same hospital having a baby. I thought about the cycle of life and death, but I didn't say anything. It would have sounded too much like a script for *Ben Casey*.

They put me in the Presidential Suite, which has its own dining room, and Jerry and Nancy and Susan and Mike and Gayle (who'd flown down from Boston) had dinner with me. The other boys, both in Utah, were keeping in touch by phone. The Presidential Suite was not very high up, and I could look out and see the news people down below with their searchlights shining up at my windows.

Jerry says he's never been so lonely as he was going home to the White House that night. He was more upset than I. I think I faced the situation rather matter of factly. I'd been through several crises in my life and always come out all right. I thought, This is one more crisis, and it will pass.

Next morning I was awake at six—unusual for me—and I found flowers from my husband beside the bed, and by six-thirty, all the family were there at the hospital. Even our friend the Reverend Billy Zeoli had come from Ohio to see me before they took me down to the operating room. I tried to make them laugh about the toeless socks which were part of my operating-room costume. "Here's one for *Women's Wear Daily*," I said. Nobody so much as smiled weakly.

Right before the orderlies wheeled me away, Jerry kissed me. "Good luck," he said. "God bless you."

It had all been explained to me what this operation would entail. They would do the biopsy, and there was a possibility that the lump would be benign, and I would be shipped back to my room. But, if the lump proved malignant, they would go ahead and remove my breast while I was still under the anesthesia.

I joked with the anesthetist. "Good night, Sweet Prince," I said. I think I knew then that I had cancer, and that they would have to go ahead with the operation, but I also felt I could conquer the disease.

Susan was less confident. "We all sat around and prayed," she remembers, "but the thing I didn't realize until after you'd gone to the operating room was, that may be the last time I'll ever see my mother alive. It hit me, and I just went nuts. I really did. I didn't need that at all. I stuck around your room as long as I could stand it, and then I went down and saw Louise and the baby. It was a girl; they named her Katy. I held that brand-new baby in my arms, and fed her the first bottle she ever had, and I was scared, scared about everything.

"I guess I was the first one they told it was cancer, because I was walking down the hall, and Lukash grabbed me. He said, 'Susan, they had to go ahead.' And my knees buckled. 'But she's all right,' he said.

"I went and saw you in the recovery room. I'll never go into another recovery room. You were so white, and so doped up, you didn't look alive."

Katherine Elizabeth (Elizabeth after me; if she'd been a boy, he'd have been Gerald) Abbruzzese is four years old now. I remember the anniversary of my operation by her birthday, and when we talk on the phone she always wants to know, "Where's the President?"

I came out of the anesthesia and saw the long faces of my loved ones around me, and I said, "If you can't look happy, please go away. I can't bear to look at you."

I was connected to tubes, and mumbling words I thought were crystal clear, but I was really okay. When I woke up, I wasn't in the least surprised to have the doctor tell me my intuition had been correct, the growth had been malignant, and they'd had to remove the right breast.

It was over, but certainly life wasn't over.

Hume Cronyn, the actor, had a tumor in one eye and lost the eye, and in an interview given by him and his wife, Jessica Tandy, to the *New York Times*, Miss Tandy told how she'd responded. "It does sound when you first hear about it a ghastly thing to happen to anybody, and to anybody close to you," she said, "but at the end of it, you have a whole man and somehow you find yourself saying, 'It was only an eye, you know, and life is much more important than anything else.' So there you are, you see, it was all right."

That's exactly the way Jerry and I felt. We were both just so grateful the doctors had got the cancer in time so that I was going to live. There was no way of predicting how *long* I was going to live—every checkup is a new hurdle—but you have to have a positive attitude. Again, it's a question of mental health affecting your physical health.

I got a lot of credit for having gone public with my mastectomy, but if I hadn't been the wife of the President of the United States, the press would not have come racing after my story, so in a way it was fate.

"God moves in a mysterious way His wonders to perform." Even before I was able to get up, I lay in bed and watched television and saw on the news shows lines of women queued up to go in for breast examinations because of what had happened to me.

Susan wanted to come live at the hospital, Holton Arms being only ten minutes away, but I wouldn't permit it. I knew she wouldn't get any studying done. So she visited every afternoon, came out when classes were over, spent a couple of hours talking to me, reading cards, taking calls. She was growing up, and I think she was surprised at the depth of her own feeling.

Five days after the operation, I had a delayed reaction, and broke into fits of weeping. That was all right too. Dr. Fouty sat beside the bed, and told me it was just post-operative depression. "Cry it all out," he said.

Jerry too had had a bit of a reaction. Less than an hour after my operation he'd made a speech to eight hundred delegates at an economic conference, and the newspapers said his voice broke when he told his listeners the surgery was over.

Along with the breast and some supporting muscle, the doctors had removed lymph nodes from my armpit, and traces of cancer had been found in three. That meant I would have to take chemotherapy to ensure that the disease wouldn't spread. I asked the doctors what the magic number was, how many nodes could be affected and the patient still recover. They told me four. I'm not clear about whether they really thought that, or were only trying to reassure me.

It was on a Sunday night that Dr. Lukash brought up a little brown bottle of pills for the first time. "I want you to take these for five days straight," he said. I was upset. I thought, Every time I look at these pills, it's going to remind me of the fact that I've had cancer. Also, I'd heard so many dreadful tales about chemotherapy that at first I was convinced the pills were giving me headaches. Then I pulled myself together, decided the pain was in my imagination, this medicine had to be taken, so I might as well take it and forget about it. (Five days in a row every five weeks for two years, and it was over. Now I have to have a bone scan every six months, and that's about it. I know there's public conjecture about my health, but apart from the arthritis and the pinched nerve, I'm fine. My cancer checkups show I'm clean. I can't neglect my hot packs, my physical therapy, or I wind up in bed. I don't want to be in bed; I like to go places, to see people, and I'll do anything in the world to keep from becoming an invalid.)

In the hospital, they kept sending me downstairs for scan-type X-rays, and I had to sit in one position for oh, maybe ten minutes. They'd put me on a metal stool, and I remember thinking my bones were going to go straight through my skin, and when I stood up I would surely be bleeding from my bottom, which has never been very well endowed. The nurses were so good, though, so protective. I can still hear a nurse named Jeannie scolding one X-ray technician. "She cannot raise her arm that high!" she said crossly, and when I had to stand up for a picture, she watched me like a hawk. I could see it in her eyes: she was waiting to catch me if I dropped.

Here's another passage from the Hume Cronyn interview: "The only really bad time was when they put you in the hospital to go over the whole of your system to see whether or not this is the site or whether this is simply a reflection of it somewhere else," Hume had said. "That's an ugly time to wait through. Apart from that, once it was decided, I had the world's greatest blessing. I had a big job to go to, right like that. I didn't have *time*. I just went back and did it as though nothing had ever happened."

It was the same for me. The question in my mind was how fast I could get on my feet and get back to being First Lady, and doing my job. I worked hard at exercising. I worked my hands in something they called a spider walk, where you make your fingers crawl up a wall. I was lucky because the doctors had left me some strands of muscle so my right arm didn't swell, and it could be used, although very slowly at first. If I jerked, it hurt. The first day I could pick up a cup of tea with my right hand I felt triumphant, and one week after the operation I walked out to the elevator to meet Jerry. (I'd kept watch from the window to see when he was arriving; we were always forewarned because the press gathered ahead of him.)

There were Marines all up and down the stairs and Secret Service agents in the hall, and Jerry stepped off the elevator and blanched. "What in the world are you doing out here in the hall?"

"I came out to surprise you," I said.

He handed me a football. "I brought you a present." It was from the coach of the Washington Redskins, George Allen, and all the players had signed it after a game with Denver, which the Redskins had won 33 to 3.

As we started back down the hall, Jerry was a little bit in front, and I was holding the ball. I drew my arm back, said, "Here, catch!" and threw a pass at him. Poor Dr. Fouty just about dropped to his knees right then and there, but Jerry, who was equally shocked, still showed good reflexes. He caught the ball, saying as he did so, "Okay, dear, that's enough." Then he put his arm around me and we walked to the suite. "Let's go in and sit down," he said. "I think you've had your exercise for tonight."

I never felt a psychic wound, I never felt hopelessly mutilated. After all, Jerry and I had been married a good many years, and our love had proved itself. I had no reason to doubt my husband. If he'd lost a leg, I wouldn't have deserted him, and I knew he wouldn't desert me because I was unfortunate enough to have had a mastectomy. Neither of us could walk away from the other. When I say we've had an ideal marriage, I'm not just talking about physical attraction, which I imagine can wear pretty thin if it's all a couple has built on. We've had that and a whole lot more.

I stayed in the hospital longer than I needed to because Jerry went on a campaign trip, crossing the country to speak on behalf of various Republican candidates for Congress—elections were only a few weeks away—and he didn't want me to come back to the White House until he got home. I had to have all those tests run anyway, and it was a forty-minute trip from Washington to Bethesda, which would have meant that as an outpatient I'd have to get up every morning at the crack of dawn. (Hospitals do everything during the hours when sane people are still pounding their ears.)

My sister-in-law Janet came from South Carolina to be with me, and she and Nancy Howe were there all day long, day after day, and the flowers kept arriving, and we kept sending them out as fast as they came in, sending them all over the hospital, sharing them with other patients. There wouldn't have been enough room for them and us in the suite.

It was wonderful, that outpouring of feeling from all over the United States. Letters, cards, prayers arrived (eventually fifty thousand pieces of mail were counted). There was so much mail some of my friends set up an answering service, and we finally had to have a card printed extending appreciation to each person who'd remembered me. I got a couple of exasperated phone calls from intimates who'd received printed cards, but they didn't realize I saw only half the letters, and got reports about the rest.

The volunteers who worked on the correspondence said they laughed a lot and cried a little, too, as they read. Women—from a teenager to a lady of ninety-three—wrote in saying they'd had breasts removed, offering hints about exercise and underwear, suggesting cancer could be cured by everything from eating asparagus to standing with your hands on your hips while wearing a compress made of rhubarb leaves. I'm not making that up. One lady advised me to alternate drinking carrot and apple juice while massaging the instep of my foot. That, she said, would prevent a recurrence of disease.

We got donations of money, and thousands of dollars were turned over to the American Cancer Society. Some of the good wishes came from kind souls who didn't even put return addresses on the envelopes; they weren't looking for replies, they just wanted me to know they were thinking of me.

Men wrote too. Men married to women who'd had mastectomies tried to buck me up by telling me they still loved their wives.

They did buck me up. I was touched, and overwhelmed.

Two weeks after I'd checked into the hospital, Jerry came to Bethesda to pick me up in a helicopter. I remember flying away from the hospital and looking down over the houses and the trees, and how brilliant the leaves were, how absolutely beautiful the world was. Because I was coming home.

27

SO LONG, BAD TIMES

They were lined up by the Diplomatic Entrance, everyone who worked in the White House, with signs saying, WE LOVE YOU, BETTY, and long banners printed with legends in bright colors welcoming me back.

Janet and Susan and Liberty (the golden retriever puppy Susan and David Kennerly had bought for Jerry to cheer him up during the time I was away) came running across the lawn to meet me, and I had no words for the joy I was feeling. I could only look, and touch, and smile, and hold on.

Four days later, Jerry and I celebrated our twenty-sixth wedding anniversary. He planned a special treat. Usually, he took his lunch on a tray in the Oval Office, but this day he had the whole thing set up in the Red Room. As a surprise, Tennessee Ernie Ford and his group—just back from a State Department tour of Russia where they'd represented the United States marvelously well—were supposed to come in and have lunch with us, and then they were going to serenade me.

As the hour approached for me to get dressed, somebody on my staff tipped me off about the party, and I said no. "I'm not going downstairs for anything. I don't want the publicity."

Silly thing for a President's wife to say? Well, I just didn't feel emotionally ready for a big dramatic appearance. I phoned Jerry in his office and said I was sorry. "I'd love to have lunch with you if you want to come up here, but I'm just not up to the other thing yet."

He came, and we had a private lunch in the family dining room (Heinz Bender, the White House pastry chef, sent us two hearts sculpted out of ice cream) and then we went out on the Truman balcony, me still in my bathrobe, and Tennessee and his group were gathered below on the south lawn and they sang "The Anniversary Waltz." It was a fantastic anniversary. Just to be well and alive and home was wonderful. I was a very happy person on the fifteenth of October in 1974.

Which didn't mean I could quit doing my exercises or taking the pills in the little brown bottles.

Some of my mail had been from women who'd said they couldn't stand to look at their own bodies after their mastectomies, but I was curious about my scar, from the minute the doctor started changing my bandages. I examined it every day to see how it was healing. The one thing that worried me was whether I'd be able to wear my evening clothes again. Jerry said I was silly. "If you can't wear 'em cut low in front, wear 'em cut low in back." By the time I was able to try the dresses on, I found I could wear just about everything. With the exception of gowns which were sleeveless. Because of the excess amount of skin the doctor left so I could have free use of the arm, I had to choose things that came at least down to the elbow. But I think in most women of my age the upper arm has begun to fade anyway, and they don't look particularly well in sleeveless dresses.

My doctors never suggested reconstructive surgery. Even if they had, I doubt that I'd have wanted to go through more operations. Again, it may have been the fact that I was secure in a long, affectionate relationship with my husband which kept me from feeling the need for a breast implant.

(Once in a while, of course, if you wear a prosthesis, which I do, you have an embarrassing moment. There was a tag football game in Vail one summer. The Secret Service had divided up, with the Presidential detail playing against the family detail, and I was coaching the family detail. It was a rough game, played with lots of spirit, and afterward the press were trying to get some pictures. The press were with us wherever we went. I said okay, I'd pass the ball, but that didn't suit the photographers. "We'd like a picture of you centering the ball." I said centering the ball wasn't nearly so ladylike as passing the ball, but if that's what was wanted, I'd cooperate. I was wearing white slacks and a navy blue jersey T-shirt with a White House insignia on it, and because it was so hot, I hadn't tucked the T-shirt in my pants; it was hanging loose. Talk about whoops! When I bent over to center the ball, I felt this kerplop! as the prosthesis slipped out of my bra, and I thought, Oh, oh, when I stand up, it's going to fall right smack on the ground at my feet. How am I going to get out of this? Holding my arm tight across my waist, so the falsie couldn't slide any lower, and trying to appear nonchalant, I half sauntered, half crouched over to the sidelines and hissed at Susan, "For heaven's sake, come help me." Immediately, she realized what had happened, and the two of us ducked behind some cars and got the thing back into position without anyone's being the wiser.)

Right after the mastectomy, people kept saying how thin I was. I had lost a tremendous lot of weight. I came to the White House wearing a size ten, went down to a six, and am now stabilized at an eight. Despite reports to the contrary, I am *not* a fragile person. I stay size eight because I want to.

I don't think it was more than a month after my operation that Happy Rockefeller had hers. The country was completely shocked. First the President's wife, then the wife of the Vice President. Nelson Rockefeller said on television that my having told the world I had cancer had helped save Happy's life because it had caused her to go—in time—for a checkup. During our convalescence, Happy and I were always planning to spend some time together at the Rockefellers' place on Foxhall Road, just go into the woods and walk, but it never happened; we were both too busy.

I was impatient with the recuperation period. I felt I had lost precious time being ill, and needed to get my First Lady act together. Never having had the traditional three months' transition period a President's family is generally heir to, I'd been going through what one reporter called "on the job training" in the seven weeks before I'd been laid low.

Lying in the hospital, thinking of all those women going for cancer checkups because of me, I'd come to recognize more clearly the power of the woman in the White House. Not *my* power, but the power of the position, a power which could be used to help.

I felt I hadn't even begun to work effectively for the causes— the Equal Rights Amendment, mental health, the fight against child abuse, the fight against the abuse of old people and retarded people—that I cared about. Even so, I'd been given all kinds of credit for such straight talking as I'd already done. Betty Friedan told reporters I'd been so good for the women's movement she hoped "some of our strength can flow back to her."

I went to Camp David for a couple of days, got still another Welcome Back. The whole staff hugged and kissed me when I came in the door of Aspen. I walked the grounds with Liberty, ate food that was good for me (liver and onions, ugh) whether I liked it or not. I think it was that weekend that Jerry broke the news to me that Steve had enrolled in a school for rodeo riders in Wyoming. I said we should stop him. "I don't want him all broken up in rodeos."

"He's too old to stop," Jerry said. "And you know how well he's taken our advice on everything else."

Situation normal, generation gap. What Martha Graham had been to me, horses are to Steve, and a mother interferes with true love at her peril.

The last two months of 1974 were furiously busy, which is to say they were ordinary White House months.

On the night of November 5, Jerry and I watched the election returns on television, as the Democrats gained four Governors, three Senators and forty-three Representatives. The Nixon pardon, added to the issue of Watergate, had soured the voters on Republicans. Jerry was sad but philosophical. "The people have spoken," he said in a statement delivered by his press secretary, "and for twenty-six years, I have accepted the verdict of the people."

The next week, I tried to pull together a state dinner for Austria's Chancellor, Bruno Kreisky, who was coming to visit on November 12. It was being done in a great rush and should have been organized earlier. Every orchestra we called was booked, and so were all the entertainers. We couldn't corral a soul. Then I found out that singer Vicki Carr, who'd been in Washington for the American Lung Association, had visited Jerry's office and made quite an impression on him. We got him to phone and invite her to the party, and she came.

I don't know how Chancellor Kreisky felt about Vicki Carr, but she clicked with my husband. It was right after the WIN button had come out. (Jerry had a Whip Inflation Now campaign which was supposed to encourage everybody to pull in our belts and get the economy straightened out, but people thought his program wasn't far-reaching enough—except for the ones who thought it was too far-reaching—and they tended to laugh at the buttons; the whole thing sort of flopped.) At Chancellor Kreisky's party, Vicki Carr tried to pin a WIN button on the almost nonexistent front of her dress, and Jerry beamed and kissed the little lady on the side of her head. (I'm not saying I'm jealous; I'm just saying that the next time I went into the west wing and found a large picture of Vicki in a beguiling dress hanging there, I laughed and turned her to the wall.)

I couldn't lure Jerry off the dance floor until one A.M. on the Kreisky-Carr night, and I had to be up at seven the next morning for a meeting with my staff. That was probably the point at which I realized I was recovered, well again.

Justice William O. Douglas had also come to Chancellor Kreisky's dinner, healing a breach which had existed since 1970, when Jerry had called for the Justice to be impeached. He'd taken the strong stand because, as a conventional, conservative Midwesterner, Jerry thought the four-times-married Douglas (or, for that matter, *any* Supreme Court Justice) shouldn't have been writing for *Evergreen Review*, a magazine full of nude photographs. At the time, I completely agreed with my husband. (I don't approve of politicians putting articles in *Playboy*, either, no matter how well it pays. I like *Playboy*, I'm not stuffy, but I think men like Andy

Young and Jimmy Carter could find a better setting for their ideas. It's like the wrong frame on a picture. Magazines are getting worse and worse. *Playboy* and *Evergreen Review* must seem like Mother Goose compared to some of the newer publications. I'm shocked when the newspapers tell about sex magazines that use little children as models. Some of their parents are *selling* those children. It makes me sick. I think we've fallen to a new low.)

Jerry came to think he'd been wrong in his attacks on Justice Douglas—"Impeachment would have been too harsh," he said later—and since neither he nor Douglas was a rancorous man, they shook hands in reconciliation on the night of Chancellor Kreisky's fête.

Less than a week later, Jerry left for Japan, Korea, and a quick visit with Leonid Brezhnev in Vladivostok in the Soviet Union.

I always went out on the Truman Balcony to wave goodbye when he took off on a trip without me. There were usually press people around taking pictures, and a crowd of citizens who were interested too; the helicopter coming in on the south lawn never ceases to draw people, it's such a neat thing. Sometimes Jerry would be leaving fairly early in the morning—nine-thirty, ten o'clock—and there were occasions when, I blush to confess, I wasn't dressed by nine-thirty or ten o'clock. (Unlike me, my husband had always been an early riser. In the White House, he got up at five-fifteen every morning, went over to the Oval Office about seven, often didn't come back until seven-thirty at night; there was just that much to do, and even then he couldn't see all the people who wanted to see him.) When I'd hear the helicopter coming in to fetch him, if I didn't have time to put my clothes on, I'd quickly take off my robe, slip into shoes and a coat, tuck my nightgown up under the coat, and go out on the balcony and smile at the world, just as confidently as if I were dressed. (In hot weather, it was more difficult; it looked sort of strange to see me buttoned up to my chin in July.)

Jerry would look up at the balcony and wave, and I'd wave back and say a little prayer. Please, dear God, keep him safe and bring him back to me.

(My anxiety deepened in 1975. After the first attempt on his life, by Squeaky Fromme, I couldn't watch him leave without thinking, What's going to happen this time? The worry was always there.)

It was during that November visit to Japan that Jerry was photographed with Emperor Hirohito in a picture that made history. The Emperor is a little bit of a man, and his pants were so baggy they were hanging on the ground, and Jerry's pants were way up above his ankles. I didn't know whether to laugh or cry. My husband hangs on to his clothes. He still has jackets with narrow lapels. He doesn't wear them out in public, but he wears them around the house. And when I get after him, he says, "Well, I'm not going anyplace, nobody's going to look at me." "*I* look at you," I say, but that doesn't make a big impression.

I think those tails he was sporting on that Japanese trip were left over from college. He hadn't worn striped trousers in ages, and I'd been trying, without success, to get him to try them on before he left so we could see if they still fit. Finally, it was nearly time for him to pack, and I brought the subject up again. "You've got to try those pants on." He was getting ready for bed, and he tried them on in his bare feet, and they looked fine. I didn't notice they were too short; without shoes, you couldn't tell.

He took a beating in the press, they made such fun of him. To think the President of the United States would show up with high-water pants! (Jerry told me later that the suspenders were wrong, they hiked the pants up still shorter, and nobody could find him a longer pair of suspenders.)

Well, if you're going to assume the office, you have to assume the striped pants that go with it. The public expects a President to dress well; he just can't say to hell with protocol. Remember the flap when President Carter tried his first fireside chat in a cardigan sweater?

My fashion plate was back home before Thanksgiving, and suddenly we were plunged into our first holiday season in the White House, which meant that while my right hand was shaking the hand of West German Chancellor Helmut Schmidt and welcoming him to our country, my left eye was watching out for the arrival of the giant White House Christmas tree, which comes in all wrapped up in cord and burlap, on a truck. I don't mean the tree literally followed the Chancellor up the red carpet, I just mean events rushed past so thick and fast that memory blurs them together.

While the Christmas decorations were going up on the State floor, the White House was closed to the public for three days. The decorations were fabulous; the State floor became a fairyland. In the Dining Room, there was a gingerbread house made by the pastry chef, and in the East Room a beautiful crêche, framed in gilt, with wax dolls. (An electric fan plays on the crêche the entire time it's up in order to keep the wax figures cool enough so they don't melt.) The crêche was donated by Jane Engelhardt, who also donated a stage—large enough for a ballet company—to the White House. (The stage takes a day to put up and a day to take down.)

We'd been hoping to find donors for the White House tree trimmings too. We'd started out thinking we'd like handmade Christmas ornaments from all over the United States. (Each year the tree is different; once it was entirely trimmed with cookies.) But what groups to approach? There are thousands. Whom are you going to eliminate? We'd have liked to ask the aged to contribute. Old people have time to sit and make things. Yet we didn't want to cut out the young people. And if you get the Girl Scouts into it, the Boy Scouts want to get into it too.

In 1974, we were lucky. The Colonial Williamsburg Foundation (the restoration project in Virginia, funded by Rockefeller money) offered to do the whole tree with thousands of antique hand-carved wooden ornaments. I breathed a great sigh of relief.

The same day the giant tree arrived and was hauled into the Blue Room, the Harlem Globetrotters arrived and were ushered into the waiting room outside the Oval Office. They'd come to call on Jerry, who had a conference which was running late. I was dying to meet them (I'd watched them on TV whenever I got a chance) so I went over and introduced myself, and accosted Meadowlark Lemon. "I played football," I said, "but I never could manage to dribble a basketball. Will you teach me?"

"Sure," he said, "it's easy, you just go like this—" And he took a basketball and started dribbling it real fast, and tossed it to me. I fumbled, got lower and lower to the ground trying to keep the ball going, and I was squealing, "Oh, I'm hopeless, just hopeless, I can't do a thing about it—" when all of a sudden around the corner came Don Rumsfeld with word that the President said there was too much noise in the outer office, and whoever was carrying on, would they please stop. Cease. Desist from their activities.

I ran over and put the basketball on Nell Yates's desk. Nell, who was Jerry's secretary, shook her head. "*I* don't want the blame."

"Oh, Nell," I said, "he won't blame you. He knows you wouldn't do a thing like that. He knows it would probably be me."

The Christmas parties started, and I didn't think they'd ever stop. There was a party at the Hospital for Sick Children, and I went and helped Santa Claus distribute gifts. There was a White House party for the children of the diplomatic corps, and after that, a practically identical party for the children of the cooks, maids, and anybody else who worked in the White House.

There were parties for kids, and parties for grownups. We gave a Christmas party for the members of the White House press. The press party started at seven, was supposed to be over by nine. Jerry and I had to leave to go to the Senate for Nelson Rockefeller's swearing-in as Vice President. (The two little Rockefeller boys, Mark and Nelson, were photographed with their mother—for the first time in public—that night. They were such obvious targets for kidnapers that they had always had a guard with them who took them to school, picked them up, dogged their steps.)

When Jerry and I got back to the White House, it was 11 P.M., and the last members of the press were just straggling out into the night. Once we'd left for the Senate, and formality could be thrown to the winds, our guests had really had a blast.

We gave an honest-to-goodness ball that season too: the first Annual Christmas Ball in years for the Cabinet and members of Congress. It had occurred to me that the White House looked so beautiful during the holidays that it would be an ideal time to entertain the Congress with a great black-tie gathering. And it was. In the Blue Room, Jerry pointed to the magnificent tree that stretched clear to the ceiling and told the thousand guests—from the Hill, the Cabinet, the senior White House staff—that he and the Christmas tree, also from Michigan, had a lot in common. "A few months ago, neither one of us expected to be in the White House."

On the twenty-second of December we left for Vail. And on New Year's Eve, at the Basshaus, our friends gathered—everyone had to come before midnight, so he or she would have the glass of champagne in his or her hand when the bell tolled—and we toasted 1975. There's a picture of the whole crowd of us looking sloshed, as the New Year came slipping in.

Jerry and I had made it; we had come through. Watergate and the mastectomy were behind us, our children and our friends surrounded us, and outside, through the picture windows on either side of Dick Bass's two-story fireplace, we could see fresh snow covering the ground, clean, white, new.

28

◆◇◆

CAUSES AND EFFECTS

From *Susannah of the Mounties*, 1939 movie:

> Small Indian boy, eight or nine years old, to Shirley Temple:
> "Squaw, keep quiet and walk behind."
> Shirley Temple, also eight or nine years old, indignantly:
> "Walk behind! I will not!"

It took the people who drafted the Equal Rights Amendment nearly forty years to catch up with Shirley, who never *did* walk behind. (She served her country in the UN and as Ambassador to Ghana, and even a mastectomy didn't slow her down.)

As wife of the Vice President, I was already involved with the Equal Rights Amendment, and when Jerry became President, I kept pushing, trying to influence him. I used everything, including pillow talk at the end of the day, when I figured he was most tired and vulnerable. I championed the idea of women in high places. Carla Hills came into his Cabinet as HUD Secretary, Anne Armstrong was named Ambassador to Great Britain (I thought she should have been Jerry's Vice Presidential running mate in 1976), but my big disappointment is I never got him to appoint a woman to the Supreme Court. I probably didn't do enough research, and I lost that battle.

A woman who made it to the highest court would have to be very well qualified in judicial matters, but if we'd stayed in the White House, it might have happened. Because Jerry's changed. I heard him talking on the radio the other day—he was speaking from somewhere in Texas—and he said he thought there would be a woman Vice President within the next ten years, and maybe a woman President in twenty.

I've worked hard on my husband, so that pleased me. Back in January of 1975, Jerry signed an executive order establishing a National Commission on the Observance of International Women's Year, and while this order didn't have any legal or legislative force, it had moral force; it meant a President of the United States was standing up for women and the ERA, and against "legal inequities between sexes."

At the ceremony in the Cabinet Room, he turned to me. "Before I sign this, Betty, if you have any words of wisdom or encouragement, you are welcome to speak."

Through the laughter of the audience, I spoke. "I just want to congratulate you, Mr. President. I am glad to see that you have come a long, long way."

Mr. President shook his head. "I don't know how to take that," he said.

Maybe I ought to explain that my views on women's rights don't extend to believing that all women need to work outside the home. A housewife deserves to be honored as much as a woman who earns her living in the marketplace. I consider bringing up children a responsible job. In fact, being a good housewife seems to me a much tougher job than going to the office and getting paid for it. What man could afford to pay for all the things a wife does, when she's a cook, a mistress, a chauffeur, a nurse, a baby-sitter? But *because* of this, I feel women ought to have equal rights, equal social security, equal opportunities for education, an equal chance to establish credit.

When your daughter goes out and finds a job, even if she's had the same education, it's very likely she would be paid less for the job than your son would be. That's wrong.

Maybe some women *aren't* equal to some men. I don't say I'm equal to my husband; I certainly couldn't have done what he's done. But there are a good many women in this world who are brilliant, and I think we're going to get one of those brilliant women on the Supreme Court in the near future.

As this is written, ERA still has to be okayed by the voters in three more states before it can be brought before the Congress for enactment (it's already been defeated in some important states like New York and New Jersey), but I keep hoping.

In the White House, I was picketed by ERA opponents. Phyllis Schlafly, who managed to rally battalions of housewives against ERA, went around the country talking about motherhood. Well, I was a mother. I thought motherhood was swell. But I wasn't so sure mothers shouldn't have *rights*.

I've been asked if I'd be interested in debating Mrs. Schlafly. I wouldn't be. She contends that women's place is in the home, yet she's out touring all over the United States in order to bring women that message. I wonder how often she's home to greet *her* husband when he comes in for dinner.

A lot of men around the White House had to be educated about ERA (some of them vaguely believed it to be an outfit called EAR) and Dick Hartwig who, at the time I'm talking about, was head of my Secret Service detail, thought it was strictly for the birds. I was always teasing him (I bought him a male chauvinist pig necktie), and when we rode together in a car, and I mentioned ERA, he'd turn around from the front seat and look at me as if to say, "You're nuts."

"It's not the duty of the Secret Service to censor the conversation," I would say loftily. Hartwig, Rick Sardo, and I were constantly bantering about ERA.

Which is how I came to get my very own ERA flag.

It began because of the flags flying on diplomats' cars. When diplomats present their credentials to a President, the arrangements have been made beforehand. Since the White House has to bring in troops, line them all up in the driveway, and produce trumpeters to blow a salute, four or five of these diplomatic calls are scheduled in the same hour, spaced a few minutes apart. Each ambassador or minister drives up in a car sporting his country's flag, he's met at the diplomatic entrance by the Chief of Protocol, and he's taken into the Oval Office, where he spends about ten minutes with the President. Then he's escorted out again, and he gets into his car and goes.

I used to look down from an upstairs window and watch the parade, one diplomat driving away as the next one's car pulled up, pennants waving in the breeze.

When a President goes anyplace, flags fly from the front of his car too, the American flag from one side, the Presidential flag from the other.

One day I took this up with Hartwig and Sardo. "I have a nice car," I said, "but no flag. If the President gets flags, why shouldn't the First Lady?" I pointed to some troops who were just marching away as my limousine pulled up to the diplomatic entrance. "And look at that. They could at least wait for *me* to arrive. I sure do get second-class treatment around here."

A week later, Sardo came in with a flag. A girlfriend of Hartwig's who knew how to sew had put it together, and it was made to fit on one of the fender poles of my car. It was blue satin, trimmed with lace and braid, and decorated with red, white, and blue stars. In the middle of it, carefully stuffed, shaped, formed, was a pair of red and white calico bloomers, in honor of my maiden name, and the legend above these fat little pantaloons read, "Don't tread on me." Down below the bloomers were the letters ERA.

Gorgeous. I wrote and thanked Hartwig's friend, and told her the flag should be in a museum. I think I'm going to have it framed, or put in a glass case.

I did a lot of stumping for ERA. I phoned legislators, I wrote to them, I made speeches. All I wanted was for the amendment to come to the floor so that Congress could vote its conscience. The struggle goes on. Last winter, having been out of the White House for a year, I went to Houston to attend a women's conference. I sat on a platform with Lady Bird Johnson and Rosalynn Carter, and I got up and said a few words. I'm still hearing about it. Letters pour in. Many are addressed jointly to Mrs. Carter, Mrs. Johnson, and me, and I'm sure each of us gets a copy. "How can you women be up there promoting a bunch of lesbians?" is the question most often posed.

We *weren't* promoting a bunch of lesbians. I can't even say we were in step with the lesbian faction of the women's movement, although I do think lesbians are entitled to free speech, the same as anybody else. God put us all here for His own purposes; it's not my business to try to second-guess Him, and I think Anita Bryant's taking action against the gay population was ill considered. I don't believe people should lose their jobs because of their sexual preference. On the other hand, I'm not sure I'd want my small children being taught by gay teachers. I also think it's about time for sex—of any and all kinds—to get back in the closet. I'm tired of everyone's flaunting what should be a private matter. Whether people are straight or gay, I don't want to see them making time on the street corner. I feel like that Englishwoman who said she didn't mind what her weekend guests did, "so long as they don't do it on the lawn, and scare the horses."

There is no way I'm going to stop fighting for women's rights. Phyllis Schlafly suggests that people like me, who lie in bed in the morning instead of making their husbands breakfast, are pushing America toward unisex toilets and drugs, and as if that weren't bad enough, soon we'll have brought an end to alimony and Bible reading.

I'm still lying in bed in the mornings, and my tongue is still wagging—although I believe my reputation for outspokenness is partly due to my having come after Mrs. Nixon, who was very quiet and never thrust herself forward.

I tried to be honest; I tried not to dodge subjects. I felt the public had a right to know where I stood. Nobody had to feel the way I felt, I wasn't forcing my opinions on anybody, but if someone asked me a question, I gave that person a straight answer.

I've been told that I didn't play it safe enough, but my husband has always been totally supportive. He's never stepped on my toes; he's never turned around and complained, "Well, *that* was a dumb thing to say."

Even after he decided he liked being President and was going to try to hold on to the job (I had released him from his promise to quit politics), he made no effort to muzzle me.

Which brings me to the *60 Minutes* show on CBS, the one that made so many headlines. Morley Safer caught me off balance. Out of the blue, he asked me what I would do if my daughter came home and told me she was having an affair with a man. The cameras were on, and I couldn't just stand up and leave. "Well, I wouldn't be surprised," I said. "I think she's a perfectly normal human being, like all young girls. If she wanted to continue it, I would certainly counsel and advise her on the subject. And I'd want to know pretty much about the young man." I added that Susan was young to be having an affair. Safer said she was eighteen—a fact I was aware of. What I'd been trying to say was that while I couldn't condone an affair I wouldn't kick my daughter out of the house for having one.

Lord knows, there are parents who disagree. I remember Bing Crosby declaring that he *would* kick his daughter out. "It would be aloha on the steel guitar," he said.

(Drunk with the controversy, reporters polled all manner of public figures. One of the people they bearded was Jimmy Carter, not so well known in 1975 except as the ex-Governor of Georgia. Asked how he would feel if his daughter told him she was having an affair, Carter said he'd be "shocked and overwhelmed," and added, "My daughter is seven years old.")

Safer and I talked about many subjects on that show, not only premarital sex (I said it might lower the divorce rate) but also abortion (I was on the side of the Supreme Court's decision to legalize it) and drugs (I said I didn't think my children were very interested in drugs).

My stock with the public did not go up. It went down, rapidly. Letters, wires, phone calls to the White House, two-thirds of them against me. How could a woman like me be the wife of the

President of the United States? Even Susan admits now that she wasn't sure she liked what I'd said. "It put me in a tight spot as far as dating guys. They thought, 'She's easy, her mother'll let her have affairs.' "

Anyway, Susan told reporters she had no affair to confess, Mike told reporters he didn't agree with all of his mother's views, Jack told reporters he'd smoked marijuana but had never used hard drugs, and Steve told reporters nothing. He just dropped out of Utah State and headed for California to try to get a part-time job raising horses.

The thing about the dope question was that I'd been burnt by it earlier, long before *60 Minutes.* I'd been down South visiting a Catholic hospital, and when I came out of the place, some news people were waiting, and they asked me whether any of my children had smoked marijuana. I said I didn't know, but that since it was a thing kids did, I supposed they'd probably tried it. That time, my children were furious with me and announced they'd never gone near the stuff.

I'm not sure what I believe about marijuana. At this point, I think some of my children would vote for legalization. As for me, I just don't know. If you legalize it, aren't you going to make it that much easier for dealers to sell dope to youngsters who want to feel grown up? And when marijuana doesn't thrill them any more, won't they go on to more powerful drugs like heroin?

I think it's a sin to start a child on marijuana. But I think it's a sin to start a child on alcohol. They're having a big problem in the schools now with liquor, and you don't hear about so many drug overdoses and suicides. The pendulum swings from one extreme to another, just the way it swings in government from right to left and back again.

The furor after *60 Minutes* terrified me. I was afraid I might have become a real political liability to Jerry. I don't want to compare it to the Nixon tapes, but it was practically as crucial to me at that point in my life. Ron Nessen, Jerry's press secretary, gave out a statement saying the President had "long ceased to be perturbed by his wife's remarks," and that caused another round of fire. A

New Hampshire publisher wrote an editorial saying the immorality of my comments was "almost exceeded by their utter stupidity. Involving any prominent individual, this would be a disgusting spectacle. Coming from the First Lady in the White House, it disgraces the nation itself." He attacked Jerry with the same fury. "President Ford showed his own lack of guts by saying he had long ago given up commenting on Mrs. Ford's radio [sic] interviews. What kind of business is that?"

Jerry remained his usual dear funny self. He told the press that when he first heard what I'd said he thought he'd lost ten million votes. "Then when I read about it, I raised that to twenty million."

All of a sudden, the mail turned around. The people who wrote first were the people who disagreed with me. People on my side didn't bother to write until it looked as though I needed their support. After a while, my popularity in the opinion polls was said to have climbed up to around seventy-five percent. Jerry, who was still paying for the pardon (and the economy and the Vietnam War), used to joke about his wife's rise to public favor. In the middle of a speech, he'd say, "If I could just get my rating up to hers—"

When we'd come to the White House, the first question reporters asked me was "What is your program going to be?"

I hadn't had time to think about my program. I came from dance, and was interested in opera, writing, photography, so I knew I wanted to help support creative arts, but I also wanted to work with children, retarded children, crippled children, handicapped children.

I think, because of the power of the White House, I was able to do more for the Washington Hospital for Sick Children than a private citizen could have done. Everybody knew about Children's Hospital, which was highly publicized, but few people knew—or cared—about the Hospital for Sick Children. Most of its patients were retarded, and some had been abused. I remember a baby in a crib who'd been savagely burnt. The mother had been out working, the father couldn't stand the baby's crying, so he'd pressed his lighted cigarette in her ears.

I started going to that hospital, and I got other people interested. Our friend Milton Hoffman, a New York City businessman, donated two brand-new rooms, one in memory of his wife, the other in my honor. So many of the children there had been abandoned. Relatives never came to see them because retardation seemed such a stigma to the families. Out of sight, out of mind. I used to sit there holding children on my lap, talking to them, and sometimes, after they got to know me, they would try to talk back. Their little faces would twist with the effort of getting the words out—"muh-muh-muh-Mrs. Fyooooord—" but when they managed it, they were so pleased. Tiny children, a few white, mostly black, some dragging around heavy braces, some wearing helmets to protect their heads if they fell down, some completely out of it, six-year-old vegetables.

You ask yourself, Why? What's the design? I've never been able to come up with a good answer, except maybe that it's to make those of us who have healthy children appreciate our blessings, and give of ourselves to those less fortunate.

Throughout the time that Jerry and I were in the White House, I worked for an organization called No Greater Love, which is active in helping children of soldiers lost or missing in action; I was also involved with the Heart Association, and Goodwill Industries (which employs handicapped workers), and the cancer and arthritis foundations. I posed for pictures with the Easter Seal child and the Multiple Sclerosis child, hoping some good, however small, might result from the publicity.

It was safe to be on the side of sick children, but coming out for abortion was another matter. Even though the Supreme Court had said a woman's body was her own business, the pendulum swung back fast. The Carter administration has supported efforts to cut off Medicaid funds for abortions, and that upsets me. What happens to a poor woman who's on welfare, or a married woman who already has four or five children and who just can't afford to take care of any more? Now she can't have the abortion because no federal funds will be available to her, and there's no place she can go to find a friend.

I read a statement by a member of the National Organization for Women who said that in her state, Connecticut, where almost all federal funding for abortions had been cut off, more than a third of the females who came looking for assistance were teenagers. "They are children having children," she said, "and we can't allow them to have back-alley abortions."

It's the same old story: the helpless are the ones who will suffer, poor people and twelve-year-old girls who aren't old enough to assume responsibility for bringing babies into the world.

My own daughter is just twenty-one, but I honestly don't think she's anywhere near ready to get married and have a baby. If she came to me pregnant, I would want to take her to a good psychiatrist and see what he thought about how she could handle an abortion. Emotionally, I mean. Susan loves babies; I don't think she could have a child and give it up for adoption. But girls like Susan aren't the point. She would have access to help, whether psychiatric or surgical. It's the teenagers, and the older women without resources, and the unwanted babies, whom I worry about.

(Right to Life people used to come around the White House carrying signs with pictures of fetuses on them. I didn't know what to do, so if I passed them, I'd just smile and wave. I must say, they never screamed at me, and sometimes when I'd run into a whole crowd of anti-abortion pickets, they'd hoist their placards over their shoulders, rest them, pick up their cameras and take my picture, or ask me for autographs.)

Jerry never got into any abortion arguments. He left that to me. Very wise.

While he was President, my old friend Mary Adelaide Jones, now Mrs. Ralph Mendelsohn, came to me to ask for help in trying to stop the abuse of the elderly in nursing homes. It's as bad as child abuse, and almost as prevalent. At least there's some sort of legislation against child abuse, but until the past few years nobody's paid much attention to the old people left to wither in nursing homes. Mary Adelaide got involved because her mother had been in a nursing home where the family had paid fabulous fees to keep her, and one day Mary Adelaide came into the place and found her perfectly alert mother sitting in her wheelchair with a welt on her forehead. She had been hit by an aide, and had no idea why.

That proud, beautiful woman who had once protected her polished hardwood floors against our muddy feet couldn't protect herself from the indignities visited on her by her own worn-out body, and the casual cruelties of strangers.

Because I was in the White House, I was better able to lend Mary Adelaide a hand; we saw to it that some light—and some heat—were directed into a few shameful dark corners.

Since for the most part I did what came naturally, I was somewhat astonished to find I'd become one of the most popular women in the world.

I loved it. I'd be dishonest if I said it didn't please me. I hadn't expected it, but so long as it was forthcoming, I enjoyed it. Though it bothered me that while I was getting so much praise Jerry was getting criticism. He was a good sport. He was proud of me and even in cases where he didn't agree with my views, he was all for my spouting them.

Some of the causes I worked for made me sad—you can't spend time with the maimed and the blind and not feel somewhat guilty—and some of them made me happy. I had taken it upon myself to see to it that Martha Graham was awarded a Presidential Medal of Freedom, which is the highest award a President can give to a civilian. Jerry hadn't handed out very many (one, I remember, had gone to Artur Rubinstein), so he and I talked about it and talked about it and talked about it.

"Let's give a few of them at a big party," he said, "rather than just do an individual dinner for Martha Graham."

I said no, and stuck to my guns. "Dance should be recognized as an art, and Martha is the first lady of modern dance, still choreographing new works in her eighties. She's done so much for America and the whole world of dance, and the Medal of Freedom should go to her."

I kept after him until Martha got her dinner and her medal. You know, if you bring up a subject long enough with a man, why finally he gets so tired of it he agrees to anything. There might be a woman on the Supreme Court now if I'd just brought it up more often.

29

SUZE

When Morley Safer asked me about the possibility of Susan's having a love affair, I felt fairly sure it was nothing I had to worry about. For one thing, she was living with us in the White House, so it would have been pretty hard for her to carry on an affair without my getting a hint of it. The other thing was, she and I were close enough so that I knew if she'd come to care deeply about anyone she'd have told me.

Which, to my chagrin, is exactly what happened.

Right before Thanksgiving of 1975, Susan came to me and said she wanted to move to Vail. "Brian and I would like to get married," she began, "but before we do that, I'd like to go and live in Vail and find out if it's really what I want."

Oh boy, I thought, this is a dandy one. What am I going to do now?

I knew Brian, I didn't dislike him, but my daughter was eighteen years old, a little young to be making the decision that she wanted to marry a member of the ski patrol and settle down in Vail for the rest of her days.

(If I was more concerned about Susan than I had been about

The Empress of Japan and Mrs. Ford
arrive for the State Dinner

After the State Dinner for Queen Elizabeth II, the
guests enjoy entertainment by Bob Hope (from right,
President Ford, Queen Elizabeth, Mrs. Ford,
Prince Philip)

President and Mrs. Scheel of West Germany share laughter
with President and Mrs. Ford

Mrs. Ford and General Franco,
during the state visit to Spain
in May 1975

Mrs. Ford joins Chinese ballet dancers during the
visit to China in December 1975

Greeting a Chinese child
during the visit

En route to the Philippines on Air Force One,
Mrs. Ford dons King Neptune's crown for her
first trip across the equator

Martha Graham and Betty Ford, on the stage of the
Uris Theatre, New York, June 19, 1975

A light moment with
Bob Hope in the
East Room of
the White House

Mrs. Ford greets
Pearl Williams,
106 years old,
at Pepperdine
University

Visiting a model Day Care
Center during the International
Women's Year Congress in
Cleveland, October 1975

Vice President and Mrs. Rockefeller greet the
Fords at the White House after the second
attempt on President Ford's life, on
September 22, 1975

Mrs. Ford arrives at the LBJ Library in
Houston in April 1976 and is welcomed
by Lady Bird Johnson

Greeting crowds during the Holland (Michigan) Tulip Festival Parade, May 1976

Betty Ford campaigning in the West, September 1976

The Ford family at the Republican National Convention in Kansas City, August 1976

Gerald and Betty Ford at the Convention, after the President's nomination on August 19

Early on election night,
the President and Mrs. Ford
watch election returns
on television

Later the same evening,
Gayle and Susan Ford
join in the vigil

Betty Ford reads the President's
concession statement in the
White House Press room as he
and the family listen.
The President lost his voice
after the heavy final week
of campaigning

The President and Mrs. Ford return to the White House after
their first visit to the office on Jefferson Place that
he will use after leaving office

the boys when it came to dates and drinking, it was because she was our only girl. I harangued her about being careful, even when the only thing that was going down was beer. "Because when you drink, you lose control, and what may seem like a romantic moment that night turns out to be a terrible afterthought the next morning." She knew the speech by heart.)

Because of David Kennerly's being constantly on the scene, Susan had got interested in photography. She enrolled in a workshop given by Ansel Adams, and the great man said she had an eye. I believed it when she came back with her pictures. There was one of sunlight coming through some trees and hitting certain leaves, making them white, and another of a stream. Susan had got out in the middle of the stream, just to watch the water move, and to try to catch on film its rushing currents.

In June of 1975, she was graduated from Holton Arms and had her prom at the White House. She didn't find it much fun. "We couldn't serve beer because we'd have had to get a slip from each student's parents saying they approved, which would have been a pain in the neck," she recalls. "Our headmaster was a pain in the neck too."

I may have mentioned before that my daughter speaks her mind. She took to heart the advice offered by Alice Roosevelt Longworth, who'd lived in the White House when her father, Teddy Roosevelt, was President. "Have a helluva good time," Mrs. Longworth wrote to Susan.

Having a good time involved Susan's realizing that she couldn't make everybody in the United States happy, and she might as well stop worrying about it. "I got used to criticism when Daddy was in office," she says. "I was criticized for everything from wearing blue jeans to dating Brian, who was nine years older than I, to being given a muskrat coat [as a high school graduation present] because muskrats are trapped, not bred. The family even got criticized for Liberty's having puppies. You know, 'Why bring more dogs into the world when you think of all the dogs that are being put away at the ASPCAs?' You can't do 100 percent right, and you just accept it."

Susan had met Brian McCartney in Vail when we'd been out

there skiing, and the romance had flourished through telephone calls—the separation made the whole thing more intense—and occasional reunions. Brian and his buddies, Arvin and Bruce, came to Washington for Susan's eighteenth birthday, and because the boys were sharing the third floor of the White House with my daughter, I laid down the law.

"I want no trespassing," I said. "By which I mean you don't go into one another's rooms. If you want to spend time together, you can spend it in the solarium. And if there *is* any trespassing, and I hear about it, you boys are going to be thrown out on your ears."

I wasn't being funny, I meant every word I said. I didn't want one single bit of monkey business, and I'm sure there wasn't any. I had no reports to the contrary.

The birthday party was everything the prom hadn't been. "My eighteenth birthday party was the best party in the world," Susan says flatly.

This is her memory of the events:

"The night before the party, the fourth of July, we watched fireworks from the balcony of the White House, and stayed up late cavorting in the solarium, so the next day started very slowly.

"We held the party on the fifth (even though my birthday is on the sixth) because the fifth was a Saturday. We didn't really get going until about three in the afternoon. There was a dance floor laid out on the south lawn under a clump of trees, and picnic tables all around, and we had hamburgers and hotdogs on a grill, and beer in plastic cups. Heinz Bender had made me a birthday cake in the shape of a camera—a tribute to my hoped-for career—and a rock band, friends of mine from Vail, played a song with lyrics dedicated to me.

"Brian was wearing kind of rumpled yellow pants and a blue shirt, and I had on a long green dress with an apron. I called it my nursing mother's dress. I was a lot heavier then.

"That night, we went down to Winston's, which is a bar in Georgetown, where I had a pie thrown in my face. It's a Winston's tradition on your birthday to have a pie thrown in your face.

"I stayed out all night. When you're having that good a time, and you're with friends, who cares about going home to bed? But I drank myself into the gutter, which was horrible, because next day I died. I thought I might fall asleep and never wake up."

(That toot lasted Susan for two years; she never again stayed out so late until her twentieth birthday came around. We were in Vail for the twentieth birthday, and I was awake until 4:30 A.M., waiting for her to come home. She'd gone from a discothèque to breakfast with about twenty pals, and when she finally showed up safe and sound, I felt not only relieved but foolish. Because I knew that when *I* was twenty years old I was staying out until four o'clock in the morning, then catching a few hours' sleep and getting up at eight to go to work, and thinking nothing of it. But mothers will be mothers.)

The summer of her eighteenth year, Susan went to Topeka, Kansas, to work for six weeks as a photographer on a newspaper, the *Capitol Journal,* so even though she thought she was very much in love with Brian, it didn't occur to me to be anxious about it. Before Brian, she'd been in love with a boy named Gardiner, and that had passed. Besides, she was busy and she seemed happy.

In the fall, she entered Mount Vernon, a girls' college in Washington, for her freshman year. Again, she appeared to be enjoying herself. (After Jimmy Carter was elected, and Jerry and I left Washington, she transferred to Kansas University. "I had more fun at Mount Vernon than I did at Kansas," she says. "Sure," I say. "That was because you and your girlfriends spent all your time at Winston's." My daughter is unrepentant. "Mount Vernon, the college of no knowledge," she crows. "I had a blast.")

Susan was wary of dating Washington boys because of the press. There were rumors about her and David Kennerly, but they had no basis in fact. "I adore him because he gave me my career," she says, and David says when he considers everything that was written "with nothing going on, I can only imagine what it would have been like if anything *had* gone on."

Irritated by what she called the Washington passion for pairing people off, Susan tried to show up with a different boy for every state dinner she attended ("except when I was dating Gardiner") and avoided escorts who lived in Georgetown. When I was ready for bed at night, robe on, face off, I'd go up to the third floor to check on whether or not my chick had got in. If I found nobody home, I'd leave a note: "12:30. I was here, where were you? See you in the morning. Love, Mom." She always got a kick out of it, and I didn't want her thinking I was too busy to care.

And then, that Thanksgiving, I got the word. My daughter wanted to move to Vail.

I walked softly. If Susan thought she was in love with Brian, the last thing in the world for Jerry and me to do was say we didn't approve. I really didn't think Brian was as serious as Susan was, yet he'd asked her to quit school, move to Vail, get a job out there as a photographer.

An idea came to me. "Why don't we have an engagement party? We'll be in Vail at Christmas, and we'll have this great big gorgeous party, and Brian can give you a lovely ring. If he can't afford a diamond, he can get you one of those nice handmade silver ones."

"I don't know," Susan said doubtfully, "whether he really wants to do that sort of thing."

"Talk to him about it," I said. "After all, I can't just let you stay out there in Vail and be gossiped about. I have too much respect for you. On the other hand, if you're engaged, it makes more sense. You could take a quarter off from school, and really get to know each other."

You can't argue with an eighteen-year-old. They're of age, and you have nothing much to say about what they do. The only thing I could try was letting her see with her own eyes what it would be like to live in Vail under the suggested conditions. Luckily, she had a girlfriend who also wanted to take a quarter off from Mount Vernon, so when we went to Vail at Christmas, we found an apartment for the two girls. Much against Jerry's wishes, let me say.

Susan had of course been talking to Brian on the phone, telling him her parents' terms, and she must have scared the life out of him. She can laugh about it now. "On Christmas Eve, he sat me down and told me he'd been dating another girl. Lovely, I thought.

My folks have rented me a place, I have a friend coming out to live with me, and he's trying to upset me so much I'll go home. Not Susan. My parents had found out that trying to tell me no was like beating their heads against a wall, and Brian discovered the same thing. Susan has to learn everything for herself. Susan sticks it out. I wanted him so badly and I was so determined to have him that I fought a losing battle until the end of the following February. He'd backed out totally by that time. I sat home a lot of nights while he was out with other girls. I was tagged as Brian's baby, so nobody else asked me anywhere. Brian had me wrapped."

Susan was hurt (she phoned me and said she'd had it—"I've enjoyed the skiing, but, Mother, I don't want to live in Vail"), yet we all have to go through those first love affairs. You look back at the guy later and wonder. What in the world did I find attractive about *him?*

Brian and Susan still see one another. She says that's what's nice about people in Vail. "Once you end a relationship, it's not 'I hate you and I'll never see you again.' Brian's in love with somebody else, and probably going to marry her. But next summer a bunch of us may all go camping; he'll be with his dolly, and I'll be with somebody else. We had a good time together, and that's all that matters."

Susan worries about letting me and Jerry down. She knew we weren't happy over the Vail interlude and when, two years later in the spring of 1977, she quit Kansas U., she wouldn't even tell her father. She phoned me and asked me to pass along the news. I said okay. "I'll tell him, but he'll call you anyway."

He couldn't reach her at home that night, so he woke her at eight-thirty the following morning. The way she remembers it, he said, "I'm really disappointed in you," and she said, "Daddy, tell me anything but that. Tell me you're mad at me, tell me you've thrown me out of your house, but don't tell me I've disappointed you. That really hurts."

(It isn't quite fair to say Susan quit: she was asked to withdraw from K.U. because she'd got a D in Public Relations. That baffled me. "I'd think you'd be good at Public Relations," I said. "Yeah," she said, "I thought it was going to be a cinch too, but it turned out to be rather difficult."

Her other marks were all right, but the dean said he'd just turned down a boy who had a D on his record, and who wanted to come back to school, so it wouldn't be fair to keep Susan. She was delighted. She'd wanted to leave anyway, but Jerry and I had given her the "You just don't start something and then—" lecture.)

Sometimes Susan is asked if she feels insecure because she got her start as a photographer through family connections. She is very level-headed about that. "I think maybe for a year or so people would hire me because of who I am, but when that year was over, they'd have to say, 'She's a hardworking girl, she did a good job,' or else they wouldn't keep me around. I'm a little bit scared, but I work very hard, and I think I'll prove myself."

Of late, she's been so busy proving herself that she hasn't seemed particularly interested in dating. When one of the men she goes out with begins to press, she backs off and comes running to Mother. "What am I going to do? He says he loves me." Once in a while, her father hears her complaining that men are a pain in the neck (still her favorite phrase for the opposite sex) and he says, "Ah, we're not so bad. I supported you for twenty years." To which she answers, "*Young* men. I'm talking about *young* men."

If you catch her in a dark room these days, it isn't romance that's developing, it's eight-by-ten glossies.

While she was at K.U., one of the national women's magazines printed a "White House Scrapbook" full of family photographs taken by Susan. There was a picture of Susan herself, shot by somebody else, made up so she looked as if she was about thirty-five years old and had been through the mill, and one of the then President of the United States in his bare feet and pajamas (he wasn't so sure about the propriety of that), and one of me all curled up asleep in my bathrobe and looking just terrible. When I saw it, I said to Jerry, "I'm going to call Susan and ask if I can sue her."

Our Apple Blossom Queen, our Queen of the Azalea Festival, our daughter who loves dogs and horses and babies. In addition to being a daughter, Susan has been a friend. She's not only close to

Jerry and me, but she likes the closeness; when we're separated, she misses us as much as we miss her. Like Clara, she's sentimental; she saves all the cards and letters we've ever sent her, and she's convinced I'm a delicate flower. Going through crowds, I often feel her hands on my waist, trying to make certain nobody knocks me over or pushes into me.

I tend to be equally overprotective where she's concerned. One night a group of us were out to dinner, and I saw a couple kissing on the dance floor. I thought it was our friend John Purcell with Susan, so I had my partner fox-trot me over to this couple, and I gave the man a good shot in the back. "Listen, Purcell," I said, "keep your hands off my daughter."

The man turned around, and he wasn't Purcell at all. The girl he was dancing with wasn't Susan either. "Hey, lady," he said, very aggrieved, "I've been trying to get a kiss from this girl for six months."

He didn't recognize me, or if he did he didn't care. I was still saying, "I'm sorry, oh, I'm so sorry, I thought you were someone else," as I backed out of the restaurant.

30

LET ME ENTERTAIN YOU

I know I said this book wasn't going to be about how to set the tables at a state dinner. But since the responsibility for the comfort of state visitors—kings and queens and shahs and shabanous—falls on the shoulders of the First Lady and her staff, I think it might be in order to do one chapter about a First Lady's gang, and what they do. Or: Entertaining at the White House and How It Works.

First, the staff. A President's wife has twenty-eight people, give or take a couple, working for her. The press secretary, the social secretary, the corresponding secretary, the scheduling secretary, all have secretaries of their own. The calligraphy department is large, and so is the mail department because the mail which comes in—to *any* President's wife—is heavy.

I had helped out in the East Wing on other First Ladies' projects, so I knew something of how it all operated, but it's different when you're the one in charge. I'd inherited Mrs. Nixon's people, and I liked Lucy Winchester, Pat's social secretary, very much. I replaced her anyway. Every time a state dinner came up, Lucy and her aides would say, "This is the way we do it," and I thought, Maybe that's the way you do it, but frankly I want to do it another way. Lucy couldn't go along with my ideas, and we parted company. No hard feelings. She got a good appointment as Assistant Chief of Protocol.

Same thing with Helen Smith, Mrs. Nixon's press secretary. I'd gone to Chicago to make my first big speech at a fundraiser for Republican women, and I was nervous. Helen had promised me I wouldn't have to deal with reporters until the whole thing was over, but on the plane to Chicago she let all these journalists cluster around me and I had to talk to them or seem surly. I wished Helen well—she got a better job too—and went out and hired my own press secretary, a woman named Sheila Weidenfeld.

I'm talking now about people with the kinds of jobs which are subject to change with the coming of a new administration. (There is also a large permanent staff. White House maids, for instance, have permanent jobs, and are very good. While I'd have brought Clara with us if she'd been available, I certainly didn't need more or better household help than was provided.)

Every time there's a new President, there's turnover. Some Ford people would have liked to stay on and work for the Carters, but the Carters didn't want them, so they had to go.

Even the social aides at the White House aren't carried over; each administration hires its own. Social aides are handsome, good dancers, and they've been trained in the proper way to escort a lady or make a gentleman guest comfortable, but no matter how well trained people are, you've got to keep checking if you want things to go right. Maria Downs, my last social secretary, had an eagle eye when it came to spotting a wallflower and dispatching an aide (we had aides of both sexes) to ask a man or a woman to dance.

I held regular meetings with my staff every Monday, and when these first began, I told the Chief Usher, Rex Scouten, that I was going to depend on him for guidance. "When they get to talking about certain things, I'm going to try and catch your eye, and I'll expect you to tell me whether the plan under discussion is the right plan or the wrong plan to go ahead with." Mike Ferrell, who was in charge of all White House tours, would be there too, and all the secretaries would report what their calendars looked like for the coming week, and we'd decide how everything would be managed.

Because she gets involved in more than state dinners, a President's wife, who has to serve as a symbol for *all* citizens, sometimes finds herself talking out of both sides of her mouth. One day, I'd be greeting women stockbrokers in the Map Room, congratulating them for having got out of their kitchens and into the stock market. The next day, in the same room, I'd be greeting a Homemakers Seminar, and congratulating housewives for having stayed *in* their kitchens; it had its funny aspects.

Sometimes the simplest program could give you a headache. The White House Garden Tours took place on spring and fall weekends, which meant people streaming through the house and gardens most of the day Saturday and Sunday while military bands played. You could practically go out of your mind, hearing this martial music while you were trying to work. I remember one garden tour day when I was newly home from the hospital, after the mastectomy. I kept going out on the balcony and waving to the crowds. I'd never seen so many cameras in all my life. When you're living in the White House, you wish you had stock in the film business.

That whole period, the two and a half years Jerry was President, was so full, and made such a complete change in our lives, that it's almost hard for me to remember specific events. Things came too rapidly, one on top of another, but somehow we managed.

Though we certainly didn't please all of the people all of the time. We thought it was great, for instance, to ask Ann-Margret to the party for the Shah of Iran because we'd heard he had a propensity for pretty girls. Well, Betty Beale came out with a column in the Washington *Star* that ripped us up and down for having made that choice.

And Julia Child criticized us for not feeding the Queen of England French food. I didn't want to give her French food, or English food either; I thought we should give her American food. I wouldn't want to go to another country and have them feed me southern fried chicken. That same evening, the Captain and Tennille sang something called "The Muskrat Love Song," which many critics deemed unsuitable entertainment for Queen Elizabeth, although she seemed to enjoy it thoroughly.

Even the workmen who set up our portable stages used to put in their two cents' worth. One carpenter, enjoying the Grand Ole Opry–Tennessee Ernie rehearsal (for a West German dinner), announced to a reporter, "We don't usually get this good a show." That carpenter hadn't cared for Ann-Margret any more than Betty Beale had, and he was no opera fan either. "Beverly Sills?" he said. "Forget it."

(The government pays for entertaining foreign dignitaries, but the President pays his family's expenses, and one of the things that interested me was the way the White House staff kept such precise accounts of food, every pound of chicken and lamb and beef itemized on sheets and sheets of paper. Once a month, we'd write a check for the total amount we owed. There were records of who ate what, three times a day. "Breakfast was served to the President at such and such a time, to Jack at such and such a time." If we went to Camp David on a weekend, the kitchen listed the names of every guest and the number of meals he packed away.)

Inviting a Beverly Sills or a Van Cliburn to a party for a foreign visitor can make a huge difference to the success of the evening. Sure, you can always make up a guest list, but the guest list has got to be good. I tried to have people from sports, from the theatre, from industry, from the labor unions. I wanted a cross-section. I wanted to be able to say, "This is one of our best tennis players, one of our greatest doctors." I asked Eddie Arcaro and Warren Beatty and Saul Bellow.

With prime ministers and heads of state you invite people you know they like in Washington. You take suggestions from anyone you trust, and sometimes you have to get a bit tough. The State Department used to send over proposed guest lists, and they were so dreary we hardly ever used them, because State tried to hold back all the glittering people for themselves, for Henry Kissinger's famous luncheons.

Henry's a smart man, and a funny man. I don't think anybody

can get the better of him in a battle of wits. A while ago, a newsman told him a poll showed that seventy-five percent of the American people still thought he was Secretary of State, and Henry said, "What's so odd about that? My father and I still think so too." But I wasn't going to take his people's leftover guest lists, and I have the feeling he'd understand that very well.

I wanted to get along, but I could be firm when it was essential. We were having all sorts of problems with the State Department over Queen Elizabeth's visit. Everybody seemed to think this would be the social event of the century, and they all wanted to stir the broth. So many people were running around making commitments for the Queen and Prince Philip that one day I just phoned Brent Scowcroft, head of the National Security Council, and told him the hysteria had to stop. "General," I said, "I want this visit to be completely handled by my staff, so would you please name someone from your staff for us to have as liaison with the State Department?"

A lot of people were unhappy with me about that, but I didn't care.

We put up a tent for the Queen's dinner. There were so many state events coming up one right after the other that without the tent we'd probably have had to close the White House to the public for a good portion of the summer, and it was the Bicentennial year and the influx of tourists was heavy. A tent over the Rose Garden would be the answer, just a great white tent which would also enable us to invite more guests than we could have served indoors. (For indoor dining, the White House can handle 150 people at one time, and that's pushing it.)

An hour and a half before the Queen's dinner, there was a sudden downpour with torrential rain, thunder, lightning. Three trees on the White House grounds were struck. Fortunately, I'd insisted that our tent have a floor. (I'd been thinking of an outdoor party the Nixons had given for some newly released prisoners of war and their wives. It had been raining for three days, and the chairs just gradually sank into the ground. And all those poor wives, who'd gone out and bought beautiful new shoes, ruined them in the mud.) "We'll have a floor and a carpet," I'd said. "It will be just like a room."

I'd seen it done at the French Embassy and been very impressed, a room added right onto the building beyond some French doors. It was heated and had red velvet walls and crystal chandeliers hanging from tent poles and paintings against the velvet, and you couldn't believe you were outside.

I went to Rex Scouten, because he knew what could be done, and what funds were available to do it with, and which people we could ask for more money. Americans were generous during the Bicentennial year, and so were numbers of foreign visitors, who wanted to pay their respects to the country on its two-hundredth birthday. Lots of them made donations to the Kennedy Center and to the White House.

For the Queen's dinner, we had violinists stationed along the paths, and to be out in the gorgeous night air, with the moon shining down and the violins playing as you walked by, was unforgettable.

The Queen was easy to deal with. She was very definite about what she wanted and what she didn't want. She loves Bob Hope and Telly Savalas, so we invited Bob Hope and Telly Savalas—both came—and if I hadn't kept mixing up Your Highness and Your Majesty (he's His Highness, she's Her Majesty) I'd give myself four stars for the way that visit went off.

Although, on the night of the dinner, I had a nervous moment or two, one of them because of my son Jack. He'd had to rent tails, but the rental place hadn't sent studs for his shirt front (knowing Jack, I'll bet they *had* sent studs, and he just couldn't find them) and he'd come down from the third floor to our bedroom and was rummaging through Jerry's top drawer.

It was just a few minutes before the Queen and Prince Philip were due to arrive, and I was exasperated. "You're *never* going to be ready," I said, and left to go down and greet the Queen and the Prince.

Jerry and I were bringing the royal couple upstairs in the

elevator when it stopped on the second floor, the doors opened, and Jack came flying in, still fiddling with his shirt front. Why he hadn't sprinted up the back stairs, I don't know. He stood there, mouth open, gaping at the four of us, and the Queen of England turned to me and smiled sweetly. "I have one just like it at home," she said.

During the time that we were in the White House, I tried to feature American art at state dinners. Our centerpieces were the talk of the town. Once I borrowed a complete Steuben Glass crystal collection; another time I borrowed an exquisite collection of American-made silver from a museum in New York; and another time a collection of priceless antique Indian baskets. There was a theme for each party, a theme compatible with the tastes of the guest of honor. Prime Minister Sadat of Egypt, for instance, is a Western buff, he loves everything about the American West, and we found a museum in Texas—the Eamon Carter Museum—which loaned us an entire collection of Remington and Russell bronzes. We set the dining tables with the Russells, which were smaller, as centerpieces, and we put the Remingtons around on pedestals and mantels. (I'd decided on this theme business because for years Jerry and I had gone to White House dinners, and always I'd see the same white tablecloths and the same floral pieces.)

Often people who dine at the White House are grouped with strangers, and they sit down and dart surreptitious glances over their shoulders—who's sitting on my right? who's sitting on my left?—and there's a kind of stiffness. With these centerpieces, you could immediately start a conversation. "What in the world do you suppose that is?" "Isn't it beautiful?" or "What an ugly thing!" It didn't matter what was said; the aim was simply to put people at their ease.

I preferred round tables which could seat eight to the more formal E-shaped table; I think round tables lend themselves to friendlier evenings, and they also permitted me to seat more women at the President's table, which, if you followed strict protocol, you could never do. (I don't mean women whose husbands were Senator This or That, but women who needed a leg up.)

In line with the western motif for the Sadat dinner, we'd asked Johnny Cash to entertain, but he got sick, and at the last minute I phoned Pearl Bailey, who was playing *Dolly* in Boston. She closed her show for the night and flew down to help us out. My luck was really holding. Unbeknownst to me, Pearl was already the holder of a high award from the Egyptian government, and President Sadat was very fond of her.

That was a wild evening. I remember Pearl's borrowing Vice President Rockefeller's glasses so she could read the words to "Lara's Theme" from the movie of *Dr. Zhivago;* she wanted to serenade Omar Sharif, who was a guest. Pearl couldn't drag Sharif onto the dance floor, but she managed to pull President Sadat out, and the Egyptian Ambassador was amazed. He said the President had never danced before.

(The Muslims' strictures against dancing and drinking alcoholic beverages can be confusing to a Westerner. One night I was seated between a head of state and his prime minister, and one didn't drink any wine but the other did. After dinner, the drinker didn't dance, but the nondrinker did, so apparently there is some degree of choice.)

Pearl, who's my very good friend—we call each other Sister—ended the Sadat evening by running after President Sadat's limousine, trying to give him a pipe which somebody had told her was the President's (it turned out to belong to Jerry), and asking Nelson Rockefeller if she could go along when he took a trip to China. Nelson said he wasn't planning any trip to China. "I only go to ribbon cuttings and funerals," he said.

Sometimes, when a party was small and didn't require the State Dining Room, we'd have dinner in the Red Room, with dancing in the Blue Room afterward. I liked the Red Room best when it was done up with red flowers, pink linens, and candles giving a soft glow. No contrast, all reds.

Because it would take a whole separate book to cover two and a half years of welcoming guests to the White House, I'm not even going to attempt to deal comprehensively with the subject. What follows is just a handful of my recollections about some of the people who came to visit and, in some instances, the reasons for their coming.

Art Buchwald. He'd written a book called *I Never Danced at the White House,* and his publisher had posters made up showing Buchwald in top hat and tails and cane. As soon as Jerry became President, I invited Art to dinner. He said he had a speaking engagement. This happened so many times he became embarrassed that I might not believe him. It got to the point where he'd send me a copy of his contract to prove he honest and truly had to give a lecture. He finally came to a dinner, asked me to dance, and later sent me one of his posters—framed—with the word *Never* crossed off.

Queen Margrethe of Denmark. She has to be one of the tallest women in the world, and I remember her arriving for a luncheon dressed in a big hat with flowers all around, accompanied by Henry Kissinger, who's short. It looked as though the flowers on the Queen's hat would engulf and devour Henry.

Peter Graves. Peter (of *Mission Impossible*) and his wife had flown in from California to attend a dinner, and they phoned us from Dulles Airport. The airline had lost their luggage. "We're going to turn around and go back," Peter said. I said that was nonsense; he could rent formal gear, and Mrs. Graves could wear something of mine. "Have her come over here. I'll pull out six or eight dresses, and she can choose one." That's what happened. I laid out the dresses in the Queen's Room, Mrs. Graves arrived, picked a dress, wore it, and Jerry, while dancing with her, complimented her on her lovely gown. He had no idea it belonged to me.

Tony Orlando. He and his wife were invited to one of the summer dinners in the tent. He wasn't entertaining that night, George Shearing was, but afterward I asked Tony if he'd like to sing. He was uncertain. "Oh, gee, I don't have any music with me."

He and Maria Downs went over to the bandstand and talked to the conductor of the Marine Band, and then Tony put on the most marvelous off-the-cuff exhibition you can imagine. He pulled me and Susan into the act, and eventually Jerry and Jack were onstage too, our arms locked, singing our heads off. And believe me, I can't sing.

Fred Astaire. He came to a dinner at which we had a lot of big-time show people. Fred Astaire was very elegant, very proper. I begged him to dance, but he said he wasn't a ballroom dancer, that he had to have a routine. I wouldn't let up. I'd dreamed all my life of spinning around the room with Fred Astaire while everybody stood back watching us. Just as he gave in, my husband walked out and tapped me on the shoulder. "I'm sorry to interrupt, dear, but our guests of honor are leaving." I excused myself, gave the departing guests short shrift, and rushed back, hoping to find Fred Astaire waiting. No soap. He was wheeling around the floor with a nice little old white-haired lady of the press, mind you, and I never got near him again. I was crushed.

President Kekkonen of Finland and Foreign Minister Cosgrave of Ireland. Two more dancing stories. President Urho Kekkonen was a great, tall, handsome man way up in his seventies. He still jogged several miles every day, and dancing with him was like jogging; he was heavy on his feet. When we danced together, our waltz seemed to last an hour and a half. Jerry's good right arm, Bob Barrett (who's now our Chief of Staff, which means he runs both our lives), used to say, "Mrs. Ford danced with everybody. Even if they didn't dance, she danced with them." Well, Barrett and Susan were watching me struggling with President Kekkonen, and out of the corner of my eye I could see my daughter laughing. The very next dance, President Kekkonen invited Susan onto the floor. I prevented Barrett from cutting in and rescuing her. "Let *her* see how funny it is," I said cold-heartedly.

But the suffering at Foreign Minister Cosgrave's party was done by Jerry. Jerry likes to dance to old Glen Miller-style numbers like "In the Mood" (some members of the press have written that he does the same two-step no matter what the music is) and the first tune the band played at the Cosgrave gala was some far-out jazz thing. Dancing with Mrs. Cosgrave, Jerry looked unhappy. Then the Foreign Minister asked Barrett if the band could play a jig. Jerry was still waiting for "In the Mood" when this dump-de-diddley-diddley-dum-dump-de-diddley started, and that was another trial for my husband. After a few more selections with which he was out of sympathy, he called Barrett over and said—Barrett vows this is true—"If they won't play some music I can dance to, I'm just not gonna come to these things any more."

I loved the idea of a President's refusing to attend state functions, but Barrett, anxious to end Jerry's misery, approached the leader of the Marine Band. "No sweat," he said, "but you've got to play 'Stardust' or 'Bad Bad Leroy Brown.'" The bandleader got huffy and stood up very tall in his scarlet coat. "I've been playing at the White House for twelve years, and I just don't understand . . ."

Barrett, with the seldom-expressed wrath of the President still ringing in his ears, explained to the sergeant that he could either play the music requested from inside the White House, or play the music of his choice outside on a street corner.

The bandleader understood that, and Jerry got some different music, but he wasn't totally pacified. "He was still sulking when he went upstairs," Barrett says. "He smiled as he said goodnight to his guests, but the minute he got into the elevator, he turned to me. 'Now listen, Barrett,' he said, 'I'm the President of the United States, and I should be able to have some music I can dance to.'"

President Walter Scheel of the Federal Republic of Germany. Our White House parties, if I may be permitted a moment of immodesty, had become so popular that we had almost too many acceptances to the Scheel state dinner. We had to put one hundred guests in the State Dining Room with President Scheel and Jerry, and fifty more in the Red Room, where Henry Kissinger played host.

President Scheel, himself a pop music star—he'd made a best-selling record for charity—was enchanted to meet Harry James, who'd come over from the Kennedy Center, where he'd been in concert, and sat in as trumpeter with the Marine Band. That was really something, Harry James playing "Sheik of Araby" and "You Made Me Love You," and Helen O'Connell singing a duet of "Hey, Good Looking" with Tennessee Ernie, and Jerry calling out a request for "Hello, Dolly," in between efforts to rescue President Scheel from the reporters who surrounded him.

At that dinner, President Scheel made one of the most moving toasts I was to hear during my time in the White House. "Where else in the world," he asked "is there a republic which for two centuries has made liberty and equality of all citizens its law of life, which has not even shirked a civil war in order to remain true to the ideals upon which it entered world history?" And he added, "Those ideals are still the most important, the most powerful, the most vital of all. Europe is—who would doubt it?—the mother of the United States. But the United States is—and who could doubt that?—the mother of European democracy."

The night of the Scheel do, I couldn't get Jerry upstairs. He was dancing with the pretty actress Elke Sommer. And Henry Kissinger couldn't get his wife, Nancy, to go home either. She was talking about one more square dance when Henry marched himself toward a side door. "I'm leaving right now," he said.

If Walter Scheel made one of the nicest toasts to America, a Third World leader delivered one of the most excoriating. It seemed to me he talked for about an hour and a half, and his speech was nothing but criticism of the United States. Some people actually fell asleep, it went on so long, and I had trouble knowing how to behave. You can't laugh, but you aren't sure how to respond. Here's a guest reviling his hosts; what are you supposed to do, raise your glass cheerily? What's the protocol for that?

Thomas Stafford, Donald Slayton, Vance Brand. At a luncheon in the Yellow Oval Room for these astronauts, Jerry said, "We honor three men who have risen a hundred and thirty-seven miles above this earth, looked down at all the turmoil, pollution, the confusion and the problems, and still decided to come back. I think it gives all of us—the rest of us—some hope."

The Emperor and Empress of Japan. Theirs was the first state visit to the United States by reigning Japanese monarchs, and Americans loved them. The Empress was like a little doll; she smiled and bowed and waved at everyone. She and the Emperor traveled all around the country, once they got here, and Americans smiled and waved back. At the state dinner, we were determined to be formal because we thought that was what they were used to, with the E-shaped arrangement for the dining table (the only other times we were so formal were for the Shah of Iran and the Queen of England), draped white linen tablecloths, silver candlesticks holding long white tapers, crimson blossoms around the candle holders, and the guests in white tie and tails. And then it turned out that the Emperor and Empress were more interested to know about the informal, relaxed ways of the Americans. They wanted to learn our customs. Still, they rose to the occasion, the Empress in tiara and jewels and long white gloves. I think about Jerry and me guiding them around, holding on to their elbows, a dear fragile couple who could speak almost no English. The seventy-four-year-old Emperor tended to say, "Ah, so," just like in the movies, but the Empress's giggle didn't require translation; when she giggled, everyone around her laughed with delight.

Supreme Court Justice John Paul Stevens. We were giving what's called a "Judiciary Dinner," which would be attended by federal judges from all over the country. This was before Jerry had announced Judge Stevens as his choice to succeed Justice Douglas, who had finally retired, leaving a vacancy on the high court. Jerry had been close-mouthed about his intention, but while we were dressing, he slipped and said, "Well, the man I'm going to appoint will be at the dinner tonight," and my heart sank. It was the first inkling I'd had that he wasn't going to name a woman. Whoops! I thought, lost that one.

I could describe a hundred other incidents. When you're in the White House, every day demands that you make decisions, most of them petty. You're going to greet three hundred wives of heads of colleges from all over the United States. Should you have a receiving line? Should you let them tour? Will you come down and give them tea? Or join them after they've had their tea? Should they have their tea in the East Room?

Every social event comes with built-in questions. How much do you do? How little? Do we bend over backward for these people, or do we just stand up straight?

Sometimes it's easy: for the children of the diplomatic corps, you invite *Sesame Street*'s "Big Bird"; for Chancellor Helmut Schmidt of West Germany, who loves opera, you ask the opera star Phyllis Curtin; for France's piano-playing blues-loving Giscard d'Estaing, you bring in Earl Hines. Sometimes it's hard. But always it's educational, and often it's fun.

31

GUNSHOTS

State dinners provided some of our more dazzling moments in the White House. But there were grim times too. The first year that Jerry was President, people with guns altered—or tried to alter—our lives and the lives of friends.

Nancy Howe has been mentioned by me in earlier chapters. She came to the White House as my personal assistant, and for a time she was a very close friend.

In April of 1975, Nancy's husband, James W. Howe, shot himself to death.

I wouldn't tell this story except that I've heard there are other books by other people which are going to deal with it, so I would like to state, as simply as possible, the facts as I remember them.

Nancy left the White House four days after Jimmy's death, and the press had a field day. "At the time, Mrs. Howe was under investigation by the White House (in connection with reports that she and her husband had been entertained in the Dominican Republic by international businessman Tongsun Park) to determine whether there had been any violation of the federal code of ethics and conflict of interest laws for government employees," wrote journalist Myra MacPherson. "Mrs. Howe said, when asked whether it was not rather callous of the First Lady to let her best friend go, 'You said it, I didn't. I just don't want to talk about it.' "

Well, I didn't fire Nancy Howe. When I was told she had to leave, I cried. Her own psychologist and another psychologist met with Dr. Lukash and decided that she wasn't in shape to stay on. There was a feeling that the circumstances of Jimmy's death would make it difficult for her to handle a sensitive and burdensome job, and the Secret Service picked up her White House pass.

I was there at Jimmy's funeral. Nancy held up fine until I walked to the car with her, and then she broke down. I remember Pearl Bailey's saying, "Now, Nancy, come on, girl, this isn't the time to fall apart."

But what I could do as a private person and a loving friend, and what I could do as the wife of a President, were entirely different things. The minute I heard that Nancy couldn't come back to work, I drove straight out to her place and we sat upstairs and talked for I don't know how long. After that we couldn't speak for a long time. It broke my heart.

They say that when a wife or a husband commits suicide, the surviving partner goes through various stages. You feel loss, and hate, you want to get back at the person who's deserted you, and then at anybody else you can blame. You are resentful and frightened.

I wanted in the worst way to be with Nancy through that period. It wasn't permitted.

I didn't even mind the press's labeling me disloyal; that seemed unimportant in the face of such real trouble. Eventually, Nancy got over her resentment about leaving the White House—she even campaigned for Jerry—and I still think of us as friends, but of course there was no going back to the way it had been.

It was a nasty, nasty news story. (It's still a nasty story, the whole Korean payoff scandal. Tongsun Park was supposedly more than generous in supplying parties and plane trips to various Congressmen, and no matter how it's done, that sort of thing can't be hidden; it always comes out. Nobody working in government is permitted to accept a personal gift worth more than fifty dollars from a representative of another government. I remember as First Lady touring the International YWCA Fair—it was held in a Washington hotel—which featured booths representing foreign countries, and at each booth the Ambassador's wife, or some other official person, offered me a trinket, a little ring, a bottle of wine. But the gift from Mexico, a valuable antique, I couldn't keep. It was obviously worth more than fifty dollars, so it had to go in with the state gifts, become the property of the government. Caesar's wife has to avoid even the hint of a bribe.)

Nancy Howe used to call me Petunia, because I said petunias were the only thing that could stand the heat of Washington in the summer. I meant not only the heat of the sun but the heat of Congress, when all the members want to go home and they start racing through legislation and fighting and getting disagreeable.

But in that early spring of 1975, long before the summer came, I found the heat of Washington pretty hard to take.

And then as the summer ended, two different women tried to kill Jerry.

On September 5, in Sacramento, California, he was crossing the street from his hotel to the State Capitol when Lynette Alice Fromme, a member of the Charles Manson family, pulled a .45-caliber pistol from a leg holster she was wearing under her long red dress and pointed it at Jerry. Larry Buendorf, a Secret Service agent, grabbed the gun and forced it out of Fromme's hand. Why had she wanted to kill the President? Later, she said she was upset by his "attitude toward nuclear power plants."

The second attempt on Jerry's life came seventeen days after the first, outside the St. Francis Hotel in San Francisco, and this time Sara Jane Moore, wielding a .38-caliber revolver, actually got a shot off. (One day earlier, she'd been arrested for carrying a handgun, questioned by the Secret Service, and let go.) The bullet missed Jerry, passing right between David Kennerly and one of the Secret Service men, and by then a bystander named Oliver Sipple had reached out and knocked Moore's arm down.

I didn't know anything about the San Francisco shooting until

hours later. Jerry and I had been in Monterey for the weekend—
there was a golf tournament—and when he left for San Francisco
on Monday morning I saw no reason to go. *I* didn't have to give a
television interview from the St. Francis Hotel. (Phyllis Schlafly
notwithstanding, I never even speak to my husband early in the
morning. He has his mind on so many things, the minute his feet hit
the floor his day has started, and my metabolism doesn't work that
way.)

So I was still en route from Monterey on the afternoon that the
Sara Jane Moore business happened. The schedule called for me to
get to San Francisco in time to board Air Force One before Jerry, so
that, as soon as his motorcade arrived from the St. Francis, he could
whip up the stairs and be airborne. Normally, when a President gets
into his car or on his airplane, it goes.

All the time we were flying north, Dick Hartwig and Pete
Sorum (who was in the Presidential Advance Office, and planned
lots of campaign trips for me and the children) were trying to make
radio contact with San Francisco. The channels had been closed out;
they couldn't raise anybody. Finally, a voice came on Pete's
receiver. "Move Pinafore to Angel with all possible speed," it said.
That was all.

Pete went to Hartwig. "I don't know what's going on, but we
got to move her." "We're moving her," said Hartwig. They weren't
particularly concerned. They thought maybe Jerry had finished his
lunch speech and interview early, and wanted to be under way.

There wasn't a lot of time to think. We arrived at the airport in
San Francisco, and I noticed the motorcade cars weren't pulled up
in order as they usually would be; they'd just been parked any
which way. Pete grabbed my bags, threw them at an Air Force One
steward. A bunch of Secret Service agents were standing around,
but they didn't pay any attention to me, so Dick Hartwig said to
Pete, "Cover the left, will you?" and Dick got on one side of me and
Pete got on the other and they rushed me, practically picked me up
by my arms and lifted me up the stairs and onto Air Force One.

I still didn't know what was happening. I hadn't had time to
realize anything was wrong, and even though I knew Pete and Dick

had been having trouble making radio contact, I figured there had just been a lot of static or confusion.

So I walked into the Presidential cabin, and here were all these people sitting around with Jerry—Ron Nessen, Bob Hartmann, Don Rumsfeld, a big group. And I smiled brightly and said, "Well, how did they treat you in San Francisco?"

They looked at me as if I was absolutely out of my mind, these stunned faces registering one message: this must be the most stupid woman in the world.

Then Jerry said, "You mean you don't know?" and they all started to talk at once, to tell me what had happened. After the fact, there had been a bit of black humor. Once the shot had been fired, Jerry ducked, and his people pushed him into his limousine, and down on the floor, and then everybody piled on top of him, and the car took off, sirens wailing, for the airport. A minute or so later, Jerry spoke up plaintively from the bottom of the pile. "Will a couple of you guys get off me?" he said. "You're going to smother me to death."

I was so grateful, grateful Mr. Sipple had tackled the Moore woman, grateful my husband was still sitting there able to announce that he intended to go right on appearing in public and shaking everybody's hands.

Jerry had been fortunate. Pat Golubin wasn't.

We had known the Golubin family for years. Their twin daughters, Reagan and Elison, sweet, smart girls with lovely manners, had been Susan's closest friends since childhood and right through Holton Arms. There were three other Golubin children, but Jerry and I knew the twins best because they and Susan had been inseparable. After Holton Arms, the twins had gone off to Atlanta, to Emory College, while Susan stayed in Washington and began classes at Mount Vernon.

Pat Golubin, the twins' mother, was separated from their father and earning her living selling real estate. She had recently moved into a house in a new section of town, almost on the border of Maryland and D.C., and one day her estranged husband came out there and shot and killed Pat, and Pat's mother, before he turned the gun on himself. Brion, the youngest Golubin girl, got off the school bus that afternoon and walked into the house and found the three bodies on the floor.

A relative phoned Reagan and Elison and told them to come home, but didn't say what had happened. Susan and I went to the airport to meet the twins, who knew, when they saw us there, that something was terribly wrong. I brought them back to the White House. I took in all the Golubin children—even Greg, who was twenty-eight years old, and had his own apartment—and tried to care for them and keep their minds off what had happened.

We sat up all night and played games. I've blanked it out, but Susan remembers. "We were in the solarium, playing 'How's Yours?'" she says. "You sit in a circle and somebody leaves the room and everybody else gets together and chooses something everyone has in common. Like if everyone has a scar or a birthmark. Then the person who's been out of the room comes back and sits in the center of the circle and starts questioning the others, saying, 'How's Yours?' One player will say, 'Well, mine's long,' and the next will say, 'Well, mine's pink,' and it can be very suggestive until the person in the center figures out what they're talking about. We got some good laughs. It helped."

The funeral was the next day, one of those still, gloomy fall days when the leaves dropped off the trees and you couldn't tell why because no wind was stirring.

Friends sent me press clippings about the Golubin tragedy. I threw them away. It was something I never wanted to think about again. But I think about it anyhow.

32

LIGHTER MOMENTS

I don't want to sound as though a First Lady spends all her time in the White House serving tea to the Queen of England or thinking grimly about the number of potential assassins in the country.

Sometimes she has her portrait painted.

People in public life are forever having their portraits painted, whether they like it or not. In 1954, the wife of Sir Winston Churchill actually destroyed a portrait of Sir Winston painted by Graham Sutherland, which portrait, commissioned by Parliament, had been presented to the former Prime Minister as an eightieth birthday present. It, said Sir Winston, "makes me look half-witted, which I ain't," and the new picture was never seen publicly again.

Or privately either, it turns out. Lady Spencer-Churchill took care of the matter, never mind that the work was worth more than a hundred thousand dollars.

When Jerry became Vice President, I sat for a portrait by John Ulbricht, who said he liked to work in large figures. I didn't realize *how* large. The painting of me turned out to be about three times bigger than life size, and covered an enormous canvas. This didn't matter, because it was scheduled to hang in the Vice President's office, where there was tremendous wall space.

When Jerry was kicked upstairs, we hung the portrait outside the Yellow Oval Room, before inviting the staff to come for a look and a glass of sherry. (Some of the people were more thrilled to see our private quarters than to see the painting. "I've worked in the White House for fifteen years," one man told me, "and I've never been on the second floor before.")

I love my Ulbricht. It's strong, and has a nice Monet quality, but a lot of my friends thought it was too serious. Among my friends I have a reputation for mischief. For years, they've seen me offguard, on vacations, where I could strut around in sexy pants, wave a long cigarette holder, do a takeoff of Marlene Dietrich, the kind of silly thing you only attempt in Puerto Rico or Jamaica or Hawaii, when United Press isn't on your tail. I've tried to explain to these friends that the wives of Important Government Officials aren't supposed to be silly. I never get away with it. Some smart aleck always reminds me about the time I borrowed a skeleton from a hospital and dressed it in my hat and coat, and sat it in a bedroom chair to welcome Jerry home. (He'd been nagging me about being too thin.) And that was in the White House.

Jerry's dog Liberty was never painted by Ulbricht but she's been photographed to a fare-thee-well; even our 1977 Christmas cards featured her and her daughter Misty, each with a new litter of puppies. Misty and eight siblings were born in the White House on September 7, 1975. Up until shortly before the babies came, Liberty had spent her nights in a kennel on the ground floor. That way, she could be with Jerry in the Oval Office during the day, and when she wanted to go out, all she had to do was stand at the door. It was more sensible than trying to have her live upstairs with us. A dog can't go to the elevator, reach up, and press the button, and when we did take her up into the family quarters—we never took her on the state floor—we had to remember to keep track of time, so there wouldn't be any accidents.

But, with motherhood imminent, we were afraid she'd deliver at night, so we moved her inside, and for a short while she slept on the third floor with a trainer. One night the trainer had to be away, and he left Liberty with us. "If she wants to go out," he said, "she'll come and lick your face."

About three o'clock in the morning, she came and licked Jerry's face. Like a good daddy, he got up, pulled on a robe and slippers, took the dog downstairs and out onto the south lawn. When they were ready to come back, Jerry rang for the elevator. But at night the elevator goes off. You have to get it charged up or something. Secret Service agents are in a room in the basement (they have a mirror and closed-circuit TV and there are lights all over the grounds), and usually they notice anything that moves, so I still don't understand how they missed the scene with the odd couple. Maybe somebody dozed off.

Anyway, Jerry decided to try the stairs. He opened the door to the stairwell, said, "Come on, Liberty," and up they climbed to the second floor, Liberty waddling from side to side, her stomach with nine puppies in it practically hanging on the ground. They got to the second floor, and the door to the hall was locked. You can get out, but you can't get back in. They went up again, to the third floor. Also locked. And there they were, a President and his dog, wandering around in a stairwell in the wee small hours of the morning, not able to get back to bed. Finally they came all the way down again, and by that time the Secret Service had been alerted, and somebody got the elevator started.

We prepared for Liberty's *accouchement* by stripping a room on the third floor and making it into a hospital. We put down plastic sheets, and a tarp on top of the plastic, so there would be no possibility of damaging the floor, and we built a whelping box.

I sat on the floor and held Liberty's head for eight hours, until the first puppy came, and then I just went on stroking her and talking to her while the vet and Susan and the trainer were working, drying off the baby dogs, laughing at all the barking. I could see there was only one blonde, and I decided I wanted to keep her. Sometimes I feel guilty because Misty grew into a big, strong, husky animal who ought to be a working dog, not just a house pet, but I don't think I could part with her now.

The pups were two months old before I permitted a photograph. The vet and I were strict about this because we didn't want their eyes damaged by flash bulbs. (We protected their lungs too.

We posted a sign, saying, NO SMOKING, AND THIS MEANS YOU, GRANDPA, above a sketch of Jerry with his pipe on the door to the puppy room.) In human babies, the eyes are open, but they don't focus. In puppies, the eyes aren't even open; they don't see until they're about two weeks old, and before that they're so funny. They wiggle around with those little shut eyes and little smashed noses. Then the noses begin to push out, the eyes begin to open, they try to walk without falling down or running into each other.

David Kennerly shot the puppy picture and it took forever. To keep nine puppies still long enough to get a picture of all of them with their mother was practically impossible. We'd have them artistically arranged, and one of them would wander off, or roll over, or try to leave the room.

We gave them all away, except for Misty.

While we lived at the White House, Jerry, who'd been missing his swimming—he'd swum every day in Alexandria—became the recipient of a brand-new pool. Once there had been an indoor White House pool, but the room was hot and steamy and musty smelling; and President Nixon had ordered the pool covered over, and turned the place into a press room, which was sorely needed. If you tried to take the press room back now, the reporters would never forgive you. They used to have to come to the west entrance, pile their coats on tables in the hall, and sit around outside waiting to be called in.

The new outdoor pool was located behind the Oval Office and built with donations from the public. Jack Stiles was on the fund-raising committee. One little paper boy sent in all the money he'd earned in a week of delivering papers. "I want the President to have a swimming pool," he wrote.

Jerry used the new pool all year round. No matter how late he worked, if he had a chance, he'd take a swim afterward. In the winter, even when there was snow on the ground, he could just roll back two strips of plastic covering and make a kind of racing lane. The water was heated, too.

Jerry loves sports, and as you may have gathered, I love clothes. Jerry has never said boo when the bills came in. "If you like it, get it" is his motto. He's always been generous. I like gold, and when we were in Italy he bought me a gold bracelet that says "I love you" in Italian. I also have a gold charm bracelet that has a Bicentennial Liberty Bell with a little diamond clapper, a model of the White House, the insignia of the town of Vail, Jerry's and my initials, and a handmade globe to signify all the traveling we've done. The globe is so soft it's out of shape. There's a sermon in there someplace.

My very favorite piece of jewelry was given to me by Jerry's mother. It's a man's little-finger ring which had belonged to his great-great-grandfather, Gardner Varnum Ayer, and goes back about five generations in Jerry's family. It's an onyx square, monogrammed, set in gold and surrounded with diamond chips. I had it cut down and I wear it almost all the time. Once I almost lost it. It was on a trip to California. I had gone to the San Diego zoo, so the press could photograph me wearing a white smock and feeding a baby chimpanzee in the baby chimp's nursery.

Then some genius thought it would be cute if I would feed an elephant. He was a very nice elephant; he held his trunk up high and opened his mouth, and I put an apple in it. Now an elephant's mouth is full of saliva. It's very soft in there—you don't have to worry about getting hurt—but it's very wet. All of a sudden, the apple slid out of my fingers, and I could feel my ring sliding off too. I thought, Grandmother Ford will smite me from the heavens. I could just hear her saying, "Betty, I trusted you to pass that ring on to the next generation. You weren't supposed to lose it."

I snatched my hand out of the elephant's maw, asked somebody to please give me a towel, and made a resolution. If ever I had to feed an animal again, I would do it with my gloves on; you can always buy a new pair of gloves, but the ring was irreplaceable.

As First Lady I needed more changes of wardrobe than I do now, and I used to like to fly up to New York and see what was available. Once I sneaked away to the city with Nancy Howe and Susan, and I didn't even tell my press secretary that I was going. Only the Secret Service knew. Somehow, word leaked out, and reporters started phoning Sheila Weidenfeld and asking if I was in New York. "No indeed," Sheila said. "She's right upstairs." She wasn't, she was on Seventh Avenue.

That was fun. To avoid the press, we left one building by the freight elevator, and it stopped on every floor on its way to the lobby, which made Dick Hartwig nervous. "Take this elevator straight down," he told the operator. The operator was unimpressed. "I can't take this elevator straight down," he said. "I got people waiting for deliveries, and they're very important people. Bill Blass, Oscar de la Renta, we got important people in this building." Susan and I stood there grinning at one another, relieved, at least briefly, of the awesome responsibility for being the First Lady and Her Daughter.

My daughter's really a country girl; she finds the noise, the numbers of people in New York terrifying, but I've always loved it, whether the trip was official or just to shop and go to the theatre.

Once, in 1976, I went to New York to appear on a television show as a Woman of the Year (for the *Ladies' Home Journal;* they nominate a whole bunch of Women of the Year every year), and Barbara Walters was mistress of ceremonies, and Pearl Bailey was a presenter. I was wearing a dress of Chinese red with gold trim, very straight and tight, with a slit up the front because otherwise I couldn't have walked in it. It was a new dress and I hadn't paid much attention to how high the slit really came, but backstage I started to get nervous. All I could think of was, a First Lady should not come onstage showing her thighs. When I was finally called, I made my entrance almost cross-legged, like a little kid who had to go to the bathroom.

After the show, my Secret Service agents and Pete Sorum said they were going to take me out on the town, and we got into the car and started driving. We stopped in front of a big apartment building I didn't recognize, and when I walked in, there were the two little Rockefeller boys waiting in the lobby to escort me upstairs. Happy and Nelson were throwing a surprise birthday party for me. Pearl Bailey said she'd almost given the whole thing away at the Woman of the Year bash by saying, "See you later," as I left.

There was a birthday dinner, nothing elaborate, just terribly well done. But anything the Rockefellers do is well done. And, after all, I had got used to butlers. As a matter of fact, compared to many wealthy people, the Rockefellers live simply. You're not made conscious that they've got lots, aside from the fact that when you go to visit them in Pocantico they have a golf course and all this acreage and old family retainers. I've been there, and the big house where Nelson grew up has never been renovated. In the eight bathrooms there are old tubs on claw feet, and old washbasins, and old pull-chain toilets, and everything is very large and very comfortable.

There's also a little Japanese house which Nelson built on the property for Happy. When they were furnishing the Japanese house, the Rockefellers decided that, for them at least, Chinese and Japanese antiques from his mother's collection didn't mix well, and they donated a gorgeous Chinese chest and several other fine pieces to Admiralty House.

Not only had I been unprepared for the birthday party, but, earlier in the day, when I'd arrived at the Waldorf, I'd had another surprise. There was always some king or queen or prince staying at the Waldorf. A duchess at the minimum. So when I saw the garage filled with balloons—we came in through the garage—I said to Pete Sorum, "Hmm, there must be somebody important here."

We got out of the car, and there was half the staff of the hotel lined up to greet me. Mr. Scanlon, the manager, brought out a birthday cake taller than I was (so big, in fact, that they later put what was left of it in the lobby for other guests to sample) and I was flabbergasted. I was still looking around for the duchess. (Hernando Courtright at the Beverly Wilshire Hotel in Beverly Hills makes a big fuss over me too. Once I came into the driveway between the old and the new buildings and seven thousand rose petals showered down on my head, while two violinists, dressed in white, played "I Could Have Danced All Night." If you don't believe it, I don't blame you.)

Birthdays, Thanksgiving Days, Valentine's Days, there were some nifty ones. Jerry threw a surprise party for me one Valentine's Day in the White House, and it was such a surprise the guests caught me in a negligee. Jerry had been saying, "Why don't you get a little dressed up?" and I wasn't interested. "For dinner at home?

Why?" Next thing I knew, there were fifteen couples, mostly old friends, surrounding me. We had a buffet in the private dining room, and afterward we sat all up and down the West Hall.

(I enjoyed being able to entertain old friends in the style that the White House provided. When Phoebe Stiles, who'd remarried after her divorce from Jack, had a series of heart operations, another old friend of ours, Dortha O'Connell, and I had flown to Florida—where Phoebe and her second husband, Jackson Seay, had settled—to see her. We were afraid it might be our last chance. Then Phoebe made an amazing recovery, and some months later she and Dortha and their husbands turned up for lunch at the White House. I had to order wheelchairs for both ladies, Phoebe because of her heart and Dortha because she was getting over a broken ankle, but we all had a good time anyhow. I remember Jackson wanted to know the recipe for the martinis. He said they were magical, the best martinis he'd ever had. I don't think they were any different from any other martinis; I think it was just the atmosphere that lent them enchantment.)

People love to visit the White House; they remember it always as something special.

And of course it is special. History comes alive for you under that roof. I never had time to learn as much as I'd have liked to about each piece of furniture, each picture. I picked up only a smattering of what I wanted to know.

It was the same when we were traveling. I got to see so many places when Jerry was President, always in haste and almost always at the discretion of our hosts. But that's the next chapter.

33

GLOBE TROTTING

There's an old joke which says travel is broadening, especially around the hips. Sometimes you can travel and see nothing—I think of my poor son Jack, loading and unloading a freighter through that whole long summer—and sometimes you can learn a lesson that hasn't got much to do with the places you're traveling in.

My travels with the Presidential entourage were fascinating, though I missed some of the places I most wanted to go because I kept waiting for a longer trip. Every time Jerry went to England, it was for a short stay, and I'd always say, "I'll wait till we can spend some time, do some real sightseeing." Consequently, I've never been to England.

Japan is another country I missed, though you wouldn't know it if you'd heard me talking on Japanese TV. Our plane had set down at the airport in Tokyo to refuel, and the TV reporters came over. I told them how much I loved Japan, how beautiful I thought it was, how ardently I admired the Japanese for their habit of hard work. And all I'd ever seen was the airport.

Early on, when Jerry was still in Congress, I'd begun collecting dolls from faraway places for Susan, and I kept up the practice.

Susan has a great doll collection. In Poland, I bought one exquisite doll wearing real leather boots and a real fur Cossack-style jacket, and it wasn't cheap, either. Americans always think everything's going to be cheaper in Europe, and we're always wrong.

As the wife of the President, I needed to step off a plane looking right, so whenever we left the United States I took Jim Merson, my hairdresser, along, and Jerry paid for his trip. There wasn't any time to come into a city and ask which way to the beauty salon.

Some of our journeys were incredibly jam-packed. Once we went to Brussels, were greeted by King Baudouin and Queen Fabiola (Jerry had a NATO meeting), flew from Brussels to Madrid (General Franco gave Jerry the keys to the city), traveled on to Salzburg (Jerry conferred with the visiting Egyptian President Anwar Sadat), and ended the trip in Rome (calling on President Leone and Pope Paul).

I'll never forget the arrival in Spain. There was a parade featuring elite guards on beautiful, beautiful horses, and the guards wore great shining silver helmets with red plumes, and red-and-gold uniforms. Jerry rode with Franco in an open car, and they stood up and waved to the people, which surprised me because Franco was already weak then, and old. As we moved down the avenue, mobs of people shouted, "Franc-o, Franc-o, Franc-o," and the side streets were filled with workers who'd been let off their jobs so they could come out and welcome us, but who weren't able to get onto the main boulevard because it was so crowded.

In Washington, we sometimes do the same thing, encourage government employees to go out into the street when a head of state is arriving, and we put up groups of three flags along Pennsylvania Avenue, the American flag, the District of Columbia flag, and the flag of the visiting dignitary's country, but our ceremonies are nothing so colorful as the ones they lay on in Spain.

General Franco had to have a translator in order to talk to Jerry but Mrs. Franco spoke beautiful English. At the state dinner in the Presidential Palace—that's the dinner where we counted the twenty-eight candelabra—I sat between General Franco and the

Prince, Juan Carlos, who's now the King of Spain. I remember talking to his wife, now Queen Sophia, about their wedding. She had been a Greek princess, so they'd had both Greek and Catholic ceremonies.

Less than two months later, the Fords were back in Europe again on yet another whirlwind visit. This time, we went to several Communist countries—Rumania, Poland, Yugoslavia—as well as to West Germany and Finland. There were meetings of the Conference on Security and Cooperation in Europe in Helsinki, and while Jerry was working, Jerry's wife was shopping.

That trip covered five countries in nine days, and the only place we had more than an overnight stay was Helsinki. In one of the Warsaw Pact capitals, we were met by a motorcade and a motorcycle escort. The officers riding the cycles sported snow-white gloves and snow-white boots, imperial in their elegance. They wouldn't call it imperial, but it seems to me that Communist governments love all that pomp. Another of our arrivals came at the hottest time of the day, and I stood facing into the sun while the welcoming speeches were being made. It would have been fine if we'd only had to hear them once, but each had to be translated after it was delivered, so you got both versions, and at one point I thought, I'm going to faint. Should I just stand here and crumple into a heap in front of everybody, or should I walk around behind them to fall down?

By the time we reached Rumania, our final stop, I was suffering from *turista*, and it was the real thing; I was too old to be pregnant. I sat through the state dinner that night, but begged to be excused from an excursion to Transylvania scheduled for the next day.

Mrs. Ceauşescu, the wife of the Rumanian President, wouldn't take no for an answer. She understood that I wasn't willing to take a long train ride with her husband and my husband, but she sent an emissary over to the hotel with another proposition. She and I could take a helicopter, and still catch up with the men.

I said no thank you to the helicopter.

The emissary left, and was back in a trice. How about lunch?

I said no thank you to lunch.

Finally I agreed to a little tea, hoping I hadn't breached any understandings between our governments.

Jerry and I stayed home for a few weeks, then set out across the Pacific. This was the time we took Susan with us. In Peking she did the things I'd done before, went to the Great Wall, for instance, while I caught up on things I'd missed. I went to the museums. And the ballet school.

Oriental dancing is quite different from anything I had ever tried, particularly in the hand movements, but the students asked me to join them. I took off my shoes and worked in my stocking feet, and once more I came up lucky. My picture, *en pointe*, arms outstretched, hit all the papers, and my act was hailed as having done more to cement relations between the United States and China than all the talk of the diplomats. I told Jerry that he could stop talking to the diplomats, I'd already made the world safe for détente, but he didn't listen.

It was very cold in the Republic of China in December, and from China we flew directly to Jakarta, Indonesia, where it was so hot and humid I couldn't believe it. I honestly don't think it can be good for your body to do that kind of thing.

Indonesia's President Suharto came out to greet us, and then I was taken to see his wife's famous orchid gardens. That night, after having tramped for hours (I'd been on my feet till I thought I would drop), I got back on Air Force One, and Dr. Lukash, who didn't know what I'd been up to, looked disapprovingly at my swollen ankles. "You mustn't just sit around," he said. "You must exercise, even if you have to walk up and down the aisle of the plane."

Next came Manila, where we were greeted by one hundred thousand Filipinos. That's not a misprint. Imelda Marcos, wife of the President of the Philippines, had been so worried that we might not have been treated well in China that she thoughtfully turned out the whole population of Manila. The parade was nine miles long; it stretched from the airstrip to the Presidential Palace, where we were to stay. All the nationalities of the Philippines were represented in native costumes, playing instruments, dancing, singing.

Later, we signed the guest book at the palace, and were shown to our quarters. The palace was already decorated for Christmas. That night there was a state dinner of many courses. I was beginning to feel punchy. There was a man sitting next to me, a little short fat man, his chest covered with medals. He had his glasses on and he was sound asleep behind them, the eyes just sort of drooped, at half mast. I kept thinking, Oh, if I could only do that. We were being entertained with beautiful dancing, but I was exhausted.

Jerry and I finally got to bed, knowing we had to be up early to take a boat trip out to Corregidor, which nobody in Manila calls anything but The Rock.

The Marcos yacht is a ship (you could land a helicopter on the deck) and it was set up like a night club, featuring native entertainment and drinks and dancing and a gorgeous buffet, not like a breakfast at all. And it was very hot.

At Corregidor, we paid our respects to the servicemen who died there during World War II, and a bugler blew "Taps," and after the rites I got into trouble with Mrs. Marcos.

The Marcoses had wanted to take us to the top of a mountain to see some more war monuments, but our people felt there was no time for that. We had to get back to Manila in good order because we would be flying all night to Hawaii. It was important that we reach Hawaii by seven-fifteen the next morning for a ceremony marking the anniversary of Pearl Harbor.

"Don't get in a car, no matter what happens," our advance men told Jerry and me.

Mrs. Marcos and I had split off from the men, and when she offered a car, I declined. "It's such a lovely day," I said, "why don't we walk?"

Mrs. Marcos didn't feel like walking. Under her umbrella, she looked unhappy. "Oh, it's so hot, it's so terribly hot," she kept saying.

We talked about stopping at a teahouse—tea wouldn't take nearly as long as a drive up the mountain—but Mrs. Marcos was mad. She scorned the teahouse. "There's no tea there," she said.

"Okay," said Pete Sorum, "then we'll just go straight back to the boat."

On the return trip to Manila, Mrs. Marcos got over her unhappiness and we made it to Hawaii in time for the memorial program—it was just a little past dawn on December 7, 1975—and then we had to go to a reception at an admiral's house, or a general's house, but by then I couldn't keep anything straight, and it went on like that all day. Everyone in our group was bone weary, and at the receptions you didn't dare take a drink, because if you did you'd fall sound asleep. Standing up.

Finally, Jerry and Susan flew straight back to Washington without even stopping overnight. I stayed in Hawaii, along with Bob Barrett, Pete Sorum, my agents, and a few other lucky souls. Jerry insisted on it. I was jet-lagged and cranky and needed to sleep for twenty-four hours. Or days. Or years. (I was sitting on a suitcase in the airport and smoking a cigarette, and Barrett offered to send an aide over to talk to me. Through clenched teeth, I rejected his kind proposal. "I don't want anybody to come over and talk to me. I just want to sit here all alone and finish this cigarette.")

But, after an hour's nap at the hotel, I found I couldn't sleep any more, and rang up Barrett and Sorum. "Now that we're rid of El Presidente, what are we going to do?"

I organized a dinner party, took the staff out to a restaurant, where the proprietor very generously furnished the wine. (He'd been conned by Barrett, who'd taken him aside and said, "I don't want to suggest an expensive vintage because the First Lady's paying; on the other hand, I can't order rotgut for her, so what would you suggest?" The proprietor had risen to the bait; I was horrified when I found out.)

I thoroughly enjoyed playing hooky for a couple of days. I met the Governor of Hawaii and his wife. I think they were Democrats, but I hope they're still in office; they're really super. She gave me a basket of roses, each individual rose carved out of wood. It was a great big thing, but I brought it back because it was so lovely. It went into storage. (Once we started planning the new house, I kept telling myself, New house, new house, there'll be room for everything in the new house.)

On rereading this chapter about wilting in the heat, freezing in the cold, and going sleepless, I'm afraid I may have failed to communicate how much I really enjoyed those Presidential trips. I had fun, I was privileged to travel in style and to see many wonders; and these will stay in my memory long after small discomforts are forgotten, and the souvenirs made of paper and tin and wood are scattered or broken.

34

CAMPAIGN

Nineteen seventy-six is a jumble in my head, full of days when I just went quickly from one thing to another, changing my clothes. There were all those state dinners (some of which I've already talked about) one right after another, and the Bicentennial, and campaigning. Campaigning for a solid year.

I hadn't wanted Jerry to be President, but I had long since accepted his decision to run. You plan your life one way, it goes another. When the time came, I felt he would be the best man for the job, and I was willing to take on four more years in the White House. (It wouldn't be nearly so difficult as it had been at first; our staffs had shaken down, and we were better organized.)

I had never expected to have to go out and campaign for my husband for President of the United States, but I got so I sort of enjoyed it. At first I was petrified to get up and speak, particularly without a prepared text. In the beginning I used to feel sick. After a while I became so involved I stopped thinking about my stomach and carried on like the rest of the troops.

Nothing came easy. An incumbent President is usually sure of automatic nomination by his own party, but the Republicans were fragmented and it was clear from the start that Jerry wasn't going to be handed the prize; he was going to have to battle for it. We'd known this since the spring of 1975 when a group of conservative Republican Senators had got together to agree that "as neither the President nor the Vice President was elected to office, it would be in the best interest of the Republican Party and of the country for the 1976 presidential and vice presidential nomination to be sought and won in an open convention."

This meant that, for the first ten months of 1976, Jerry would have to fight Ronald Reagan in the state primaries. Then the Republicans would come to Kansas City in mid-August for their National Convention, and if Jerry did get the nomination, his next two months would be spent fighting Henry Jackson or Morris Udall or Jerry Brown or Jimmy Carter or whomever the Democrats put up.

Sometime in April of 1975 (it was in Palm Springs, so it must have been during Easter vacation) we'd had Nancy and Ronald Reagan to dinner. Jerry and Ronnie knew one another through politics, but were not close friends. It was in the wind that Ronnie was going to announce for the Presidency, although he hadn't yet said anything publicly; he was playing it cozy. I think Jerry was hoping to dissuade him, to appeal to him to help unite the party, but of course that never happened. We were all terribly polite, nothing of any consequence was said or done, and when the Reagans left, Jerry and I both knew, without a word's having been spoken, that Ronnie was going to run.

Looking on the bright side of the Reagan candidacy, we thought a primary fight would at least stir up more interest in Republicans of every stripe. But it also put more pressure on me, because for the most part Jerry would only be campaigning on weekends. He had to stay in the Oval Office, there was business to attend to, he couldn't get out and hit all the places, so I had to go. Fortunately for our sanity, the primaries came early in the year (the last ones, in California, Ohio, and New Jersey, all took place on June 8 because by the seventh of July, the round of state dinners was beginning with the televised gala for the Queen of England).

Somewhere I still have a picture of Ike and Mamie and Jerry

and me, a picture taken from the platform of a train in 1956. Jerry was, as usual, running for re-election to the House, and the Eisenhowers were traveling through Michigan on a campaign trip, so we hopped aboard their train in Lansing, and rode with them as far as our hometown, some sixty miles along. That way Jerry would be seen pulling into Grand Rapids with the President, and some Presidential charisma might, it was hoped, rub off on the Congressman.

Twenty years later, Jerry was President, but he was still running. And so was I. At first I'd said I would participate only as a wife, appearing with my husband when he wanted or needed me to. I didn't feel qualified to be a spokesman. But after New Hampshire it was decided that we could cover more ground by going our separate ways. Particularly since, as I've mentioned, Jerry's traveling would have to be limited. The decision made me anxious. I wasn't a good politician, I usually said what was on my mind, and that could cost my husband votes. Still, I agreed to try, and I was dispatched to Florida, where I worked for five days before Jerry came to join me.

During the campaign, Pete Sorum traveled ahead of me. He would sit down with the chairman of the Republican party in the state where our next primary was coming up and say, "Okay, what do you need, and where do you want it? How can we help?" In some cases, the chairman would have ideas; in other cases, he or she wouldn't have the foggiest notion. (Half the time, even when somebody *had* an idea, we had to reject it—it generally involved my giving a major policy speech, which would not have been my long suit.)

Then Pete would come back to Washington and confer with me. I would commit to places I was willing to go, and we would work around my White House schedule to see when we could find time for the trip.

Often, I'd encounter the Reagan entourage, Ronnie, Nancy, Efrem Zimbalist—each candidate has his own road show—at a state convention where the people running things had demanded that a Ford, some Ford, any Ford, appear.

I was treated well. My popularity seemed to hold. There was a whole collection of campaign buttons that said things like ELECT BETTY'S HUSBAND, KEEP BETTY IN THE WHITE HOUSE, I LOVE BETTY.

I was amused the first time I was sent one, but thought I'd better put it away before Jerry came in. When he walked through the door that night, he laughed and said, "Look what I got today," and tossed an I LOVE BETTY button onto a table.

Ranging the country, I visited dozens of towns and cities (one weekend in New England, I covered Manchester, Salem, Boston, Concord, Durham; one weekend in Michigan, my train stopped in Flint, Durand, Lansing, Battle Creek, Kalamazoo, Niles, Grand Rapids, Saginaw) so what follows are highly selective adventures from a few of the fifty states.

New Hampshire. This was a family trip, and of course New Hampshire was our first primary. We all started out together. Jerry and I stayed overnight in some nice people's house, and foolishly shut our bedroom door, and nearly froze our toes off in a room which wasn't heated. Then we split up. Susan went north and skied, to pacify any New Hampshire voters who might have been offended by Ron Nessen's saying the Fords found the state "too icy" for their favorite sport; Jerry hit the college campuses; and I visited handicapped children and watched some senior citizens dance the hully gully and telephoned people picked at random out of the directory: "I'm Betty Ford, here in Nashua, campaigning for my husband. I hope you'll support him in the primary."

At one of the places where Jerry spoke—it was a huge gymnasium—a student group started shouting obscenities. Most of the people in the audience were embarrassed by the rudeness, and Jerry finally said, "Everyone has a right to his own opinion," but the hectoring went on. Every time Jerry started to talk, they would scream, "That's a lot of bleep!" as they say on television. The gang was organized, they showed up all over the country for a while, then they just seemed to disappear. P.S. We took New Hampshire.

Florida. My scheduling secretary, Susan Porter, and I decided that Melbourne, Florida, would be a good trip, even though

Melbourne is a small town. For three years the people there had been trying to get a public school dedicated. When I agreed to visit, the school board was so impressed with the principal's being able to produce a First Lady that they came up with a grant to enable the school to build on a wing for handicapped children.

What a celebration we had at the dedication in the school auditorium! I danced with a young boy dressed as George Washington—he bowed very low when he asked me—and a little girl who was supposed to give me a scroll got so nervous she couldn't read the words; I had to lean over and read them for her, and then she turned around and faced the audience with a big smile on her face.

I spoke to citizens in Naples, Florida, and went to Jacksonville, Florida, to appear at Stand Up for America Day. They put me in a hall that would have held eight thousand, and no more than two thousand came. Pete Sorum was furious. He'd warned the officials in charge that they ought to publicize my arrival, but they'd disagreed. "You don't know our town, people turn out, they're very patriotic."

Fact of political life: You can't just put out a press release and assume you'll draw a crowd. The only way you can get people to a political event, Sorum says, is "Tell 'em, 'You can come, you're invited, it's free,' time and time again. Also, you have to keep repeating, 'Betty Ford'—or Mickey Mouse or Louisa May Alcott— 'will be there, she's really coming, it's not just a story somebody's made up.' Because lots of times big shots say they'll show, and they don't."

Texas.   We did a lot of driving through Texas, and I had a good time with my citizens' band radio. I had an agent, Jerry Ball, who was a CBer, and he helped me. We had a book with all the different code names. My handle was First Momma. I belong to the honorary Channel 9, which saves a lot of lives. If you pass an accident, and you have a CB radio, you can put the news right on the air, and the police and an ambulance come to the scene very quickly. I know of one man who's confined to a wheelchair and who spends twelve hours a day on Channel 9 reporting emergency calls.

If you want to talk to truckers, they're usually on Channel 19, and their patter is fun. "Smokeys" means cops, and "a bear in the sky" means a police helicopter, and "ten-four good buddy" means you're coming in loud and clear.

California. We were trying to recruit celebrities to raise money for the campaign, so we gave a party for about 150 movie and television stars at a restaurant in Beverly Hills. Farrah Fawcett-Majors was there, Gordon MacRae sang, and Cary Grant was my escort. Karl Schumaker, the photographer who traveled with me, took a color picture of Cary Grant and me dancing, and when we got home, he blew up the picture and hung it on a wall right smack as you walked into the East Wing, which housed the offices of my staff. I took one look at that handsome, handsome man, and me in his arms, positively pink with pleasure, and I wrote on the picture, right across my dress, "Eat your heart out, girls."

It was another party in Beverly Hills that made me realize my terror of public speaking was not unique to nonprofessionals. There was a dinner honoring the director William Wyler, and each of us at the head table was expected to say a few words. All these other women had played Mrs. Miniver or Jezebel, they were actresses, so I assumed they'd speak extemporaneously. I didn't know how I was going to be able to offer my salute, which I had written out on cards in my bag, without feeling like a klutz. Audrey Hepburn had flown in from Rome to say a poem for Wyler, and Merle Oberon was there, and Helen Reddy, and then, when it came time to call on these different people, out came *their* cards from their purses and their pockets and I was enormously relieved. Nobody wanted to be up there without a crutch.

I campaigned in Los Angeles' Chinatown, surrounded by Chinese children. There was a wonderful fierce dragon with flashing eyes who moved to drum beats which were supposed to chase away evil spirits. (The dragon had some little boys in his belly to give him legs.) While I was talking the children started throwing confetti, and I got a mouthful of the stuff. I was given two lovely Chinese jackets and an enormous fortune cooky, which, when broken open, revealed a typewritten assurance that the Honorable

Gerald R. Ford was going to be the next duly elected President of the United States. Anyway, I've still got the two jackets.

I campaigned in San Francisco, where everybody wanted to know if I'd really called Wayne Hays (who was accused of keeping a mistress on his payroll) "a fine gentleman." Ron Nessen tried to bail me out by saying I'd been misquoted, but I couldn't let him perjure himself. "Representative Hays is a good friend of ours. I probably did call him a fine gentleman," I said. But I reminded United Press, "I also said I was glad it was his problem, not mine."

Indiana. I rode a carousel at the opening of a children's museum in Indianapolis (I was irritable because my horse didn't go up and down; it just sat there) and I christened a brand-new 747 jet plane. (First Ladies are much in demand for christening planes. In Washington I christened the Bicentennial jet, decorated by Alexander Calder. I broke a bottle of champagne over its nose, then stuck my fingers into the stuff running down the plane and tasted it to see if it was really champagne. It was, but I suddenly thought, Oh oh, how undignified, old girl; you shouldn't have done that.

The foregoing ought to give you some idea. Proceeding on the assumption that people like to see a candidate's family, a candidate's wife shakes hands, holds babies, visits with old folks, drinks gallons of coffee, gives a little speech or does a little dance, and hopes she's more of a plus than a minus to her husband.

Two of us candidates' wives were very prominently featured at the Republican National Convention in Kansas City in August of 1976. A good deal has been written about Nancy Reagan and me, and how our boosters cheered our appearances as though she and I, and not our husbands, were the contestants.

The night most people remember, I was already on the floor of the arena when the band started playing "Tie a Yellow Ribbon Round the Old Oak Tree." Tony Orlando was there with me and Susan, and Susan said, "That's your song, Tony. Come on, you and Mom get up and dance." Susan had learned a few tricks on the campaign trail. She was wearing a blue denim shirt that had FORD spelled out between her shoulder blades, and she kept turning her back to the cameras. (We were never out of camera range.) Anyhow, she egged me and Tony on, we got up and danced for the sheer silliness of it, and I had no idea that Nancy Reagan was making her entrance into the hall at the very same time. I've been accused of trying to take the play away from her. What play? My feeling was that Nancy didn't want to play. She sat in a glassed-in box, separated from the hurly-burly, throughout the whole convention, except for the time she went upstairs to the television booth to be interviewed. I wouldn't go up there to be interviewed. I sat right in the front row of the gallery. "If they want me, they can come down here," I said.

The Republicans got their open convention. Months before, Nelson Rockefeller had taken himself out of the running for Vice President. He knew the conservatives in the party would never support him, and he didn't want to be a burden to Jerry. Early on, Jerry had tried to argue—"I don't dump good teammates," he said—but the pressure had got to Rockefeller. He told Jerry he did not want to be a candidate in 1976.

Our whole family turned out for the convention. Up until then, Mike and Steve hadn't done any politicking. "Politics is not for me, it's my old man's game," Steve said, and Mike agreed. (Gayle was even more elusive. As a social worker, she continued to use her maiden name, believing if anyone knew she was a Ford it would spoil her relationship with the people she was trying to help. At Christmas, we had to have two group pictures taken, one with Gayle, for the family, the other without her, for the newspapers.)

But even Mike and Steve got involved at the convention. When their father was nominated, there couldn't have been more thumping on backs and cheering and jumping up and down.

There was cheering in Independence, Missouri, too. Darling Bess Truman wrote and told me she was thrilled. She forgot to stay up the night of the balloting, and the next morning she turned on the radio and found that Jerry had won the nomination. "I let out such a whoop and a holler that my maid came running in to find out what was wrong with me," she said in her letter.

In the two months left before the general election, Mike

actually took some speaking engagements, and he got a few of his friends, fellows who were also studying for the ministry, involved in the campaign.

Susan was a terrific asset because she put on no airs and refused to become embroiled in debates she didn't understand. One day, while exhorting a crowd of people to go to the polls and vote, she cried, "Be sure to get out there on November fourth!" then blushed. "I mean on November second. I'm having my wisdom teeth out on November fourth."

I thought that was nice; it showed she was a young girl with other things on her mind besides the election.

Jack, of course, being the only Ford child who was actively fascinated by politics, worked harder than any of the others. He never felt that his father's being President helped him a bit, in fact he felt it was a disadvantage (he had a degree in forestry, yet he insisted that every time he got a job lined up, it would turn out to involve federal funds and therefore be denied him). But he was the best speaker in the family, and he took it upon himself to see that the "real message" about Jerry got out. Jack could really do it, talk about the economy, foreign policy, energy, conservation.

After the convention, the campaign picked right up again, with a change in opponents. Now, instead of Ronald Reagan, Jerry and Bob Dole were confronting Jimmy Carter and Walter Mondale.

Events and places jostle one another in my memory. Lunch in a university cafeteria in Oregon, and three demonstrators standing on tables, yelling at me . . . a trip to Philadelphia for dedication of a Bicentennial sculpture by Louise Nevelson, and Nevelson in a stocking cap under a jockey cap, a long black gown, and chorus-girl eyelashes . . . a stop in Sioux Falls, South Dakota, five minutes to say hello to a thousand Shriners . . . a stop in Independence, Missouri, five minutes to meet in an airplane hangar with people raising money for crippled children . . . the time I got mad at Pete Sorum because he'd scheduled me through an eighteen-hour day, and I said, "I don't want to do this next speech, what I want to do is go to a hotel and take a shower," and then I went out and did the next speech, and Pete said it was the most riproaring get-out-there-and-do-the-job-for-the-President he'd ever heard from me, probably because I was so hopped up with anger.

I never throw screaming fits, but people know when I get mad. Bob Barrett says I'm fine ninety-eight percent of the time; it's the other two percent that can be miserable. I become cool and distant. It's a selfish way to fight. During 1976, I was often on a shorter string than usual because I got so tired, and because I was more sensitive to criticism of Jerry than he was. I hated people's saying he was dumb. I thought all that Chevy Chase slapstick stuff was stupid; it really wasn't funny to me. So Jerry bumped his head going through the door to a helicopter. Big deal. I watched my press secretary, who was five foot two, bump her head trying to get through the same door.

In New York, I sneaked away one night and went to a benefit for Martha Graham. Nureyev and Fonteyn were performing (Halston had made Rudi a gold jockstrap) and Woody Allen was my escort. Sort of. He also had Diane Keaton with him. He was wearing black tie and brand-new high-topped tennis shoes, and he hung back when the press asked him about his association with Martha. He said he'd given up dancing because he was so sensitive about the way he looked in leotards. Very funny man, but very very shy.

In Denver, I saw half a football game, but had to leave because I was going to Buffalo, so I could ride in the Pulaski Day Parade on the following morning. There are a lot of Polish-Americans in Buffalo. When we left Denver, the sun was shining, and the temperature was seventy-five degrees. In Buffalo it was forty degrees and raining buckets. About two hundred people, including school children, were waiting for me at the airport, every one of them, according to Sorum, expecting to shake my hand in the rain. That time I shook my head. "I don't know what you're going to do with all those people," I said, "but I'm going to the car."

Next day I redeemed myself. I'd been named grand marshal of the parade, which meant I would ride up front. The Carter forces, having discovered that I was going to Buffalo, normally a Democratic stronghold, countered by sending Senator Mondale to town. I knew he and I would wind up in the reviewing stand together before the festivities concluded, and the press would want pictures of our meeting.

I was prepared. Pete Sorum had provided me with a green-and-white "Keep Betty in the White House" button (green and white happened to be the Carter campaign colors) and I stuck it in my pocket. When Senator Mondale, a very polite man, came up on the platform, I said, "I have something for you; I believe these are your colors," and pinned the thing right on his lapel. He looked down and smiled and said thanks and I don't know how long it was before he got a chance to really read what it said and rip it off.

Of the three Ford-Carter debates, I only made it to the last one, in Williamsburg, Virginia, ten days before the election. During the first two debates, I was on the road myself, and those nights I sat in strange hotel rooms watching the two men on television, on the edge of my seat, waiting for each word, then wondering what the papers were going to say in the morning. The first debate was conceded to Jerry, the second to Carter, the third came out pretty much a draw. I think we Ford people were all surprised that Carter was as good and as well informed as he was.

I campaigned clear up till the election. November 1, I started the day in New York, flew to Harrisburg, did a Rotary Club luncheon, then flew to Detroit to meet Jerry. The two of us were scheduled to go to a Detroit suburb for the big Welcome Back to Michigan, You're Our Boy kind of thing, and then head for Grand Rapids and a torchlight parade, and the dedication of the Gerald Ford Gymnasium at Grand Rapids Junior College.

I knew the ceremonies would go on till eleven o'clock that night, and the next morning was going to be a killer. I would have to get up at five o'clock, have my hair done at six, and be ready to look alive by seven because Jerry and I had to be seen voting on nationwide television at seven-thirty-two. (Jimmy Carter was going to be televised voting at seven.)

This is the way Pete Sorum remembers our flight from Detroit to Grand Rapids. "I expressed my concern to Mrs. Ford's secretary,

Carolyn Porembka, about Mrs. Ford's going to this gymnasium thing. I was afraid she'd be wiped out, and never make the picture the next morning, and that would be awful.

"I checked with some other people and they said, 'If she's going to cut out of anything, the dedication's the one to cut out of. It's not that big a deal one way or another.'

"So Carolyn goes up to talk to her and comes back and says, 'Mrs. Ford agrees; she's not going to do the dedication tonight.' About fifteen minutes later the steward comes back and says, 'Mrs. Ford wants you.' I go up front to the President's office, and they're sitting across the table from each other, and she looks at me and says, 'My husband wants me to go with him tonight.'

"I look at the President, and he says he respects my judgment, but it's important for him to have her with him on all the Grand Rapids things. I can see a little sparkle in her eye, a kind of 'since he really wants me there, I'm going to do it' look."

That's a factual report. We went to the gym dedication, and I still managed to rise at the crack of dawn, get myself dressed and fixed up and into Jerry's limousine. I wanted to go have some breakfast before the voting-cum-TV-pictures, but Jerry was out in back of the hotel working every last hand he could find. Finally, I just picked up his microphone—the car had an internal sound system—and said over the loudspeaker, "I want to thank you all for coming out," and Jerry realized I was in his car, playing with his toy. He turned around, ran over, got in, and we drove away.

We were on our way to vote, to try to keep the thirty-eighth President of the United States in office for another four years.

35

NATURAL SHOCKS

In the madness of a political campaign, it's easy to get off the track. When you're caught up in the fever of wanting to win, priorities can become distorted.

Sometimes calamity has to strike, snap you up short, before you relearn the things that are really important.

In June of 1976, I went to the Hilton Hotel in New York for a Jewish National Fund Dinner. Milton Hoffman, a good friend of Jerry's and mine—he's the one who donated the new rooms to the Hospital for Sick Children—was on the dais with me, and Dr. Maurice Sage, the fund's president, was in charge of the festivities.

There were probably three thousand people in the ballroom, even the balconies were filled, and CBS was filming the whole affair. Dr. Sage was about to present me with a Bible from Jerusalem, a beautiful Bible bound in silver, its cover set with stones. He was speaking when, all of a sudden, he handed the Bible over to Tex McCrary, and he, Dr. Sage, sat down on the steps behind the podium. Tex McCrary went on with the presentation, and I thought it was all happening as it was supposed to happen, that, at any moment, Tex would offer me the Bible, Dr. Sage would stand up, and we would pose for the photographers.

Then Martin Hoffman, Milton's son, turned around in his chair and looked back and saw Dr. Sage reaching into his pocket, and realized the man was trying to get a nitroglycerin tablet to put under his tongue; he was having a heart attack.

Martin came to the microphone and shouted, "Is there a doctor in the house? Please come to the podium." With that, my agents, who were trained in emergency resuscitation, rushed up and pushed the tables back—it was a large dais with several tiers; more than a hundred people were seated there—and tried to bring Dr. Sage around. I can remember their pounding on his chest.

I went back to my seat to get out of the way. Everybody was pushing in, and I knew Dr. Sage would need air. The hotel was not prepared for an emergency; it seemed like forever before a woman, apparently a doctor, came to the platform and oxygen arrived from someplace. By then everybody in the ballroom was standing, trying to see what was going on. Nobody knew what to do.

I didn't know what to do either, but I felt someone had to do something. I truly believed that if I could get up there and pray, and get all those people to pray with me, we might somehow save Dr. Sage's life.

I moved to the microphone and asked the people to bow their heads, and I asked God's blessing on Rabbi Sage. It was a simple prayer, along the lines of "We know You can take care of him, we know You can bring him back to us, we know You are our leader and our strength."

After that, I asked everyone to pray silently, each in his own way.

Dr. Sage remained alive until he reached the hospital, but he died shortly thereafter.

It was a shocking business for everyone, and I've been highly praised for the way I behaved on that night at the Hilton, but I don't think praise is warranted. What I did was instinctive, not an act of will. I read a story about Jack Nicholson, the actor, being thrown from a horse while making a movie. He landed in the dirt on his face, broke his wrist, blackened his lip, and climbed back on the horse to do the scene again. "I was scared," he said later. "I wouldn't have gotten back on the horse if I were a real person."

For some people in a public situation (as opposed to private life, where you're "a real person"), an inner strength takes over, and you don't know where it comes from, and you can't take credit for it. At such times, no matter how scared I am, I seem to be able to carry on.

Even earlier in the spring of 1976, before the nightmarish scene with Dr. Sage, Jerry and I had been dealt a couple of personal blows.

First, Phoebe Stiles Seay died.

It wasn't surprising, she'd been unwell for a long time, but it was still a shock, if that makes any sense. And then the strangest thing happened. No more than three weeks later, Jack Stiles had an automobile accident.

He'd been working at Jerry's campaign headquarters in Washington, but he'd gone back to Michigan to see about filing his income-tax return, because Michigan was where he lived and voted. Driving through Grand Rapids on a bad night, his car went out of control at a railroad crossing, hit a signal, and bounced into a ditch. He was killed instantly.

Nobody found him until the next morning. He was down in the ravine, and nobody saw the car.

Our lives—Jerry's and mine—had been so interwoven with Jack's and Phoebe's lives. I thought about the skiing trips before she and I could ski, and the violinist who'd played for us in the restaurant overlooking the Bay of Naples, and the times when we'd all had too much wine and not enough sense, but it hadn't mattered because we were young, and a night's sleep was the cure for anything.

Poor Jack. Poor Phoebe. They hadn't been as lucky as Jerry and I. Whether or not my husband would win the election, we had still come out way ahead, and I knew it.

36

ELECTION
NIGHT AND AFTER

As David Kennerly remembers it:

"The trend was pretty well set around eleven or twelve o'clock. Mrs. Ford stayed up after the President went to bed. I never saw her break down in any way at all. She was the one who was actually cheering everybody up. All the kids were, you know, down, but in moments of crisis she seems to become much stronger."

As Susan remembers it:

"That night I was a basket case. I went down to Winston's for an hour or so with a couple of girlfriends, hoping to have a laugh, but it didn't work so we came back to the White House to watch the returns with Pearl Bailey and the Joe Garagiolas and Clara, the ever-present Powell, and at four-thirty A.M., I fell asleep on the floor, all dressed and waiting to go to the Sheraton, to the room where they'd been receiving the returns. We'd been supposed to go over to the party, what would have been a victory party. We never went. Somebody woke me and said, 'Susan, go upstairs and go to bed,' and I said, 'Is there a chance?' and they said, 'No,' and I just ignored that. I got into bed and turned on the TV and fell right back to sleep."

As I remember it:

There were a lot of people in the family quarters on the second floor. Senator Dole and his wife, Liddy. Janet Ford, Senator Javits, friends from Grand Rapids, as well as the friends Susan named. We had several television sets going, and Jerry wandered from his study off the bedroom to the West Sitting Hall, spending time with everyone, but not able to say much because in the last few days of campaigning he'd developed laryngitis.

At about 3 A.M., his chief of staff, Dick Cheney, and Bob Teeter, a pollster, came upstairs and asked to speak to Jerry privately. Jerry invited Senator Javits to step into a small side room with him and listen to what the men had to say. Teeter told Jerry that the way the numbers were shaping up he was probably not going to win, and Jerry asked him to come in and tell the rest of us.

Then Jerry, who was worn out, said goodnight and went to bed.

I stayed up, and Janet and the children stayed with me and waited until it was obvious that we'd lost. I was prepared for it. Still, you don't go through a fight like that without wanting to win, and you can't help but have a feeling of regret that you haven't accomplished what you set out to do. It's a disappointment with yourself; you feel if you'd only gone to such and such a place, given such and such a speech, made such and such a point. You think you've done as much as possible, but when the election is so close— 40.8 million votes to 39.1 million votes; Carter won by only two percent—you're sure that with a little more push your man could have taken it.

I mean, the Republican party doesn't have that many registered voters, so with the election that close there had to be Democrats and Independents voting for Jerry, and I believe if the campaign had gone on just one week longer he would have won, turned the thing around. It was a last-minute horse race, the candidates neck and neck, and Jerry still climbing in the polls when it was over.

I know people who said they just couldn't vote for him because he'd pardoned Nixon. The pardon, the choice of Senator Dole, who was perceived as a hatchet man, the split in the party caused by Ronald Reagan, surely all of these contributed to Jerry's defeat; but I still think the people made a big mistake when they didn't elect him. He had stabilized the country, things were moving smoothly, getting better, and he should have been given a chance to prove what more he could do.

So much for wifely noises.

Next morning, Jerry woke up and now he wasn't just hoarse, he couldn't speak at all. At about ten o'clock, after having reviewed the returns, he sent Jimmy Carter a telegram congratulating him on his victory.

Susan came into the bathroom while I was getting dressed, and she says I was singing, which so confused her that she cried, "Mom, did we win?" and I said, "No, you kids got a father back, and I got my husband back," whereupon Susan burst into tears. (She cried off and on for the rest of the day. She'd get hold of herself and then she'd meet someone who'd say, "Gee, Susan, I'm really sorry," and that would cause a fresh deluge.)

We had to decide what to do about Jerry's concession speech. He couldn't read it; he had no voice. We thought of Jack. Jack had been the most involved in the campaign, he had known the issues, been informed about the platform, had never ducked a hard question; he was obviously the person to substitute for his father. But the defeat hit Jack very hard. "No," he said. "No, no, I won't do it."

It was no good to turn to Mike, he and Gayle detested the spotlight, and Susan and Steve weren't logical candidates, so it came down to me.

The children and I went to the Oval Office and Jerry was already there. He hugged and kissed all of us, and Susan went over and stood beside a window and tried to stop crying so that she could walk into the press room with the rest of us.

In the press room, I read the speech.

My whole family was standing behind me, looking very sad, but so far as I was concerned, it was a matter of facing facts. I'd been through many elections with Jerry, I knew someone had to win, and someone had to lose, and we lost.

"She's not a great public speaker, chokes up a little bit, but she read that concession speech without a hitch," Kennerly says. "Maybe she was glad to read it, I don't know."

I'm not sure myself. If you look over what I've just said in the last page or two, you can see I was conflicted. My conviction that my husband was the better man, my dissatisfaction that we hadn't been able to win with him, these were real. But so was my vision of a soon-to-be-restored private life, and my relief that our ordeal was over.

Dinner, that night after the election, was one of the most hilarious family get-togethers in the history of the Fords. It was gallows humor, I suppose. The children were all there, and by that time everybody had accepted the idea that we'd been battered and defeated, and we were in a strange, manic mood. We talked and talked and talked (except for Jerry, who could only croak from time to time), everybody telling wild stories about what happened to him or her during the campaign, what had happened in Duluth, what had happened in Sioux City. For so long we'd been going in different directions, and we'd never before had a chance to get together and sit down and discuss our adventures.

If you'd heard us at that meal, you'd have thought we'd all gone mad, but I've never been more proud of my now speechless husband and my tough, good-hearted children. I know Jerry was unhappy about losing, he's a very competitive man, but he sat there with the rest of us, and you could see his shoulders heaving, even if you couldn't hear his laughter.

The next day Susan had four wisdom teeth pulled, and we offered her, as a treat, a trip to Palm Springs with us. We were going out to California to start looking around seriously for a place to spend our old age. We'd be living in the White House for almost three more months—Inauguration Day would be January 20—but we had to make some decisions for the future.

Thirteen years earlier, my doctor had said that someday I would probably need to live in a hot, dry climate because of my arthritis, and I'd laughed at him. Now I'd got to the point where I could predict the weather with my bones, and I understood what the doctor had been trying to tell me.

At first Susan said she wouldn't come to Palm Springs; she couldn't afford to miss ten days at Mount Vernon. Then she rethought her position. School wasn't going well for her, she was going to transfer to Kansas University in January anyway, so why not take a little vacation?

We had been coming to Palm Springs at Easter for about fifteen years. Not only did the town offer me a good climate, it featured dozens of golf courses for Jerry, and we'd made friends there, so it was a natural place for us to retire to.

Susan wasn't impressed. "If you're going to be happy here, that's fine," she said. "I'll just be visiting, and I can put up with it for ten days two or three times a year."

(I mention this only because on her spring break from K.U. in 1977 she came to Palm Springs, met a lot of young people, fell in love with the place, and hit her father for the down payment on a condominium.)

We arranged to rent, starting the following February, a house in a part of the Palm Springs area called Thunderbird Estates, where we could be comfortable until we built a place of our own. (It was up high, very secluded, with a spectacular view of the mountains. I couldn't wait to get away from all that privacy. Our new house faces the thirteenth fairway of the Thunderbird Country Club, we share a tennis court owned by our old friends Len and Nicky Firestone, and we've got room for family and guests and my wardrobe and maybe even that portrait by John Ulbricht.)

Usually an incoming President's people stay in their own bailiwick and let an outgoing President finish his term; they don't show up on your doorstep until around the first of January. But Carter's workers were with us from November on, for the entire three months. I know it bothered Jerry, and he could easily have told them, "This or that information is not yet available to you," but being the man he is, he instructed his staff to cooperate with Carter's staff.

"I want this transition made as smoothly as possible," he said.

37

AN END AND A BEGINNING

For me, leaving the White House wasn't nearly so much of a wrench as leaving our house in Alexandria. After we decided we weren't going to move back and put the house up for sale, I never went over there again. I didn't want to. We had built the place, the children had grown up there, all of our neighbors were friends. We'd been to so many block parties and Fourth of July celebrations, we'd planted gardens and put in trees, and I knew if I saw it again it would upset me. I wanted to think of my new life, to look forward.

Our children weren't in Washington on January 20, President Carter's Inauguration Day. There was no reason for them to be there. Of course, President Carter had all his family and relatives around, but that was natural.

Most of our belongings had been sent ahead of us, and what hadn't been was pretty well packed, except for the clothes we were going to wear. But our bed was still there. Rex Scouten had said, "No, your bed doesn't go. You are still President until noon, when you go out of office and President Carter is sworn in. We will move your bed after you leave the house."

On that last morning, the old blue leather chair and the

pictures were already gone. Still, the people in charge did an excellent job of leaving our possessions around until the last minute, so we didn't have the feeling of being pushed out.

The day before we left, I asked Rex if I could go down and say goodbye to the permanent staff. I didn't want them gathered in a crowd, I wanted to talk to individuals, so Rex took me through the kitchen and the furnace room and the flower room, and I spoke to everybody, all the engineers, all the carpenters. We went at a time when there was a change of shifts, and the different departments had been notified that I was coming, so people who were going off duty stayed for a few minutes longer, and the people who were just coming on were also available. I thanked them, and told them how much it had meant to me to have lived here, and how grateful I was for the care they had taken in the matter of our comfort. "Presidents come and go," I said, "but you people are the White House." I went around shaking hands with the nurses, the groundskeepers, Dale, who helped take care of our dogs, Rusty, who was the head flower arranger.

The next morning Jerry and I were both concerned with time and schedule. The Carters were coming to the White House at ten-thirty to have a cup of coffee and a chat before the ride to the Capitol.

I was just anxious to get it over with and get out. It's like when you're going to take a trip, there's all that buildup, and then when the time comes, you really want to go. I think that's the way we both felt.

Jerry had an alarm clock by his side of the bed. (If a clock wouldn't wake you, you could always leave a call with the White House operator, and sometimes when I was alone and it was necessary for me to get up early, I'd ask the operator to phone me twice.)

That morning, however, we were both awake at dawn. My husband went in and had breakfast in the dining room and read the paper just as he did every morning, and I had breakfast in the sitting room, where I had it every morning because, as I've said before, I don't talk before ten o'clock. If I have any choice in the matter.

I bathed, dressed, put on my makeup. I was already counting a blessing. This might be the last time I would have to conform to the kind of split-second schedule which was so foreign to my dilatory nature.

At ten-thirty I was ready, with coat and hat and boots on. It was cold. We wouldn't be coming back to the White House, we would be going right to California after the Inauguration.

I don't remember exactly where we served the Carters coffee. I don't think they came upstairs. I have a feeling we sat in one of the rooms on the ground floor, the Diplomatic Reception Room or the Map Room.

It was a strained situation. We were all human beings, civilized, and the thing you want to do is be as pleasant as possible. You don't charge at one another. But it's uncomfortable. I don't remember anything I said. Probably, "My, it's a lovely day" and "Do you take sugar?"

President Carter and President Ford rode together to the Capitol, a follow-up car with the Secret Service directly behind them, and then Mrs. Carter and I came along in the next car. I tried to assure her that she would love the White House, that I had enjoyed being there and knew she would too, that she'd have a lot of new experiences and be doing lots of traveling. It was just inane conversation. I was glad when we got to the Capitol.

Everybody was already in place, waiting for the four of us. The balcony of the Capitol, on the east side, where the ceremony takes place, was full. Members of Congress were up there, and former Cabinet officers and their families, and the Speaker of the House, and the Vice President. People were even standing up around the columns.

Outside the Capitol, grandstands had been built, all miked so the spectators sitting there could hear everything, and there was an elaborate television studio enclosed in a glass booth way up high on a platform.

Jerry and I were taken down the steps to our seats. Then the Carters were seated, and the thing started. It was a short ceremony.

Nelson Rockefeller stood beside Walter Mondale while Mondale took the oath of office, then Jerry stood beside Jimmy Carter while Carter took his oath. Immediately afterward, in his opening remarks, President Carter did something very nice. "For myself and for our nation," he said, "I want to thank my predecessor for all he has done to heal our land," and he offered Jerry his hand.

It almost broke my heart. Jerry had to stand up there, acknowledging the tremendous applause. After President Carter finished his speech, I got up and we were congratulating the Carters, hoping everything would go well for them, shaking hands, and all the time what was going on in my head was, Oh, let's get out of here.

Jerry and I walked back up the steps, and then instead of going off to the right where the people would be assembling for the inaugural luncheon, we cut to the left, toward the House of Representatives, and as we walked through the halls, the Rockefellers behind us, there were all these Capitol police stationed along the way, some of whom Jerry had known since he came to Congress in 1948.

We said goodbye, as we passed, and thank you, and all the while I was hoping I wouldn't cry. And then we came out on the steps at the west side of the Capitol, and again there were crowds massed at the bottom, applauding and cheering, and we had to wave some more. It was then, coming down those steps, that I really broke up inside. But I kept smiling. I didn't want anyone to know how much it really hurt. All our married life was being left there; I don't know how else to explain it. We were married, we went to Washington, looked for a place to live and found it, our children were born there, Jerry's twenty-eight years of work had been there, and I felt as if the whole thing had just gone down the drain.

The TV cameras followed us all the way to the helicopter. I was so glad when I saw the replay on television that what I was feeling didn't show. I was just waving and smiling, and I've had people say, "Oh, you were great, coming down the steps," and I thought, Thank goodness, I put on a good act.

Somebody had got special permission to bring the helicopter in and put it right down on the lawn at the Capitol. Nelson, Happy, Jerry, and I climbed aboard and the helicopter took off, leaving all those people on the ground looking after us.

On its way to Andrews Air Force Base the helicopter circled the city. The pilot flew over the White House and the Lincoln Memorial and around the Jefferson Memorial and the Washington Monument. Every time we'd flown in from Camp David, we'd gone past the Washington Monument, so close you'd feel as though you could reach out and touch it, and they were taking us by it for the last time.

There was a small honor guard waiting for us at Andrews. We put our arms around Nelson and Happy, saying goodbye to them, and then we boarded Air Force One, which was going to fly us to Pebble Beach, California, where Jerry would play in a golf tournament.

That was the best thing in the world for Jerry, to have to go right out and jump into a tournament—the Bing Crosby Tournament, which was already in progress. We'd spend a couple of days in Pebble Beach with the Crosbys and other friends, then fly straight to Houston for a dinner in memory of Vince Lombardi, the great football coach. The dinner was a benefit to raise money for cancer. Sometime before the election Jerry had accepted the invitation to be guest of honor, and now, as we flew across the country, he was brooding. Would the fundraisers be happy with an ex-President? "They thought they'd be getting a sitting President."

"Don't worry, darling," I said. "It's me they're coming to see."

38

LONG BEACH

I had thought my book was finished. I had not expected to write this chapter. But neither had I expected to wind up in the Long Beach Naval Hospital's Alcohol and Drug Rehabilitation Service. So much for my crystal ball.

Lately, some stories have surfaced about my drinking in the White House, and having behaved on certain public occasions like a "zombie." Bull. (That's part of my new Navy vocabulary.) I was fine when I was in the White House. I had no problem handling myself, despite my present conviction—painfully gained, and offered with handsight—that I'd have been better off to have thrown away my pills, turned down my glass, and gone for a long walk whenever I was hurting.

But it wasn't until after I retired to Palm Springs, and private life, that my family noticed I was in trouble. For fourteen years I'd been on medications for the pinched nerve, the arthritis, the muscle spasms in my neck, and I'd lost my tolerance for pills. If I had a single drink, the alcohol, on top of the pills, would make me groggy. In the fall of 1977, I went to Moscow to narrate "The Nutcracker" ballet for television, and later there were comments about my "sloe-eyed, sleepy-tongued" performance. Still, I can't say I knew what was happening to me. Jerry and the children were worried, but I had no idea how much I had changed.

It was Susan who first went into action. She and I had both been patients of a particular doctor, and later Susan had worked with this man on a photo assignment. I guess they got to talking about me and he decided that what I needed was an "intervention." (The thinking used to be that a chemically addicted person— whether on pills or alcohol—had to hit bottom, decide *he* wanted to get well, before he could begin to recover; but it's now been demonstrated that a sick person's family, along with others significant and important to the patient, can intervene to help him despite himself. With this new intervention method, the recovery rate has increased significantly.)

Toward the end of last March, while Jerry was in the East on a speaking tour, the aforementioned doctor, along with Susan, Clara (who was visiting us at the new Palm Springs house), and my secretary, Caroline Coventry, all came marching into my sitting room and started talking about my giving up all medication and liquor. It was brave of them, but I wasn't in the mood to admire them for their courage; I was completely turned off. I got very mad, and was so upset that, after everyone had left, I called a friend and complained about the terrible invasion of my privacy. I don't remember making the telephone call; the friend has told me about it.

That was just preamble. On the morning of the first of April, 1978—it was a Saturday—I was walking around thinking about phoning Mike and Gayle in Pittsburgh, where they had been living and working, when the front door opened and in came Mike and Gayle, along with the entire family. At first, I was just happy to see them all. I thought they'd gathered because I wasn't feeling well, and I was thrilled. We hugged and kissed and then we went and sat down in the living room, I on the couch, they in chairs in a semicircle in front of me.

For some reason, I can tell you where every single person in that room was sitting; the floor plan is burned in my brain. Besides

Jerry and the boys and Susan and Gayle, Captain Joe Pursch, the Navy doctor who's head of the Alcohol and Drug Rehabilitation Service at Long Beach, was there, and so was a Navy nurse. And they all proceeded to confront me with a second intervention. Only this time, they meant business. They'd met together, and with Captain Pursch's guidance, the family had prepared what they were going to say.

I can't remember the words. I was in shock. I've been told that Susan harked back to the days before I'd stopped drinking the first time, and said she'd had to turn to Clara when I wasn't available, and Mike and Gayle spoke of wanting children, and wanting those children's grandmother to be healthy and in charge of her own life, and Jerry mentioned times when I'd fallen asleep in the chair at night, and times when my speech had slurred, and Steve brought up a recent weekend when he and a girlfriend had cooked dinner for me and I wouldn't come to the table on time. "You just sat in front of the TV," Steve said, "and you had one drink, two drinks, three drinks. You hurt me."

Well, he hurt me back. All of them hurt me. I collapsed into tears. But I still had enough sense to realize they hadn't come around just to make me cry; they were there because they loved me and wanted to help me.

Yet I continued to resist any suggestion that liquor had contributed to my illness; all I would confess to was overmedication. Captain Pursch told me it didn't matter, and gave me the book *Alcoholics Anonymous*, and told me to read it, substituting the words "chemically dependent" for "alcoholic." A tranquilizer or a dry martini, each brings the same relief, so for drugs or alcohol you use the same book. And when I say drugs, I'm talking about legal medications, prescribed by doctors.

At first, I was bitter toward the medical profession. Fourteen years of being advised to take pills, rather than wait for the pain to hit. I had never been without my drugs. I took pills for pain, I took pills to sleep, I took mild tranquilizers. Today things are changing, doctors are being educated right along with the rest of us, but some of them used to be all too eager to write prescriptions. It was easier to give a woman tranquilizers and get rid of her than to sit and listen to her.

(The odd thing is that I had already tapered myself off one medication, and was beginning to work on letting go of another, when the intervention started. But my family felt I couldn't do it alone, and set in motion the train of events which would lead me to Long Beach. They had been concerned since the previous Christmas. I'd thought Christmas had been wonderful—lots of gaiety, lots of snow, and Vail especially beautiful—but Jerry and the children were observing danger signs. Now I realize that after my trip to Russia I began to suffer lapses of memory; there were things I couldn't seem to fit into the right consecutive slots.)

My sixtieth birthday came at the end of that week which had begun with the intervention in Palm Springs. We celebrated at a luncheon with presents and friends and family. We drank fruit juice.

Two days later, I went to Long Beach—partly because I was so impressed with Captain Pursch, partly because Long Beach was only two and a half hours from home, and I wanted to be near my family. I could have gone to a private hospital, but I decided if I was going to go all the way as far as my treatment was concerned, it was better to do it publicly rather than to try and hide behind a silk sheet.

I asked Jerry if it would be all right if I signed myself into Long Beach, and he said yes. I think it was very hard on him. When someone you love is in trouble, you blame yourself, you think it must be partly your fault that you couldn't save the other person. Jerry had been trying to save me, but there wasn't anything effective he could do until he had gotten some expert advice.

I entered Long Beach to rid myself of dependence on drugs. Even now, I think staying off medication will be harder for me than staying off liquor because I have pain which comes often. For the present, I seem to be dealing with it. It's mind over matter a lot.

I wrote out a statement which said I'd been overmedicating

myself. "It's an insidious thing and I mean to rid myself of its damaging effects." This statement would be released to the press once I was safely ensconced in the hospital.

I drove to Long Beach. There were news cameras waiting for me as I arrived. On the fourth floor of the hospital, Captain Pursch met me and took me down the hall to what I expected would be a private room. There was no reason for me to think otherwise. I'd been in hospitals before, but always had privacy. Now we came into a room with four beds, and there were clothes around, and it was obvious other people lived here.

I balked. I was not going to sign in, I was not going to release my statement, and I knew the hospital couldn't release it until I gave the okay. Captain Pursch was used to this sort of thing, and perfectly able to handle it. "If you insist on a private room," he said, "I will have all these ladies move out—"

Brilliant man. He put the ball right in my court. "No, no, I won't have that," I said very quickly, very self-consciously, and an hour later I was settled in with three roommates, and my statement was being read to reporters by Bob Barrett, who threw in a thought of his own. Mrs. Ford didn't like the drowsiness caused by her medication, Barrett said, because "she can't raise hell in that condition."

On April 15, at the end of my first week in Long Beach, my son Steve, caught by a reporter outside the hospital, said I was fighting the effects not only of pills but of alcohol. I wasn't enchanted. I wasn't yet prepared to sign off on that. It took me another few days.

It took me, literally, until the 2 P.M. meeting on the twentieth of April in Captain Pursch's office. Jerry and I were there, along with several doctors and a Navy man who was my group-therapy counselor.

Up until that point, I had been talking about medications, while everyone nodded respectfully. Now these doctors told me they wanted me to admit that I was also an alcoholic. They wanted me to make a public statement about it. I refused. "I don't want to embarrass my husband," I said.

"You're trying to hide behind your husband," Captain Pursch said. "Why don't you ask him if it would embarrass him if you say you're an alcoholic?"

I started to cry, and Jerry took my hand. "There will be no embarrassment to me. You go ahead and say what should be said."

With that, my crying got worse. When Jerry took me back to my room, I was still sobbing so hard I couldn't get my breath. My nose and ears were closed off, everything was closed off, my head felt like a balloon. I was gasping, my mouth wide open, sure my air was going to be cut off. I hope I never have to cry like that again. It was scary, but once it was over, I felt a great relief.

Afterward, I made it down to physiotherapy. Best to keep busy, best to keep moving.

That night, while Jerry lounged in a chair and read the newspaper, I sat propped up on my bed, scrawling yet another statement. "I have found that I am not only addicted to the medications I have been taking for my arthritis, but also to alcohol," I wrote. "This program is well known throughout the country and I am pleased to have the opportunity to attend it. I expect this treatment and fellowship to be a solution for my problems, and I embrace it not only for me but for all the others who are here to participate."

It was a big step for me to write that, to let it be printed and broadcast and circulated, but it was only the first of many steps that I would have to take.

The reason I rejected the idea that I was an alcoholic was that my addiction wasn't dramatic. So my speech had become deliberate. So I forgot a few telephone calls. So I fell in the bathroom and cracked three ribs. But I never drank for a hangover, and in fact I used to criticize people who did. At house parties, I would look at friends who knocked back Bloody Marys in the morning, and I would think, isn't that pathetic?

I hadn't been a solitary drinker, either; I'd never hidden bottles in the chandeliers or the toilet tanks. When Jerry was away, there had always been neighbors to have cocktails with, either at their houses or at our house, and at Washington luncheons I'd never touched anything but an occasional glass of sherry. There had been no broken promises (my husband never came to me and said, "Please quit") and no drunken driving. I worried about my children too much to risk taking them anywhere in a car when I'd been drinking. And I never wound up in jail, or in a strange part of town with a bunch of sailors.

Until Long Beach.

I love the sailors at Long Beach, because together we embarked on a great adventure. We were all on a first-name basis—everywhere I went, people called, "Hi, Betty"—and as we struggled with our dependencies and our terrors, each of us held out his hands to the others.

The drug and alcohol rehabilitation program was started in the Long Beach Naval Shipyard in 1965, in a condemned Quonset hut. This was an undercover operation, because the armed forces claimed they had no alcoholism. However, in 1974 the Navy finally faced the fact that there was a problem, and the program was moved to the fourth floor of the Long Beach Naval Hospital. It was designed to help active-duty Navy personnel and their dependents. You mix with admirals and Navy cooks and Navy nurses and children who have come there to learn how to deal with their addicted parents, and parents who are ready at last to want to know their children.

While I was at Long Beach, Jerry went through a two-week participatory course; so did Susan. They had therapy—not in my group, in other groups—and Steve spent a few days in the program too. My children worry about themselves now. Science doesn't yet know if there's a genetic factor involved—there may be, but nobody's been able to prove it—yet alcoholics do breed alcoholics. My father was an alcoholic. I never knew it until after he died; it was not something my mother wanted me to know. He didn't drink at home, only on the road, and I'd never have found out except that a friend of my mother's brought it up after my father's funeral.

It's made my children thoughtful. Steve is cautious about even having a beer any more.

I don't think everybody has to stop drinking, I just think *I* had to stop drinking. When I add up the amount of pills I was taking, and put a drink or two on top, I can see how I got to the breaking point. (Things keep coming back to me. Anyone who was around the house used to run to fix me my nightly libation because they could keep it light, whereas when I poured it I'd make it stiff. Jerry would hand me a mild vodka and tonic, and I'd sigh, "Why don't you give me a *normal* drink?")

In our society, we get to know one another over drinks, we associate feasts and celebrations with liquor. We think we have to drink, that it's a social necessity. Looking back over this book, written in all sincerity before I knew what the ending would be, I notice how often the subject comes up, from the innocence of my beery "first real fling" at Bennington, to Jackson Seay's "magical martinis" in the White House. I think of the endless toasts at political parties, I think of the European trip with Jack and Phoebe Stiles, and sipping booze out of paper cups, the liquor mixed with melted snow we'd scooped up off the windowsill of our train compartment; how romantic that seemed.

It's romantic as long as you can handle it—for years I could and did—but it's misery when you become addicted.

At Long Beach, the alarm clock of one of my roommates went off at six o'clock every morning. I got up, showered, dressed, made my bed, fixed myself a cup of tea—I never found time enough for breakfast—and then answered the shout "Muster!" which meant roll call. I was in the Navy, after all. Cleaning detail came next, each of us patients being given a housekeeping task on the fourth floor. Then at eight o'clock, for the first couple of weeks, there was something called the Doctors' Meeting. This was an hour in which patients interacted with twenty-one visiting doctors, most of them Navy officers. These doctors were being trained to recognize addiction, and not to push medication to solve people's problems. "If someone's husband or wife dies," Dr. Pursch pointed out, "that person should be allowed to mourn, and not be sedated out of all awareness. To mourn is therapeutic, it's part of living."

Some doctors responded well to the training, some responded badly. There was one who was very unsympathetic. "I resent being waked up at three o'clock in the morning to have to go and de-tox an alcoholic," he said. We didn't let him get away with that. "What if the patient had cancer or diabetes?" someone asked. "Well, that would be different," he said.

We told him it wasn't different. Addiction is a sickness, a terminal sickness; it can be arrested by abstinence, but there is no cure for the disease. (Surprisingly, when a contingent of doctors is through with their two-week stint at Long Be. .ı, a couple of them generally sign themselves in as patients, having discovered that they are alcoholics. Or drug addicts. Or both. Though it didn't happen while I was there.)

On mornings when I didn't have a Doctors' Meeting at eight, I had group therapy at eight forty-five. (And there was always a second group-therapy session right before lunch.) Each group— there are eight groups under treatment at any given time—is composed of six or seven patients and one counselor. It's in these groups that you begin to feel the support, the warmth, the comrade-ship which will be your lifeline back to sobriety. Among my group were a twenty-year-old sailor (a jet mechanic who'd been drinking from the time he was eight years old, who'd gone on the wagon as a teenager, but fallen off again with a bang; quiet, sweet-faced, his skin too gray for a twenty-year-old, his eyes too tired), a young officer (twice married, twice divorced) and a clergyman (addicted to drugs and drink, living on the thin edge of his nerves). At first, I loathed the sessions. I was uncomfortable, unwilling to speak up. Then one day another woman said she didn't think that drinking was a problem, and I became very emotional. I got to my feet. "I'm Betty, and I'm an alcoholic, and I know my drinking has hurt my family," I said. I heard myself, and I couldn't believe it. I was trembling; another defense had cracked.

Nothing you hear in the group is to be repeated outside of the group. You can talk about yourself, but you must respect the confidences of others. In group, you can admit to having wrecked your car and your liver, broken your teeth and your marriage and your dreams, and your group mates will nod and say yes, yes, but you're not alone, and after all, it could be worse, you could still be conning yourself, or cursing your genes, or your doctors, or your luck.

In the end, what it comes down to is you have to take the responsibility for yourself. Never mind that your wife kept a dirty house, or your mother didn't like you, or your husband can't remember your wedding anniversary. Everybody's had disappointments, and anyone can rationalize his actions. I read about a drug and alcohol expert named Muriel Nellis who said there were "vulnerable points in women's lives. . . . There are the stresses of being single, then there is marriage, when contemporary young women are concerned with fulfilling themselves but are frustrated because they must often address themselves to their husbands' careers and families. Then there is the menopausal 'empty nest' syndrome, a very critical time for alcohol and pills."

I've been there. I've written in earlier chapters about feeling sorry for myself when I was left alone to bring up four children, or when I had pain, but none of that matters. Blaming other people for your condition is a total waste of time.

Sometimes I would look at members of my group across a gulf of years. A new girl, the wife of an alcoholic, came in during my last week there. "I want to get my act together," she said, talking the way kids talk these days, and I thought how much I envied the youngsters in this program, the ones in their twenties, in their thirties, even in their forties, because they can get straight and still have their whole lives ahead of them.

Toward the end of my month at Long Beach, I tried to tell my group—we were Group Six, we called ourselves The Six Pack— what they had meant to me, but I couldn't express it in words. I started to cry, and one of the fellows handed me some tissues and said, "Now we know you're going to get better."

You get better when you least expect to, when you're not even trying, when you're down by the coffee machine kibitzing with two black seamen who are playing cards. In my everyday life, I would never have met these men, but they and I helped to heal one another.

Meals at Long Beach were taken in the basement, in a big

cafeteria. Lunch was at a quarter to twelve, and then in the afternoons we had to be back upstairs for a lecture or a film from one to two-thirty, and then there would be another class at two-thirty, and by three o'clock you were usually free for exercise—jogging, volleyball, a walk. After that, a little private time until dinner at five-thirty.

For the early-afternoon activities, all the patients on the fourth floor would come together in a big room full of green plastic chairs (I carried a cushion everywhere to protect my bony bottom), most of us clutching mugs of coffee or tea, secure in the knowledge that, even if we spilled something on the hideous yellow-and-brown rug, nobody would ever notice it. That rug appeared to be printed with a pattern of shredded fried eggs.

Sometimes, we'd have assertiveness training, during which we were told we had the right to be whatever kinds of hairpins we wanted to be, but that we could only change ourselves, not others. I remember a seaman with bright blue eyes sitting on the little stage, the platform, complaining that his wife was a dreadful cook. Improvising a scene with a girl lieutenant, the seaman pretended she was his wife. "Nobody could eat this slop," he began, and the therapist stopped him. "You mustn't criticize her; this is how we get in trouble."

"I'm not in no trouble," said the seaman, and we all broke down laughing, cheering, clapping, because none of us would have been there if we hadn't been in trouble. I wish I could communicate some sense of the fun we had, living moment to moment, while the great issues of the day got themselves settled without us, in the big world beyond the fourth floor.

After I came into the hospital, it was as though a dam had burst. Newspapers and magazines poured in, filled with articles about women and drugs and alcohol. Bags of mail followed, and flowers, and messages sent by well-wishers. One letter was from my cousin George T. Bryant, a gentleman of eighty-seven who lives in Evanston, Illinois.

"It has been a long while since we have communicated," wrote cousin George, "but I felt the need to say Bravo! for Betty Bloomer. I refer, of course, to your forthright and overt handling of a very common problem. If your forebears mean anything, I know you will accomplish your mission. Anna Bloomer, your grandmother and mine, showed her mettle when she lost two husbands, one by death, one by desertion, yet she raised two children to adulthood by her own resourcefulness. As for Hortense, your mother, I always thought of her not only as one of the nicest persons I ever knew, but also as a person who overcame the rough times. Life wasn't always easy for her, but she had a way of coming out on top. She had spirit."

For something to occupy his mind, Cousin George told me, he was doing "voluntary tutoring two days weekly. I work in a first grade class with a small group of slow learners, a condition probably stemming from disadvantaged homes."

I looked at a snapshot Cousin George had enclosed, a picture of him and some of his pupils, and another picture came into my head: Betty Bloomer, all those years ago, mushing out to teach dancing on the wrong side of the tracks while her stepfather, wordless and disapproving, watched her leave the house.

I was stubborn then, and I'm stubborn now, and thank God for that.

Cousin George concluded his letter by saying millions of people were pulling for me, which certainly appeared to be the case. I got compliments in high places. The Washington *Post* ran an editorial declaring that my candor in discussing my mastectomy had given heart "to countless other victims and prospective victims of breast cancer," and went on to praise me for revealing my present addiction to pills and alcohol. "Whatever combination of emotional and psychological stress and physical pain (she is arthritic) brought her to this pass, she is, characteristically, determined to overcome it. And she is unafraid and unembarrassed to say so."

I thank the Washington *Post*, but I don't deserve the accolade. I've been both afraid *and* embarrassed. I've gone through every possible emotion, suffered every possible mood, loneliness, depression, anger, discouragement. Here, for example, is a notation from a diary I kept, off and on, during my weeks at Long Beach. It's part of the entry for April 21:

Now to bed. These damn scratchy wool blankets. Little did I know when I signed in that it was going to be so rough, and I don't mean just the blankets, either. It's a good program, but mighty hard for anyone even twenty years old, let alone someone who turned sixty a couple of weeks ago. Oh well, just one week more, and I get a weekend pass. What in hell am I doing here? I've even started talking like the sailors. I could sign out, but I won't let myself do that. I want it too badly. Guess I'll just cry.

When I did get the weekend pass, I went home, had my hair cut, decided the operator had hacked it too short, and threw a temper tantrum.

Serenity is hard won, but I'm making progress.

I don't want to drink any more, and it's been a great relief to me to stop. Jerry has cocktails before dinner. It doesn't bother me. I enjoy ginger ale, I enjoy tonic with a lime in it, I enjoy Perrier water.

I've learned a lot about myself. Most of it is all right. When I add up the pluses and subtract the minuses, I still come out pretty well.

Eisenhower Hospital, in Palm Springs, is planning an active program for chemically addicted patients, and I think that's one of the things that will be strong for me; I'll be able to participate, to help others, which is the best possible therapy.

There's one more point I want to make. There are plenty of chemically dependent people like me, women who aren't recognized as problem drinkers until it's forced on them, or they crack. I've heard stories about women who are golfers and bridge experts, women who are leaders of their communities, heading up charity drives, turning in great records, but the iced tea in their hands or the coffee at their desks is laced with vodka just to keep them going.

I'm not out to rescue anybody who doesn't want to be rescued, I just think it's important to say how easy it is to slip into a dependency on pills or alcohol. And how hard it is to admit that dependency.

I'm grateful to Jerry and my children for coming to my rescue. I'm grateful to Captain Pursch and the rest of the believers at Long Beach for their skills and their caring. I'm grateful to thousands of strangers for their kindness and encouragement.

As I continue to study and learn and work toward an aware future, I'm sure more will be revealed to me, and I'm looking forward to that.

Stubborn Betty Bloomer Ford intends to make it.

ACKNOWLEDGMENTS

My thanks go to Clara Powell, David Kennerly, Maria Downs, Peter Sorum, Patti Matson, Bob Barrett, Carolyn Porembka, Captain Joseph Pursch, Sandra Eisert, and all my children, especially Susan, for helping me remember.

INDEX